Instability and Tourism

The rise of political instability and terrorism necessitates a reassessment of various tourism policy issues. This book focuses upon evaluating the impact of terrorist political conflicts and other types of instability on the tourism sector and considers the practical implications for countries being adversely affected by these episodes. Over the last decades, tourism has been adversely affected by a wide range of problems such as economic crises, social conflicts, political instability, terrorism and wars. Each of these, and their consequences on tourism, confirms the need to understand more about potential mitigating policy interventions in different contexts. This book includes six chapters exploring a wide range of themes related to instability and tourism using innovative approaches and considering different countries for their research. Precisely, countries such as Turkey, Ukraine, Jordan, Egypt and Nepal are under analysis. The articles published in this special issue were written by authors affiliated with universities in the USA, New Zealand, Spain, Egypt, Jordan and Bulgaria. All selected papers underwent a rigorous double-blind review process before final revision and acceptance.

The chapters were originally published in a special issue of the *Journal of Policy Research in Tourism, Leisure and Events*.

María Santana-Gallego, PhD, is Associate Professor in the Applied Economics Department at the University of the Balearic Islands, Spain. Her research interests include international economics and tourism economics. She has published in journals such as *Annals of Tourism Research*, *Tourism Management*, *World Economy* and *Economic Modelling*.

ShiNa Li, PhD, is Professor at Sun Yat-sen University, Guangzhou, China and Visiting Professor at Leeds Beckett University, UK. Her research interests include tourism economics, sustainable development, tourism geography, events and tourism in China. She has published in journals such as *Annals of Tourism Research*, *Journal of Travel Research* and *Tourism Management*.

Instability and Tourism

Edited by
María Santana-Gallego and ShiNa Li

Routledge
Taylor & Francis Group

LONDON AND NEW YORK

First published 2019
by Routledge
2 Park Square, Milton Park, Abingdon, Oxon, OX14 4RN, UK

and by Routledge
52 Vanderbilt Avenue, New York, NY 10017

First issued in paperback 2020

Routledge is an imprint of the Taylor & Francis Group, an informa business

British Library Cataloguing-in-Publication Data
A catalogue record for this book is available from the British Library

ISBN 13: 978-0-367-58612-6 (pbk)
ISBN 13: 978-1-138-32256-1 (hbk)

Typeset in Minion Pro
by codeMantra

Publisher's Note
The publisher accepts responsibility for any inconsistencies that may have arisen during the conversion of this book from journal articles to book chapters, namely the possible inclusion of journal terminology.

Disclaimer
Every effort has been made to contact copyright holders for their permission to reprint material in this book. The publishers would be grateful to hear from any copyright holder who is not here acknowledged and will undertake to rectify any errors or omissions in future editions of this book.

Contents

Citation Information

The chapters in this book were originally published in the *Journal of Policy Research in Tourism, Leisure and Events*, volume 9, issue 1 (March 2017). When citing this material, please use the original page numbering for each article, as follows:

Chapter 1
Special issue on instability and tourism
María Santana-Gallego and ShiNa Li
Journal of Policy Research in Tourism, Leisure and Events, volume 9, issue 1 (March 2017)
pp. 1–2

Chapter 2
Political instability and tourism in Egypt: exploring survivors' attitudes after downsizing
Ibrahim A. Elshaer and Samar K. Saad
Journal of Policy Research in Tourism, Leisure and Events, volume 9, issue 1 (March 2017)
pp. 3–22

Chapter 3
Addressing travel writers' role as risk brokers: the case of Jordan
Suleiman A. D. Farajat, Bingjie Liu and Lori Pennington-Gray
Journal of Policy Research in Tourism, Leisure and Events, volume 9, issue 1 (March 2017)
pp. 23–39

Chapter 4
Political instability and trade union practices in Nepalese hotels
Sandeep Basnyat, Brent Lovelock and Neil Carr
Journal of Policy Research in Tourism, Leisure and Events, volume 9, issue 1 (March 2017)
pp. 40–55

Chapter 5
Evaluating the dynamics and impact of terrorist attacks on tourism and economic growth for Turkey
Julio A. Afonso-Rodríguez
Journal of Policy Research in Tourism, Leisure and Events, volume 9, issue 1 (March 2017)
pp. 56–81

Chapter 6
Travel advisories – destabilising diplomacy in disguise
Aman Deep and Charles Samuel Johnston
Journal of Policy Research in Tourism, Leisure and Events, volume 9, issue 1 (March 2017)
pp. 82–99

Chapter 7
Impacts of political instability on the tourism industry in Ukraine
Stanislav Ivanov, Margarita Gavrilina, Craig Webster and Vladyslav Ralko
Journal of Policy Research in Tourism, Leisure and Events, volume 9, issue 1 (March 2017)
pp. 100–127

For any permission-related enquiries please visit:
http://www.tandfonline.com/page/help/permissions

Notes on Contributors

Julio A. Afonso-Rodríguez is Senior Lecturer in the Department of Applied Economics and Quantitative Methods at the University of La Laguna, Spain since 1996. His main research interests are time series analysis (univariate and multivariate), applied macro-econometrics and applied financial econometrics.

Sandeep Basnyat is Assistant Professor at the Institute for Tourism Studies (IFT), Macao. He holds a PhD in Tourism Research at the University of Otago, New Zealand. Areas of interest include employee relationships, human resource management in tourism and hospitality industry, tourism and work, tourism labour and sustainable development of tourism.

Neil Carr has been Head of the Department of Tourism at the University of Otago, New Zealand since 2015. Since obtaining his PhD in Tourism Geography from the University of Exeter, UK in 1998, Neil has worked as Lecturer at the University of Hertfordshire, UK, Lecturer and Senior Lecturer at the University of Queensland, Brisbane, Australia and Senior Lecturer at the University of Otago, Dunedin, New Zealand. He has also been Editor of the *Annals of Leisure Research*, since 2013.

Aman Deep is an MA (Tourism) from Swiss Hotel Management School, Switzerland and MBA graduate from Auckland University of Technology, New Zealand. He has worked as a tourism lecturer in universities in India for three years. Security has been a key interest in his developing research profile.

Ibrahim A. Elshaer received an MPhil/PhD in Management from the Business School at the University of Hull, UK and is currently a full-time Lecturer of Management in the Faculty of Tourism and Hotels at Suez Canal University, Ismailia, Egypt. He has a wide range of experience in teaching different courses in management for multicultural students and a strong advocate of how these different courses are interrelated to form a system. His professional interests focus on quality management, competitive advantage, communication skills, organizational politics, human resource management and leadership. In addition, he is Editorial Secretary of the *Journal of Association of Arab Universities for Tourism and Hospitality* and a reviewer in some international journals (i.e. *IJQRM, Total Quality Management & Business Excellence*, and *WASET*).

Suleiman A. D. Farajat PhD, is Assistant Professor in the Department of Tourism Management at the University of Jordan, Jordan. He holds a BA from Jordan, a higher diploma in Tourism Management from Austria and an MSc (Distinction) in Tourism and Hospitality Management and a PhD in Tourism Studies from the UK. Before embarking on his academic career, he worked in diverse tourism positions in Jordan, Austria and the UK. His research interests include, the relationship between heritage, tourism and national identity; destination development and management; and marketing destinations in times of crisis. He has been part of different international groups working on tourism development projects in Jordan. Besides his teaching tasks, he is currently Director of Media and Public Relations at the University of Jordan, Amman, Jordan.

Margarita Gavrilina graduated from the BA (Hons) International Hospitality Management programme at Varna University of Management, Bulgaria, with Margarita has conducted a number of tourism-related research projects during her studies. She has participated in several intensive programmes as an international exchange student in Finland and Lithuania, such as 'Conference Tourism as a Remedy for a Low-season Tourism Market' and 'Gastronomic Heritage Tourism – Entrepreneurship and Innovative Marketing'.

Stanislav Ivanov is Professor in Tourism Economics and Vice Rector (Research) at the Varna University of Management, Bulgaria. He is Editor-in-Chief of the *European Journal of Tourism Research* (http://ejtr.vumk.eu) and serves on the editorial boards of 25 other journals. His research interests include destination marketing, tourism and economic growth, political issues in tourism and special interest tourism. His publications have appeared in different academic journals – *Annals of Tourism Research, Tourism Management, Tourism Management Perspectives, Tourism Economics, Journal of Heritage Tourism, Tourism and Hospitality Research, Tourism Planning and Development, Journal of Hospitality Marketing and Management* and other journals.

Charles Samuel Johnston is a senior lecturer in the School of Hospitality and Tourism at the Auckland University of Technology, New Zealand. He is an 'old backpacker', who turned his love of travel into his profession. His main research themes currently focus on tourism in Asia and in cities, on the relationship between tourism and sustainable development and on mobility theory in relation to lifestyle migration.

ShiNa Li, PhD, is Professor at Sun Yat-sen University, Guangzhou, China and Visiting Professor at Leeds Beckett University, UK. Her research interests include tourism economics, sustainable development, tourism geography, events and tourism in China. She has published in journals such as *Annals of Tourism Research, Journal of Travel Research* and *Tourism Management*.

Bingjie Liu is currently Instructor of the Tourism, Leisure, and Event Planning Program at Bowling Green State University, USA. She is also Doctoral Candidate in the Department of Tourism, Recreation and Sport Management at the University of Florida, Gainesville, USA, under the advisement of Dr Lori Pennington-Gray. She received her bachelor's degree in Tourism Management from Sun Yat-sen University, Guangzhou, China, and her master's Degree in Parks, Recreation, and Tourism Management from Clemson University, USA. Her current research mainly focuses on crisis communication in tourism and hospitality.

Brent Lovelock is Associate Professor with the Department of Tourism. His background is in natural resource management and protected area tourism and recreation. Brent's main research interest has been the application of sustainable tourism – in its broadest sense – environmentally, socially and politically. He has undertaken research in North America, New Zealand and the Asia-Pacific region, examining collaborative planning processes for sustainable tourism development.

Lori Pennington-Gray PhD, is Professor in the Department of Tourism, Recreation and Sport Management at the University of Florida, Gainesville, USA. She also serves as Director of the Tourism Crisis Management Institute. Her research programme's common theme is tourism planning and development from a demand and supply perspective. Her other major research initiative is in tourism crisis management. Her main aim is to provide destinations with research findings, which enable them to make more informed policy choices and better market their destinations. She has worked with several stakeholders including non-profits, private sector businesses, public sector businesses and governments, as well as residents.

Vladyslav Ralko is Assistant Professor at the Varna University of Management, Bulgaria. He teaches Marketing Communications and Project Management. His research interests include sustainability, marketing and waste and energy management. His background also includes conducting field research in hotel pricing management.

Samar K. Saad is Lecturer of Management in the Faculty of Tourism and Hotels at Suez Canal University, Ismailia, Egypt. She received her PhD in Human Resource Management from Helwan University, Egypt. She has been involved in consultancy and related research projects in the fields of tourism and human resources. Her research interests include human resource planning, organizational politics, justice, and attitudes and behaviours in the workplace. She has published her work in journals such as *the Journal of Human Resources in Hospitality & Tourism, International Journal of Social Science* and *International Journal of Heritage Studies.*

María Santana-Gallego, PhD, is Associate Professor in the Applied Economics Department at the University of the Balearic Islands, Spain. Her research interests include international economics and tourism economics. She has published in journals such as *Annals of Tourism Research, Tourism Management, World Economy* and *Economic Modelling.*

Craig Webster is Assistant Professor of Event Management at Ball State University, Muncie, USA. He studied Government and German Literature at St. Lawrence University, Canton, USA, received an MA and PhD in Political Science from Binghamton University, USA and an MBA from Intercollege Limassol, Cyprus. His research interests include the political economy of tourism, public opinion analysis, human rights and comparative foreign policy. Dr Webster is Editor-in-Chief of *Tourism Today* and a Co-Editor of *The Cyprus Review.* He has published in many peer-reviewed journals internationally and co-edited Routledge's book *Future Tourism: Political, Social, and Economic Challenges.*

Special issue on instability and tourism

María Santana-Gallego and ShiNa Li

The rise of political instability and terrorism necessitates a reassessment of various tourism policy issues. This special issue focuses upon evaluating the impact of terrorism political conflicts and other types of instability on the tourism sector and considers the practical implications for countries of being adversely affected by these episodes.

Over the last decades, tourism has been adversely affected by a wide range of problems such as economic crises, social conflicts, political instability, terrorism and wars. The US 9/11 terrorist attack, the Arab Spring, the rise of Islamic State and political instability in Eastern Europe are examples of events that are seriously affecting international tourism flows. Each of these, and their consequences on tourism, confirm the need to understand more about potential mitigating policy interventions in different contexts.

As others have noted, political stability is extremely important in determining the image of destinations in tourist generating regions (Hall, 1996). Indeed, safety is one of the priorities when consumers make travel decisions; if they perceive a risk of injury or death, or a highly stressful situation, they will avoid that destination. When violence becomes widespread and prolonged, governments in tourist origin countries will advise against travelling to those destinations and commercial operators will cancel tours because of insufficient bookings and for fear of liability suits, and will promote other destinations instead (Neumayer, 2004). A further problem is that terrorist attacks and political disruption can damage infrastructure relevant to the tourism industry (Llorca-Vivero, 2008) and may damage or destroy national treasures (Yap & Saha, 2013).

In spite of its relevance, the effects of instability on tourism are still under research. This special issue provides examples of different approaches to understanding and addressing the impacts of this phenomenon on tourism. The articles contribute to, and draw upon, tourism economics, tourism management and leisure studies policy frameworks reflecting the holistic nature of the effect of instability on tourism. Additionally, the articles provide discussion of the policy implications and evaluate the impact of policies undertaken to deal with instability. Finally, the articles encourage further research and identify potentially fruitful areas of enquiry.

Elshaer and Saad in 'Political instability and tourism in Egypt: Exploring survivors' attitudes after downsizing' explore the impact of job insecurity on the attitudes of survivors in downsized hotels and tourism companies in Egypt after the instability generated by the Arab Spring in 2011. Moreover, the article provides relevant discussion of the implications of their findings. Farajat, Liu and Pennington-Gray in 'Addressing travel writers' role as risk brokers: The case of Jordan' analyse the role of travel writers as risk brokers during unstable times, considering Jordan as the case study. The article reveals that safety emerges as one of the major issues that contemporary travel articles were concerned about, and they also discuss the importance for tourism policy-makers of risk management. Basnyat, Lovelock and Carr in 'Political instability and trade union practices in Nepalese hotels' collect data through interviews to study the effect of instability on trade union practices in the Nepalese tourism industry by examining how the roles of trade unions alter after changes caused by political instability.

Afonso-Rodríguez in 'Evaluating the dynamics and impact of terrorist attacks on tourism and economic growth for Turkey' provides an up-to-date analysis of the Tourism Led Growth Hypothesis in Turkey but with the value added of considering information on terrorist attacks. The author uses different econometric specifications of cointegrating regressions to quantify the impact of terrorism on the relationship between tourism demand and economic growth, including the novelty approach of a threshold cointegrating regression. Deep and Johnston in 'Travel advisories-destabilising diplomacy in disguise' present an interesting conceptual paper to create a destabilisation-to-re-stabilisation sequence on the use of travel advisory as an attempt to politically and/or economically destabilise the developing-nation destination through disruption of tourism. Finally, Ivanov, Gavrilina, Webster and Ralko in 'Impacts of political instability on the tourism industry in Ukraine' collect questionnaires completed by hotel managers and travel agency managers to learn about how the tourism industry in Ukraine has been hit by the political instability in the country and how it has reacted to mitigate its negative consequences.

To sum up, the special issue includes six papers exploring a wide range of themes related to instability and tourism using innovative approaches and considering different countries for their research. Precisely, countries such as Turkey, Ukraine, Jordan, Egypt and Nepal are under analysis. The articles published in this special issue reveal that the authors for this special issue are affiliated with universities in the USA, New Zealand, Spain, Egypt, Jordan and Bulgaria. All selected papers underwent a rigorous double-blind review process before final revision and acceptance.

References

Hall, C. M. (1996). *Tourism and politics: Policy, power and place*. England: John Wiley & Son.

Llorca-Vivero, R. (2008). Terrorism and international tourism: New evidence. *Defence and Peace Economics*, 19(2), 169–188.

Neumayer, E. (2004). The impact of political violence on tourism: Dynamic cross-national estimation. *Journal of Conflict Resolution*, 48(2), 259–281.

Yap, G., & Saha, S. (2013). Do political instability, terrorism and corruption have deterring effects on tourism development even in the presence of UNESCO heritage? A cross-country panel estimate. *Tourism Analysis*, 18, 587–599.

Political instability and tourism in Egypt: exploring survivors' attitudes after downsizing

Ibrahim A. Elshaer and Samar K. Saad

ABSTRACT

Political unrest, framed within an array of terrorists' attacks and large demonstrations against the regime, has been considered a mainstay of the tourism collapse in Egypt since 2011. The number of tourists visiting the country has drastically declined, mainly in response to international travel alerts and warnings by many Western governments. As such, several tourism and hospitality organizations have applied downsizing strategies in their attempt to cut labor cost. Both employees who lost their jobs (victims) and who remain in the organization (survivors) have been experiencing a great fear of the future and incremental feelings of job insecurity. While a review of literature clearly shows the harmful influence of political unrest on tourism destinations, little is known to suggest such influence on employees' reactions. The purpose of this paper is to explore the impact of job insecurity on the attitudes of survivors (i.e. trust, organizational commitment and turnover intention) in downsized hotels and tourism companies in Egypt. The results indicate that survivors' perception of job insecurity within an unstable political climate has a strong positive relationship with survivors turnover intention. The results suggest that this relationship is more likely to be weakened by survivors' high perception of trust and commitment in their organization. Additionally, it is found that survivors who intend to leave their organization target to entirely change their career or seek to work abroad. Losing qualified survivors to other industries or countries may become a significant risk for the Egyptian tourism industry. The implications of the results are discussed and elaborated.

RESUMEN

El descontento político, enmarado en una serie de ataques terroristas y grandes manifestaciones contra el régimen, ha sido considerado un pilar del colapso del turismo en Egipto desde 2011. El número de turistas que visitan el país ha caído drásticamente, principalmente en respuesta a las alertas de viaje y a las advertencias por parte de muchos gobiernos occidentales. Y así, algunas organizaciones turísticas han aplicado estrategias de recorte de personal en un intento de reducir los costes laborales. Tanto los empleados que perdieron sus trabajos (víctimas) como aquellos que permanecen en la organización (supervivientes) han estado experimentando un gran temor al futuro y unos crecientes sentimientos de inseguridad laboral. Mientras que una revisión de la literatura muestra claramente la nociva influencia del descontento político en los destinos turísticos, se conoce poco para sugerir tal influencia en las reacciones de los empleados. El propósito de este trabajo es explorar el impacto de la inseguridad laboral en las actitudes de los supervivientes (i.e. confianza, compromiso con la organización e intención de abandono) en hoteles con recortes de personal y en compañías turísticas en Egipto. Los resultados indican que la percepción de la inseguridad laboral de los supervivientes dentro de un clima político inestable tiene una fuerte relación positiva con la intención de abandono de los supervivientes. Lo resultados sugieren que esta relación es más probable que sea debilitada por una elevada percepción de confianza y compromiso con su organización de los supervivientes. Además, se encontró que los supervivientes que tienen la intención de abandonar su organización se fijan como objetivo cambiar completamente su carrera o buscar trabajo en el extranjero. La pérdida de supervivientes cualificados a favor de otras industrias o países puede llegar a ser un riesgo importante para la industria turística egipcia. Se discuten y se desarrollan las implicaciones de estos resultados.

RÉSUMÉ
L'instabilité politique causée par des attaques terroristes et des vagues de manifestations contre le régime a été considérée comme l'un des facteurs majeurs de l'effondrement du tourisme en Egypte depuis 2011. Le nombre de touristes qui visitent le pays a considérablement chuté, principalement suite aux alertes aux voyageurs internationaux, aux conseils et aux avertissements émis par de nombreux gouvernements occidentaux. À cet effet, plusieurs organismes de tourisme et du l'hôtellerie ont mis en place des stratégies de consolidation visant la réduction des coûts de la main-d'œuvre. Les employés qui ont perdu leur emploi (victimes) et ceux qui sont restés dans l'organisation (résistants) ont tous senti une grande peur de l'avenir et un sentiment croissant d'insécurité à l'égard de l'emploi. Si l'analyse des données disponibles au public montre clairement les effets négatifs de l'instabilité politique sur les destinations touristiques, il est clair qu'un tel impact sur les réactions des employés est très peu connu. Le but de cet article est d'étudier l'impact de la précarité sur les attitudes des résistants (à savoir la confiance, l'attachement à l'organisation et les perspectives du chiffre d'affaires) dans les hôtels et les entreprises touristiques soumis aux mesures d'austérité en Egypte. Les résultats de cette recherche indiquent que les perceptions des résistants à l'égard de l'insécurité de l'emploi dans un climat d'instabilité politique ont une influence très positive sur les perspectives de la productivité des résistants. Par contre, les résultats suggèrent que cette relation est plus susceptible d'être faible lorsqu'il y a une forte perception de confiance et d'attachement des résistants à leur organisation. En outre, on constate que les résistants qui envisagent de quitter leur organisation affichent l'intention de changer complètement leur carrière ou veulent travailler à l'étranger. Perdre les résistants qualifiés pour d'autres entreprises ou d'autres pays peut poser un grand risque à l'industrie du tourisme égyptien. Les implications des résultats ont été discutées et mises en exergue.

摘要

政治动乱加上一系列恐怖袭击、大量的反政府示威游行被认为是埃及自2011年以来旅游业崩溃的主要原因。游客数量的急剧下滑主要是由于许多西方国家发布了国际旅游警报和警告。因此，许多旅游接待组织采取收缩战略以减少人力资源成本。因此而失业的雇员（受害者）和留下来的雇员（幸存者）都对未来充满极大的担忧，职业不安全感增加。虽然已有研究发现政治动乱对旅游目的地会产生不利影响，但是很少研究在这种影响下雇员的反应。本文研究埃及裁员的酒店及旅游企业中职业不安全感的对幸存者态度（如信任、组织认同感、离职倾向）的影响。研究表明幸存者职业不安全感的感知与不稳定的政治氛围与其离职倾向具有强烈的正相关关系。本研究认为这种强相关很有可能被幸存者较高的信任感和组织认同感减弱。另外也发现，那些打算离开目前所就职组织的幸存者，将彻底改变职业生涯或出国工作作为目标。这些有能力的幸存者流失到其他产业或其他国家可能带给埃及旅游业重大风险。最后讨论并详细阐述了本研究结果的启示。

Introduction

Safety and security are considered important concerns that influence tourists' travel decision to specific destinations. While numerous environmental and man-made disasters can considerably impact the flow of tourists, perceptions of risk and danger that come along with political instability in some destinations usually frighten potential tourists more strongly (Sönmez, 1998). According to Darity (2008), a number of signs indicate the presence of political instability in a distention. The most common are the probability of a change in regime or government, political turmoil or violence in a society (e.g. assassinations and demonstrations), and instability in policies such as policies of human and property rights (Darity, 2008). Although countries may experience different signs of political instability, their tourism and hospitality industries share similar challenges. These include a decline in demand, fall in hotels occupancy rate and accordingly cash flow, perceptions of possible hostility by potential tourists, negative image and reputation, low quality of safety and security concerns, and reduction in foreign investment (Issa & Altinay, 2006).

The recent unstable political situation in Egypt negatively influenced its tourism industry in many ways. The large demonstrations against the regime accompanied by violent incidents and terrorists' attacks have influenced the international image of Egypt as a safe tourist destination. According to Crotti and Misrahi (2015), political instability in Egypt reduced its appeal to international tourists. The volume of the tourist arrivals has severely decreased in 2014 compared to 2010 by 14.2% (Egyptian Center for Economic Studies [ECES], 2016). The number of tourist nights has decreased by 20.3% for the same period (ECES, 2016). Hotels' occupancy rate has achieved a significant downturn by 75.4% in 2013 compared to 2010 (Information and Decision Support Center, 2014). The majority of tourism companies and hotels have suffered serious financial hardships (Nassar, 2012). They have implemented alternative strategies to overcome the harsh financial situation. Cutting costs was the main applied strategy in tourism and hospitality companies. Although the common belief that human resources (HR) in tourism organizations are valuable assets, labor costs are usually the first to be cut during financial problems

(Saad, 2013). Thus, managers have reduced the salaries of staff or laid off a considerable percentage of their staff (Mohammad, Jones, Dawood, & Sayed, 2012; Nassar, 2012).

Previous literature has indicated that transitional strategies such as downsizing usually create employees' feelings of stress and insecurity (Ashford, Lee, & Bobko, 1989; Sverke & Hellgren, 2002). They get usually worried about the continuity or existence of their jobs. It may be that employees' perception of less control on their status in the organization motivates such feeling to occur (Greenhalgh & Rosenblatt, 1984).

According to Brockner, Wiesenfeld, and Martin (1995), the reactions of survivors during and after the downsizing are significant indicators of the future success/failure of organizations. This is consistent with the study of Kinnie, Hutchinson, and Purcell (1998) which argued that managers in organizations with failed downsizing strategies rarely considered survivors' attitudes and interests during and after the downsizing. Thus, the recovery strategies that the organizations conducted due to the political instability may be at risk. Understanding the possible changes in survivors' attitudes and interests may increase the downsizing chances of success (Mishra & Spreitzer, 1998). In this study, we examine perceptions of job insecurity, trust, organizational commitment and turnover intentions as potentially affected attitudes of survivors in downsized tourism companies and hotels in Egypt.

Literature review

Political instability in Egypt

Tourism industry in Egypt enjoyed a period of continuous and stable growth from the 1990s through the 2000s. Although such long period has experienced some shocking political crisis due to the terrorist attacks in famous Egyptian tourist cities (e.g. Luxor in 1995 and Sharm El Shiekh in 2005) causing a sudden decline in tourists' arrival, the tourism industry was able to have a quick recovery and the number of tourists has risen again (Crotti & Misrahi, 2015).

However, following the revolution of 2011, which resulted in the toppling of the former President Mubarak and the election of Mohamed Morsi as a new president in June 2012, several subsequent incidents turned out to be the cause of severe long political instability period. A lot of acts of civil disobedience, strikes and a series of demonstrations ended with the ousting of President Morsi after one year of ruling Egypt (Brown, 2015). After a while, bloody clashes took place between demonstrators, security forces and supporters of President Morsi in many cities in Egypt (Stacher, 2015). Since then, Egypt has been shaken by a wave of terrorists' attacks mainly in Cairo (capital of Egypt) and Sinai Peninsula (a famous tourist attraction). The majority of such attacks have targeted the security forces, usually at checkpoints and police stations and negatively impacted the tourist image of Egypt. However, the following incidents during 2015 placed Egypt's image in a critical condition. For example, terrorists attacked a famous pharaonic temple (El Karnak), assassinated the Egyptian Attorney General and blew up the Italian consulate in downtown Cairo. Moreover, 12 Mexican tourists were mistakenly killed by military and security forces (State Information System [SIS], 2016). The situation reached its peak after the crash of the Russian plane over Sinai causing the death of 224 passengers (SIS, 2016). Tourism and hospitality organizations were faced by prevalent cancellations and suspension of flights to Sharm El Shiekh and evacuation of thousands of tourists from Egypt (Middle East Monitor, 2015). Such quite long lasting political instability in Egypt made decision-makers in tourism companies and hotels encountering a continued fall in the financial situation of their organizations. Many organizations concentrated on cutting down costs as a way to survive in such economic shock.

Job insecurity

The continuous political instability in Egypt after 2011 has created severe financial disorders in organizations working in tourism and hospitality domain. According to Mohammad et al. (2012) and Nassar (2012), the intensive decrease in the number of international tourist arrivals and hotel room occupancy rates has caused a sharp decline in cash flow and revenues of such organizations. Most tourism and hospitality organizations have engaged in downsizing strategies that included labor reduction and flexible programs of using employees (e.g. part-time or temporary jobs) (Nassar, 2012). Specifically, the successive governments in the aftermath of the revolution have not placed appropriate effort to financially compensate the affected organizations (Mohammad et al., 2012). Previous literature stated that within such transitional strategies, employees probably feel insecure about the future existence of their jobs (Greenhalgh & Rosenblatt, 1984; Heaney, Israel, & House, 1994; Roskies & Louis-Guerin, 1990).

Job insecurity refers to the extent of concerns that employees have on the continuity in their jobs (Davy, Kinicki, & Scheck, 1997). Such concerns are usually induced by employees' perception of potential threat in their organizational environment (Heaney et al., 1994) in addition to feelings of powerlessness in securing their jobs (Greenhalgh & Rosenblatt, 1984). Job insecurity is based on employees' interpretations of the current work environment (Hartley, Jacobson, Klandermans, & van Vuuren, 1991) that lead them to anticipate the coming loss of their jobs (Sverke & Hellgren, 2002). Employees experiencing job insecurity due to downsizing issues are expected to have negative reactions known as 'survivors' sickness' or 'survivors' syndrome' (Dekker & Schaufeli, 1995). These include anger, depression, fear, distrust, powerlessness, guilt and loss of morale and motivation (Mishra & Spreitzer, 1998). Survivors' syndrome may cause low performance of survivors after downsizing (Dekker & Schaufeli, 1995).

Commitment

Organizational commitment is usually conceptualized as the psychological attachment to the organization, in which employees are willing to accept organizational goals and values, put forth effort in their jobs and sustain their organizational membership (Brown, 1996; Somers, 1995). This commitment can develop from positive experiences with the organization, job-related characteristics, personal and structured characteristics (Meyer & Allen, 1991). Though the few studies, literature of organizational commitment in tourism domain shows an explicit link between committed employees and their productivity and quality of services (Clark, Hartline, & Jones, 2009; Kim & Brymer, 2011). Committed employees are willing to deliver high service quality and accordingly enhance customer loyalty. However, from time to time, employees commonly evaluate organization eligibility of commitment (Hopkins & Weathington, 2006) and accordingly their level of commitment is subject to change. Hopkins and Weathington (2006) argued that lack of expected outcomes may reduce feelings of commitment toward the organization or the supervisor.

In downsized organizations, Armstrong-Stassen (2004) found that low organizational commitment is more likely to occur. Though survivors' happiness of not being displaced, they may feel less secure in their job status and sympathetic for their laidoff fellows. Survivors may think they should not count on their organization in supporting their interests. Consistent with this argument, Hopkins and Weathington (2006) found that survivors may not be interested anymore in having membership in their organization after downsizing even though they have an investment in it (e.g. retirement fund, accrued time off and seniority). The level of strain experienced from the threat of job loss may adversely influence the level of survivors' commitment to the organization (Spreitzer & Mishra, 2002). It could be that individuals' feeling of powerlessness and insecurity in the job status provides fertile ground for the decline of the organizational commitment.

In contrast, Mishra and Spreitzer (1998) and Armstrong-Stassen (2006) found that losing organizational commitment after downsizing is not always the case. Worried survivors are more likely to work harder after watching layoffs in order not to experience the risky situation that their fellows had. On the other hand, Brown (1996) stated that organizational commitment may be sustained due to organizational efforts that are made to help employees amend to the new workplace structure. Similarly, findings by Chipunza and Berry (2010) showed that survivors' motivation and commitment may be improved overtime due to the managerial effort of their organization. Based on the previous, we form the following hypothesis:

> H1: Survivors' perceptions of job insecurity is negatively related to their commitment to the organization.

Turnover intention

The major changes in the organization after downsizing cause survivors' negative feelings of anxiety and stress regarding their jobs (Ashford et al., 1989; Spreitzer & Mishra, 2002). Although being not dismissed, survivors (especially the top performers) may attempt to search for new jobs due to cuts in salary and mandatory vacations (Cheng & Chan, 2008). Moreover, Krausz, Yaakobovitz, Bizman, and Caspi (1999) stated that layoff of coworkers may motivate the turnover intention of survivors, especially when there is a close relationship between both parties. Long political instability period that financially influences organizations may also motivate survivors to reevaluate their job status and consider other career opportunities. According to Greenhalgh and Rosenblatt (1984), survivors may seek for new jobs when they are worried about employment continuity.

Researchers have found that job insecurity plays a significant role in employees' decision of quitting the organization (Ashford et al., 1989). When employees feel that the future of their organization is likely to be vague, they may consider moving to another organization. Despite the increasing consensus that job insecurity has a consistent relationship with survivors' intention to quit, other researchers indicate different outcomes. For example, Robinson (1992), Staufenbiel and König (2010) and Gilboa, Shirom, Fried, and Cooper (2008) noted that some survivors may react to job insecurity by sticking with their organization through bad times and increasing their work effort and high-quality performance. Researchers explain this behavior as an outcome of survivors' desire to attain the organization's success and accordingly job security (Gilboa et al., 2008; Robinson, 1992; Staufenbiel & König, 2010). It seems that survivors' loyalty and commitment to the organization reduce their desire to quit even in organization's hard times. Based on the previous, we hypothesize the following relationships:

H2: Survivors' perception of job insecurity is positively related to their intentions to quit (turnover intentions).

H3: Survivors' commitment to the organization is negatively related to their intentions to quit (turnover intentions).

Trust

Trust, which is a psychological state, refers to 'one's expectations, assumptions, or beliefs about the likelihood that another's future actions will be beneficial, favorable, or at least not detrimental to one's interest' (Robinson, 1996, p. 575). Previous research showed two factors combination that drives trust (Aryee, Budhwar, & Chen, 2002; Mayer, Davis, & Schoorman, 1995; McAllister, 1995). First, cognition which is determined by individual's evaluation and beliefs about the ability of another party (e.g. organization/ supervisor) to abide by its obligations and accordingly show reliability and dependability. Second, affect which develops from mutual feelings of care and concern between two parties that goes beyond any rational evaluation.

During periods of political instability, making employees dismissed due to downsizing and not replacing them with new positions may make survivors feel that they would face a similar fate in the future. Therefore, feeling job insecurity may prompt survivors to evaluate their organization as unreliable and not trustworthy (Brockner, 1988). This is consistent with the longitudinal study of Armstrong-Stassen (2002) on survivors in a downsized organization, which found a significant decline in trust during and past downsizing periods. On the other hand, survivors' feelings of uncertainty and confusion about their new responsibilities after downsizing and what is expected from them may accumulate their low feeling of trust in their organization (Spreitzer & Mishra, 2002).

Evidence suggests that low perceptions of trust can lead to an increase in negative survivors' perceptions and feelings. According to Mishra and Spreitzer (1998), if survivors do not trust their organization in its ability to uphold their goals and concerns, they are likely to engage in withdrawal behaviors. In tourism and hospitality literature, Hon and Lu (2010) and Chiang and Wang (2012) claimed that cognitive-based trust is positively related to employees' commitment. These attitudes usually form when employees have a strong belief and confident in the management of the organization. Such belief leads them to accept any change proposed for the good of the organization (Hon & Lu, 2010). However, survivors experiencing low trust in their organization are more likely to seek other career opportunities (Aryee et al., 2002; Hopkins & Weathington, 2006). Having less confidence in the management's ability to guide and facilitate organization's success probably make employees evaluate their career in an unfavorable manner and accordingly seek for other opportunities. Based on these arguments, we hypothesize the following:

H4: Survivors' perception of job insecurity is negatively related to survivors' trust in their organization.

H5: Survivors' trust in their organization is positively related to their organizational commitment.

H6: Survivors' trust in their organization is negatively related to their intention to quit (turn-over intention).

Figure 1 shows the model we propose and test in this research.

Research methods

Job insecurity operationalization

Scholar's work of job insecurity is mainly inspired by Greenhalgh and Rosenblatt's (1984) theoretical paper, where they defined job insecurity as 'perceived powerlessness to maintain desired continuity in a threatened job situation' (p. 438). Other researchers described job insecurity as 'expectations about continuity in a job situation' (Davy et al., 1997, p. 323) and as 'an employee's perception of a potential threat to continuity in his or her current job' (Heaney et al., 1994, p. 1431).

Based on Greenhalgh and Rosenblatt's (1984) theoretical article, Hellgren, Sverke, and Isaksson (1999) differentiated between two aspects of job insecurity: quantitative (worries about leaving the job) and qualitative (worries about losing some job features) job insecurity.

Hellgren et al. (1999) scale of job insecurity has demonstrated good psychometric properties and has been widely employed in different empirical studies (such as those by Cheng & Chan, 2008; De Witte et al., 2010; Låstad, Berntson, Näswall, Lindfors, & Sverke, 2015; Mauno, Leskinen, & Kinnunen, 2001), quantitative job insecurity was measured in our study by employing three items developed by Hellgren et al. (1999). These items (e.g. 'I am worried that I will have to leave my job before I would like to') reflect worries

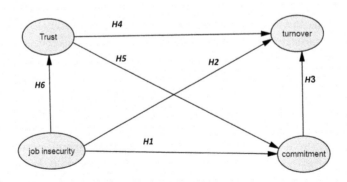

Figure 1. Research framework.

about the continuity of the job. A 4-item scale, also introduced by Hellgren et al. (1999), was employed to measure qualitative job insecurity (e.g. 'I worry about getting less stimulating work tasks in the future') capture a worry about losing some good job features. The Cronbach's alpha in this sample found to be .94 for quantitative job insecurity, and .95 for qualitative job insecurity.

Commitment operationalization

In its primary stages, organizational commitment was defined and conceptualized as a global model. These models assumed that organizational commitment is one-dimensional in nature, rather than the more advanced models that operationalize commitment as a multi-dimensional construct. The most widely employed global measure is that introduced by Mowday, Steers, and Porter's (1979) Organizational Commitment Questionnaire (OCQ). This 15-item self-report scale questions participants the degree to which they agree/disagree with questions that measure their organization commitment. The OCQ is considered to be a measure of attitudinal commitment (Salanick, 1977; Staw, 1977), which is comparable to what Meyer and Allen (1991) describe as affective commitment (will be illustrated below).

Several researchers have employed organizational commitment as a multi-dimensional construct. Rather than a one-dimensional construct, Meyer and Allen (1991) observed similarities between the several measures. They determined that these many measures can be categorized into one of three categories – an emotional relationship with the organization, beliefs about the rewards and costs of staying with or leaving the organization, and a feeling of moral responsibility towards his organization. Accordingly, Meyer and Allen introduced three dimensions of organizational commitment: affective, normative and continuance. Affective commitment explains the degree to which an employee wants to be a part of the organization. Normative commitment describes the degree to which an employee feels that he/she ought to stay at his/her present job. Continuance commitment explains the degree to which an employee feels that he/she needs to stay at the organization.

In the current study, we employed the 18-item measure of commitment as developed by Meyer, Allen, and Smith (1993). A sample item for each of the three dimensions includes: 'I would be very happy to spend the rest of my career with this organization' (Affective commitment); 'Right now, staying with my organization is a matter of necessity as much as desire' (continuance commitment); 'This organization deserves my loyalty' (normative commitment). The Cronbach's alpha in this sample found to be .84 for affective commitment, .95 for continuance commitment and .94 for normative commitment.

Turnover intention and trust operationalization

We employed a 5-item scale to measure turnover intention to. These items were adapted from several sources (Karatepe, 2009; Kickul, Lester, & Finkl, 2002; Meyer et al., 1993; Sjöberg & Sverke, 2000), a sample item being 'It would not take much to make me leave this hotel.' The Cronbach's alpha was found to be .74 in our sample.

Finally, we employed a 6-item scale to measure trust. These items were adapted from Podsakoff, MacKenzie, Moorman, and Fetter (1990). Podsakoff et al. (1990) trust scale demonstrated good psychometric properties and has been widely employed in different empirical studies (such as those by Bartram & Casimir, 2007; Deluga, 1994; Jung & Avolio, 2000; Rich,1997; Zhu, Newman, Miao, & Hooke, 2013), a sample item being 'I feel quite confident that my leader will always treat me fairly.' The Cronbach's alpha was found to be .89 in our sample.

Sample

A survey method was employed to collect data from the managerial positions (i.e. front office managers, rooms division manager, food and beverage manager, account managers, sales manager, director-marketing) working in hotels (178 five star hotels) and travel agents (100 class A travel agents) in Egypt. Managerial positions were our target as they have good years of experiences making the intention to leave the organization, not an easy option. We obtained data from a survey of 900 employees (managerial positions). The number of participants from each hotel ranged from 3 to 5 in order to avoid the under/over-representation of certain hotels/travel agents. A total of 560 responses were attained. Sixty uncompleted questionnaires were excluded leaving 500 usable with a response rate of around 55.5%. A continuous scale from 0 to 10 was used to measure the study variables where 0 means completely disagree with this question and 10 means completely agree.

Data analysis techniques

We used some successive phases to analyze the current study data. In Phase 1, we used Cronbach's alpha and the Corrected Item-Total Correlation (CITC) to assess the reliability of the measures, then in Phase 2, exploratory factor analysis (EFA) was employed. Finally in Phase 3, structural equation modeling was used to test the causal relationship between the research variables. It is the only data analysis technique that permits simultaneous and complete tests of all relationships for the multi-dimensional and complex phenomenon (Tabachnick & Fidell, 2007). To test a structural model's goodness of model fit, we employed the following measures: (a) measures of absolute fit: χ^2/df, and Root Mean Square Error of Approximation (RMSEA); (b) measures of incremental fit: Comparative Fit Index (CFI) and Normed Fit Index (NFI); and (c) measures of parsimony fit: Parsimony Comparative Fit Index (PCFI) and Parsimony Normed Fit Index (PNFI) (Hair, Black, Babin, Ralph, & Ronald, 2006; Byrne, 2010).

Results

Test of dimensionality and reliability

The aim of EFA in the current study was to purify and summarize the data. Our data fulfill the requirements for factor analysis, more specific, Bartlett's test of sphericity is significant which supports the factorability of the data set and suggests the presence of non-zero correlation between the items and a high level of homogeneity between variables (Field, 2006). Bartlett's test of sphericity displays an approximate Chi-square of 21133.831 with 295 df and significance .000. The overall measure of sampling adequacy (Kaiser–

Meyer–Olkin) is 0.887 which is higher than the cut-off point of 0.6 as recommended by Field (2006) and Hair et al. (2006). Overall, these data satisfy the requirements for factor analysis (Hair et al., 2006)

The EFA generates a seven-factor solution. A seven-factor solution is suggested using the criterion of an eigenvalue greater than 1 and the extracted factors account for 81.12% of the total variance. Table 1 contains a summary of the factor analysis and reliability analysis for the study constructs. Factor loadings are all higher than 0.6 on their own factors as recommended by Hair et al. (2006). All the 35 items employed in the question-naire to measure the study constructs retained and load highly on the expected factors (with no cross loading). This agrees with the 'simple structure' view of Thurstone (1947), where the scholar hopes to find each of the variables loading strongly on only one factor, and each factor being represented by a number of strongly loading variables.

More specifically, the factor loadings for the retained items are as follows: Trust (0.71, 0.77, 0.84, 0.80, 0.87 and 0.61, respectively), Quantitative Job insecurity (0.84, 0.86 and 0.86, respectively), Qualitative Job insecurity (0.92, 0.92 and 0.91, respectively), Affective Commitment (0.83, 0.86, 0.82, 0.88, 0.72 and 0.71, respectively), Normative Commitment (0.70, 0.85, 0.83, 0.84, 0.857 and 0.91, respectively), Continuance Commitment (0.85, 0.83, 0.84, 0.85, 0.91 and 0.70, respectively) and Turnover Intention (0.70, 0.69, 0.86, 0.87 and 0.91, respectively) (see Table 1). Furthermore, composite Cronbach alpha value scores for the seven factors reflect satisfactory internal consistency for those items. The reliability scores (Cronbach alpha or α) of each construct *exceed* 0.70 (see Table 1), which is above the usual cut-off level of 0.7 as recommended by Nunnally and Bernstein (1994) (see Table 1). Additionally, the CITC was used as one indicator of internal consistency among variables' items which reflects the degree of correlation between each item and the total score. CITC is used to evaluate whether all measures demonstrated a dominant loading on the hypothesized factor and did not have significant cross-loadings. The results of CITC ranged from 0.96 to 0.42. These results are satisfactory and are above the threshold of 0.4 as recommended by Nunnally and Bernstein (1994).

Structural equation modeling

The current study takes a confirmatory approach in which the researcher hypothesizes a specific theoretical model (from reviewing the literature), gathers data, and then tests whether the data fit the model (Schumacker & Lomax, 2010). In this approach, the theor-etical model is either accepted or rejected based on a chi-square statistical test of significance and meeting acceptable model fit criteria. The data for the model were entered in AMOS v18 by employing the ML estimation technique and AMOS Graphic is employed to draw the structural and measurement paths collectively in the model as drawn in Figure 1.

The goodness-of-fit measures indicate that our model fit the data well, χ^2 (98, $N = 500$) = 219.52, $P < .001$ (Normed χ^2 = 2.24, RMSEA = 0.029, CFI = 0.99, NFI = 0.96, and TLI = 0.99, PCFI = 0.83, and PNFI = 0.81).

The factor loading values for all the study dimensions exceed the cut-off point 0.7, con-firming a high degree of a positive relationship among scale items (see Figure 1).

After obtaining a satisfactory fit of our model, research hypotheses were assessed. Each path in the structural model among the latent variables makes a specific hypothesis (see Figure 1). According to the suggested research model, six hypotheses represent the

Table 1. Statistical summary: factor analysis (with the principal component as an extraction method) and reliability analysis for the study constructs.

Factors and variables	Factor components and loading							Reliability	
	1	2	3	4	5	6	7	CITC	α
Trust									.89
Trust1 I feel quite confident that my leader will always treat me fairly	.71							.76	
Trust2 My manager would never try to gain an advantage by deceiving workers	.77							.83	
Trust3 I have complete faith in the integrity of my supervisor	.89							.74	
Trust4 I feel a strong loyalty to my leader	.86							.89	
Trust5 I would support my leader in almost any emergency	.87							.69	
Trust6 I have a strong sense of loyalty toward my leader	.61							.42	
Job insecurity									
Quantitative job insecurity									.94
QUNJN1 I am worried that I will have to leave my job before I would like to					.84			.86	
QUNJN2 I worry about being able to keep my job					.86			.89	
QUNJN3 I am afraid I may lose my job in the near future					.86			.88	
Qualitative job insecurity									.95
QUALJN1 I worry about getting less stimulating work tasks in the future						.92		.90	
QUALJN2 I worry about my future wage development						.92		.91	
QUALJI feel worried about my career development in the organization N3						.91		.91	
Commitment									
Affective Commitment									.94
ACommitment1 I would be very happy to spend the rest of my career with this organization.		.83						.80	
ACommitment2 I really feel as if this organization's problems are my own.		.86						.86	
ACommitment3 I do not feel a strong sense of 'belonging' to my organization.		.82						.84	
ACommitment4 I do not feel 'emotionally attached' to this organization.		.88						.92	
ACommitment5 I do not feel like 'part of the family' at my organization. (R)		.72						.75	
ACommitment6 This organization has a great deal of personal meaning for me.		.71						.72	
Normative Commitment									.94
Ncommitment1 I do not feel any obligation to remain with my current employer.				.70				64	
Ncommitment2 Even if it were to my advantage, I do not feel it would be right to leave my organization now.				.85				.85	
Ncommitment3 I would feel guilty if I left my organization now.				.83				.83	
Ncommitment4 This organization deserves my loyalty.				.84				.86	
Ncommitment5 I would not leave my organization right now because I have a sense of obligation to the people in it.				.85				.85	
Ncommitment6 I owe a great deal to my organization.				.91				.96	
Continuance Commitment									.95

(Continued)

Table 1. Continued.

Factors and variables	Factor components and loading							Reliability	
	1	2	3	4	5	6	7	CITC	α
Ccommitment1 Right now, staying with my organization is a matter of necessity as much as desire.			.85					.81	
Ccommitment2 It would be very hard for me to leave my organization right now, even if I wanted to.			.83					.87	
Ccommitment3 Too much of my life would be disrupted if I decided I wanted to leave my organization now.			.84					.82	
Ccommitment4 I feel that I have too few options to consider leaving this organization.			.85					.90	
Ccommitment5 If I had not already put so much of myself into this organization, I might consider working elsewhere.			.91					.80	
Ccommitment6 One of the few negative consequences of leaving this organization would be the scarcity of available alternatives			.70					.85	
Turnover Intention									.74
Turnover1 I often think about leaving that hotel							.70	.61	
Turnover2 It would not take much to make me leave this hotel							.69	.61	
Turnover3 I will probably be looking for another job in the same career (in Egypt) soon							.86	.64	
Turnover4 I will probably be looking for another job in the different career (in Egypt) soon							.87	.65	
Turnover5 I will probably be looking for another job (outside Egypt) soon							.91	.67	
% of cumulative variance	18.07	32.93	46.80	60.05	70.00	78.09	81.12		

Note: Kaiser–Meyer–Olkin (KMO) Measure Sampling Adequacy = 0.887; Bartlett test of sphericity = 21133.831 with df295; Bartlett test, significance = .000. CITC, Corrected Item-Total Correlation; α = Cronbach's alpha.

suggested relationships among research variables: job insecurity, trust, organization commitment and turnover intention.

An inspection of the path coefficients and its related P-value of the model's variables reveals four negative and significant paths coefficients as well as two positive and significant path coefficients (see Figure 1). More specifically, job insecurity was negatively and significantly related to trust (path coefficients = −0.17, $P < .05$); and organization commitment (path coefficient = −0.26, $P < .05$). This result supports H3 and H1. Furthermore, trust was found to have a negative and significant relationship with turnover intention (path coefficient = −0.24, $P < .05$). Similarly, the model results indicate that organization commitment has a negative and significant relationship with the turnover intention (path coefficient = −0.19, $P < .05$).

While the study results show two positive and significant relationships as follow: job insecurity has a positive significant relationship with turnover intention (path coefficient = 0.64, $P < .001$), and trust has a positive significant relationship with the organization commitment (path coefficient = 0.36, $P < .001$) (Figure 2).

Discussion

We investigated the relationships between perception of job insecurity and work attitudes (i.e. trust, organizational commitment and turnover intention) among survivors in

15

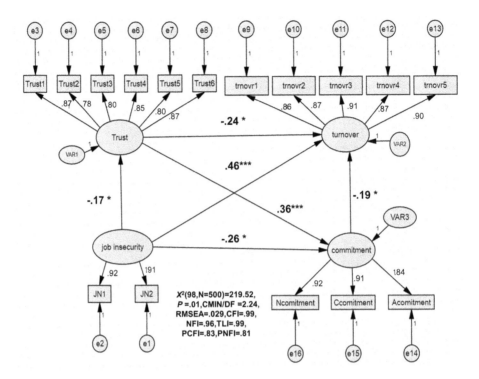

Figure 2. Structural and measurement model. Trust1–Trust6: Measures of trust dimensions; Trnovr1–Trnovr5: Measures of turnover intention dimension; JN1: Quantitative job insecurity variables as a composite average score; JN2: Qualitative job insecurity variables as a composite average score; Ncomitment: Normative Commitment variables as a composite average score; Ccomitment: Continuance Commitment variables as a composite average score; Acomitment: Affective Commitment variables as a composite average score; ***Correlation is significant at the .00 level; **Correlation is significant at the .01 level; *Correlation is significant at the .05 level.

downsized hotels and tourism organizations. The study was conducted in a tourism destination that is seen as politically unstable; Egypt.

The study hypotheses (H1 and H4) received support as we found strong negative relationships between survivors' perception of job insecurity and two variables; survivors' trust in the organization and organizational commitment. Our results suggest that feelings of uncertainties accompanying the period of the political unrest in Egypt, in addition to conducting downsizing strategies in hotels and tourism organizations, incremented the feelings of job insecurity among survivors. The relations found between job insecurity and such survivors' attitudes provide support for past studies (Armstrong-Stassen, 2002, 2004; Brockner, 1988; Hopkins & Weathington, 2006; Spreitzer & Mishra, 2002) indicating the negative consequences of the insecure job situation. Survivors with negative work attitudes cannot reverse the financial decline and make the organization more profitable and effective (Brockner et al., 1995).

Consistent with previous studies (Cheng & Chan, 2008; Greenhalgh & Rosenblatt, 1984; Krausz et al., 1999), the results support H2 which suggests the positive relation between job insecurity and turnover intentions. Such significant relation has an important influence on the inefficiency of the downsizing strategy. Dekker and Schaufeli (1995) suggested that turnover of core and qualified survivors, as a response to feeling job insecurity, is a direct antecedent of low organizational effectiveness. Specifically, qualified and experienced survivors can easily find new jobs and, therefore, are more likely to quit the organization when they experience job insecurity (Cheng & Chan, 2008). In addition, the results indicated that survivors seek for new opportunities not only in their destination but also abroad. Some of them made arrangements to change their entire career to a more stable one in another industry. It seems that survivors gradually lose faith in the ability of the organization to achieve success within continuously unstable political conditions. The movement of qualified survivors to other industries or countries may become a considerable risk for the Egyptian tourism industry.

However, the relationship between job insecurity and turnover intention may not be as clear-cut as previously indicated. The findings show that some work attitudes may buffer the strength of such relation. First, the results support H5 indicating the positive relationship between survivors' perception of trust and commitment in addition to H6 indicating the negative relationship between perception of trust and turnover intention. This implies that though political instability in some destinations, survivors may still have trust in their management. They probably gain the belief that their organization is competent and reliable from their past experiences. Moreover, feelings of trust are more likely to increase when employees perceive HR decisions to be based on fair procedures (Brockner et al., 1995; Hon & Lu, 2010). Mishra and Spreitzer (1998) stated that feelings of trust in management diminish survivors' feelings of threat towards their jobs and, in turn, lead to more positive work reactions. With this in mind, it is not surprising that survivors with high trust in their organization are more committed to it and have less intention to quit even though the political unrest is continuing.

Second, the results support H3 and previous studies (Gilboa et al., 2008; Robinson, 1992; Staufenbiel & König, 2010) indicating the negative relation between commitment and turnover intention. The findings suggest that survivors' emotional attachment to the organization has a great value in lessening their intention to leave the organization after downsizing. Such emotional attachment is derived from survivors' trust in the organization, their acceptance of its goals and plans and their readiness to exert effort for the good of the organization. Therefore, though the uncertain organizational situation, survivors prefer to keep their organizational membership and not to quit.

These results are especially interesting because survivors with feelings of job insecurity are expected to experience negative attitudes towards their organization. However, they may remain with it and work for its good because of the strength of their emotional relation with the organization. Such emotional relation can be explained in terms of survivors' trust in the organization and commitment to it. The area of work attitudes that may moderate the negative consequences of job insecurity represents rich directions for further research.

Conclusion

Although the impact of political instability on tourism destinations is fairly well documented, research on the influence of such phenomena on employees' attitudes in tourism and hospitality industry is surprisingly lacking. Using Egypt as a case study of unstable tourism destination and adapting a quantitative methodology, this study explored the influence of survivors' perception of job insecurity on their attitudes (i.e. trust, commitment and turn-over intention) within downsized hotels and tourism companies.

Based on data gathered from 500 survivors, the model of relationships between job insecurity and outcomes suggests some of the organizational costs job insecurity may bring. These costs concern the psychological attachment bond between survivors and their organizations. Job insecurity is associated with declines in trust and commitment, and increase in turnover intentions. Such harmful relationships are expected to adversely influence the organizational effectiveness after the downsizing period. However, the significant positive relationships found between trust, commitment and low turnover intention may weaken the strength of the negative outcomes of job insecurity. Future research should examine such relationships as this may represent a significant step in the area of the organizational effectiveness within periods of instability.

In addition to the theoretical results, the study also proposes some practical implications for managers in the tourism and hospitality field. The results suggest that for decision-makers, being perceived as trustworthy has an important influence on diminishing negative survivors' attitudes (i.e. low commitment and high intentions to quit) in the workplace. Managers are responsible for many practices that make individuals gain faith in their organization (Dirks & Ferrin, 2002; Hon & Lu, 2010). For example, the fairness of performance evaluations, guidance and assistance with work assignments and sharing information on the progress done within the organization are impressive HR practices (Saad, 2013). Their conduct can develop positive attitudes and behaviors among survivors which can, in turn, benefit the manager and, finally, the organization as a whole.

It is also important, for managers, to understand possible changes in survivors' every-day work interactions and their effect on the organizational goals. This may guide managers to the need to change or develop current HR practices or programs to suit survivors' new attitudes and behaviors at work. Direct supervisors can provide the management with insights related to employees' attitudes because of their involvement in the daily work life (Saad, 2013). Maintaining survivors' feeling of safe and trust in the management through suitable HR practices (e.g. training programs and participation in decision-making) probably creates positive attitudes towards their organization. When employees believe that their organization is trustworthy, they are likely to be more committed to their work, more receptive to new ideas, more willing to follow tough decisions and less intending to quit. Securing survivors' trust in the organization may help in ensuring consequent positive responses of them, avoiding the critical risk of losing the core employees, and protecting the future of the organization.

Disclosure statement

No potential conflict of interest was reported by the authors.

References

Armstrong-Stassen, M. (2002). Designated redundant but escaping lay-off: A special group of lay-off survivors. *Journal of Occupational and Organizational Psychology, 75*(1), 1–13.

Armstrong-Stassen, M. (2004). The influence of prior commitment on the reactions of layoff survivors to organizational downsizing. *Journal of Occupational Health Psychology, 9*, 46–60.

Armstrong-Stassen, M. (2006). Determinants of how managers cope with organizational downsizing. *Applied Psychology: An International Review, 55*, 1–26.

Aryee, S., Budhwar, P., & Chen, Z. (2002). Trust as a mediator of the relationship between organizational justice and work outcomes: Test of a social exchange model. *Journal of Organizational Behavior, 23*, 267–285.

Ashford, S., Lee, C., & Bobko, P. (1989). Content, cause, and consequences of job insecurity: A theory-based measure and substantive test. *Academy of Management Journal, 32*(4), 803–829.

Bartram, T., & Casimir, G. (2007). The relationship between leadership and follower in-role performance and satisfaction with the leader: The mediating effects of empowerment and trust in the leader. *Leadership & Organization Development Journal, 28*(1), 4–19.

Brockner, J. (1988). The effects of work layoffs on survivors: Research, theory, and practice. In B. M. Staw & L. L. Cummings (Eds.), *Research in organizational behavior* (pp. 213–255). Greenwich: JAI Press.

Brockner, J., Wiesenfeld, B., & Martin, C. (1995). Decision frame, procedural justice, and survivors' reactions to job layoffs. *Organizational Behavior and Human Decision Process, 63*, 59–68.

Brown, N. (2015). The transition: From Mubarak's fall to the 2014 presidential election. *Adelphi Series, 55*(453–454), 15–32.

Brown, R. (1996). Organisational commitment: Clarifying the concept and simplifying the existing construct typology. *Journal of Vocational Behaviour, 49*, 230–251.

Byrne, B. (2010). *Structural equation modelling: Basic concepts, applications, and programming.* London: Lawrence Erlbaum Associates.

Cheng, G. H. L., & Chan, D. K. S. (2008). Who suffers more from job insecurity? A meta-analytic review. *Applied Psychology, 57*(2), 272–303.

Chiang, C. F., & Wang, Y. Y. (2012). The effects of transactional and transformational leadership on organizational commitment in hotels: The mediating effect of trust. *Journal of Hotel & Business Management, 1*(103). doi:10.4172/2169-0286.1000103

Chipunza, C., & Berry, D. (2010). The relationship among survivor qualities-attitude, commitment and motivation-after downsizing. *African Journal of Business Management, 4*(5), 604–613.

Clark, R. A., Hartline, M. D., & Jones, K. C. (2009). The effects of leadership style on hotel employees' commitment to service quality. *Cornell Hospitality Quarterly, 50*(2), 209–231.

Crotti, R., & Misrahi, T. (2015). *The travel & tourism competitiveness report 2015.* Geneva: The World Economic Forum.

Darity, E. (2008). *Indices of political instability* (2nd ed.). Detroit, MI: Macmillan Reference.

Davy, J., Kinicki, A., & Scheck, C. (1997). A test of job security's direct and mediated effects on withdrawal cognitions. *Journal of Organizational Behavior, 18*, 323–349.

De Witte, H., De Cuyper, N., Handaja, Y., Sverke, M., Näswall, K., & Hellgren, J. (2010). Associations between quantitative and qualitative job insecurity and well-being: A test in Belgian banks. *International Studies of Management & Organization, 40*(1), 40–56.

Dekker, S., & Schaufeli, W. (1995). The effect of job insecurity on psychological health and withdrawal: A longitudinal study. *Australian Psychologist, 30*, 57–63.

Deluga, R. J. (1994). Supervisor trust building, leader-member exchange and organizational citizenship behavior. *Journal of Occupational and Organizational Psychology, 67*, 315–326.

Dirks, K., & Ferrin, D. (2002). Trust in leadership: Meta-analytic findings and implications for research and practice. *Journal of Applied Psychology, 87*(4), 611–628.

Egyptian Center for Economic Studies. (2016). *Egypt's economic profile and statistics*. Retrieved from http://www.eces.org.eg/Publication.aspx?Id=605&Type=7

Field, A. (2006). *Discovering statistics using SPSS* (2nd ed.). London: Sage.

Gilboa, S., Shirom, A., Fried, Y., & Cooper, C. (2008). A meta-analysis of work demand stressors and job performance: Examining main and moderating effects. *Personnel Psychology, 61*(2), 227–271.

Greenhalgh, L., & Rosenblatt, Z. (1984). Job insecurity: Toward conceptual clarity. *Academy of Management Review, 9*(3), 438–448.

Hair, J., Black, B., Babin, B., Ralph, A., & Ronald, T. (2006). *Multivariate data analysis* (6th ed.). London: Prentice-Hall.

Hartley, J., Jacobson, D., Klandermans, B., & van Vuuren, T. (1991). *Job insecurity: Coping with jobs at risk*. London: Sage.

Heaney, C., Israel, B., & House, J. (1994). Chronic job insecurity among automobile workers: Effects on job satisfaction and health. *Social Science & Medicine, 38*, 1431–37.

Hellgren, J., Sverke, M., & Isaksson, K. (1999). A two-dimensional approach to job insecurity: Consequences for employee attitudes and well-being. *European Journal of Work and Organization Psychology, 8*, 179–195.

Hon, A., & Lu, L. (2010). The mediating role of trust between expatriate procedural justice and employee outcomes in Chinese hotel industry. *International Journal of Hospitality Management, 29*(4), 669–676.

Hopkins, S., & Weathington, B. (2006). The relationships between justice perceptions, trust, and employee attitudes in a downsized organization. *The Journal of Psychology, 140*(5), 477–498.

Information and Decision Support Centre. (2014). *Egypt on the map of world tourism*. Retrieved from http://www.idsc.gov.eg/IDSC/Publication/View.aspx?ID=1399

Issa, I., & Altinay, L. (2006). Impacts of political instability on tourism planning and development: The case of Lebanon. *Tourism Economics, 12*(3), 361–381.

Jung, D., & Avolio, B. (2000). Opening the black box: An experimental investigation of the mediating effects of trust and value congruence on transformational and transactional leadership. *Journal of Organizational Behavior, 21*(8), 949–964.

Karatepe, O. (2009). An investigation of the joint effects of organizational tenure and supervisor support on work-family conflict and turnover intentions. *Journal of Hospitality and Tourism Management, 16*, 73–81.

Kickul, J., Lester, S., & Finkl, J. (2002). Promise breaking during radical organizational change: Do justice interventions make a difference? *Journal of Organizational Behavior, 23*, 469–488.

Kim, W., & Brymer, R. (2011). The effects of ethical leadership on manager job satisfaction, commitment, behavioral outcomes, and firm performance. *International Journal of Hospitality Management, 30*(4), 1020–1026.

Kinnie, N., Hutchinson, S., & Purcell, J. (1998). Downsizing: Is it always lean and mean? *Personnel Review, 27*(4), 296–311.

Krausz, M., Yaakobovitz, N., Bizman, A., & Caspi, T. (1999). Evaluation of coworker turnover outcomes and its impact on the intention to leave of the remaining employees. *Journal of Business and Psychology, 14*, 95–107.

Låstad, L., Berntson, E., Näswall, K., Lindfors, P., & Sverke, M. (2015). Measuring quantitative and qualitative aspects of the job insecurity climate: Scale validation. *Career Development International, 20*(3), 202–217.

Mauno, S., Leskinen, E., & Kinnunen, U. (2001). Multi-wave, multi-variable models of job insecurity: Applying different scales in studying the stability of job insecurity. *Journal of Organizational Behavior, 22*, 919–937.

Mayer, R., Davis, J., & Schoorman, F. (1995). An integrative model of organizational trust. *Academy of Management Review, 20*, 709–734.

McAllister, D. (1995). Affect- and cognition-based trust as foundation for interpersonal cooperation in organizations. *Academy of Management Journal, 38*, 24–59.

Meyer, J., & Allen, N. (1991). A three-component conceptualization of organizational commitment. *Human Resource Management Review, 1*, 61–89.

Meyer, J., Allen, N., & Smith, C. (1993). Commitment to organizations and occupations: Extension and test of a three-component conceptualization. *Journal of Applied Psychology, 78*(4), 538–551.

Middle East Monitor. (2015). *Russia, Britain evacuate stranded tourists from Egypt.* Retrieved from https://www.middleeastmonitor.com/20151111-russia-britain-evacuate-stranded-tourists-from-egypt/

Mishra, A., & Spreitzer, G. (1998). Explaining how survivors respond to downsizing: The roles of trust, empowerment, justice, and work redesign. *Academy of Management Review, 23*(3), 567–588.

Mohammad, A. A. A., Jones, E., Dawood, A. A. A., & Sayed, H. A. (2012). The impact of the Egyptian political events during 2011 on hotel occupancy in Cairo. *Journal of Tourism Research and Hospitality, 1*(3). doi:10.4172/2324-8807.1000102

Mowday, R., Steers, R., & Porter, L. (1979). The measurement of organizational commitment. *Journal of Vocational Behavior, 14*(2), 224–247.

Nassar, M. (2012). Political unrest costs Egyptian tourism dearly: An ethnographical study. *International Business Research, 5*(10), 166–174.

Nunnally, J., & Bernstein, I. (1994). *Psychometric theory* (3rd ed.). New York: McGraw-Hill.

Podsakoff, P., MacKenzie, S., Moorman, R., & Fetter, R. (1990). Transformational leader behaviors and their effects on followers' trust in leader, satisfaction, and organizational citizenship behavior. *The Leadership Quarterly, 1*(2), 107–142.

Rich, G. (1997). The sales manager as a role model: Effects on trust, job satisfaction, and performance of sales people. *Journal of the Academy of Marketing Science, 25*(4), 319–328.

Robinson, S. (1992). *Retreat, voice, silence, and destruction: A typology of behavioral responses to organizational dissatisfaction and an examination of their contextual predictors* (Unpublished doctoral dissertation). North-western University, Evanston, IL.

Robinson, S. (1996). Trust and breach of the psychological contract. *Administrative Science Quarterly, 41*, 574–600.

Roskies, E., & Louis-Guerin, C. (1990). Job insecurity in managers: Antecedents and consequences. *Journal of Organizational Behavior, 11*, 345–359.

Saad, S. (2013). Contemporary challenges of human resource planning in tourism and hospitality organizations: A conceptual model. *Journal of Human Resources in Hospitality & Tourism, 12*(4), 333–354.

Salanick, G. (1977). Commitment and control of organizational behavior. In G. Salanick (Ed.), *New directions in organizational behavior* (pp. 1–54). Chicago, IL: Sr. Clair Press.

Schumacker, R., & Lomax, R. (2010). *A beginner's guide to structural equation modelling.* London: The University of Alabama.

Sjöberg, A., & Sverke, M. (2000). The interactive effect of job involvement and organizational commitment on job turnover revisited: A note on the mediating role of turnover intention. *Scandinavian Journal of Psychology, 41*, 247–252.

Somers, M. (1995). Organizational commitment, turnover and absenteeism: An examination of direct and interaction effects. *Journal of Organizational Behavior, 16*(1), 49–58.

Sönmez, S. (1998). Tourism, terrorism, and political instability. *Annals of Tourism Research, 25*(2), 416–456.

Spreitzer, G., & Mishra, A. (2002). To stay or to go: Voluntary survivor turnover following an organizational downsizing. *Journal of Organizational Behavior, 23*, 707–729.

Stacher, J. (2015). Once upon a revolution: An Egyptian story by Thanassis Cambanis (review). *The Middle East Journal, 69*(3), 474–475.

State Information System. (2016). *Tourism conclusion* 2015. Retrieved from http://www.sis.gov.eg/Ar/Templates/Articles/tmpArticles.aspx?ArtID=116425#.V3BuxtJ97rc

Staufenbiel, T., & König, C. (2010). A model for the effects of job insecurity on performance, turnover intention, and absenteeism. *Journal of Occupational and Organizational Psychology, 83*(1), 101–117.

Staw, B. (1977). *Two sides of commitment.* The annual meeting of the Academy of Management, Orlando, FL.

Sverke, M., & Hellgren, J. (2002). The nature of job insecurity: Understanding employment uncertainty on the brink of a new millennium. *Applied Psychology: An International Review, 51*, 23–42.

Tabachnick, B., & Fidell, L. (2007). *Using multivariate statistics* (5th ed.). New York, NY: Pearson Education.

Thurstone, L. (1947). *Multiple factor analysis.* Chicago, IL: University of Chicago Press.

Zhu, W., Newman, A., Miao, Q., & Hooke, A. (2013). Revisiting the mediating role of trust in transformational leadership effects: Do different types of trust make a difference? *The Leadership Quarterly, 24*(1), 94–105.

Addressing travel writers' role as risk brokers: the case of Jordan

Suleiman A. D. Farajat, Bingjie Liu and Lori Pennington-Gray

ABSTRACT

Recent international events such as Brussels bombing and the terrorist attacks in Paris have stressed the importance of issues related to terrorism, personal safety, and instability on tourism. Jordan, as a major tourism destination in the Middle East, is relatively safe. However, its tourism industry has been negatively impacted by the political instability and the constant occurrence of on-going geopolitical crises in the Middle East region. One of the main strategies to respond to this challenge is to invite western travel writers to experience Jordan and to promote the destination via travel articles. Thus, using Jordan as the case, the purpose of this study was to examine the representation of Jordan as a travel destination within travel media and to discuss travel writers' roles as risk brokers during unstable times. A qualitative framing analysis was conducted on travel feature articles published in five national newspapers from five countries (US, Canada, UK, New Zealand, and Australia) over a 10-year period. Results of the analysis revealed that Jordan was framed as a typical heritage tourism destination, with natural and cultural resources featured. Findings further revealed that safety emerges as one of the major issues that contemporary travel articles were concerned about. Based on the findings, travel writers' role as risk brokers was addressed. The article also discussed the importance for tourism policy-makers to emphasize risk management during unstable times.

RESUMEN

Recientes acontecimientos internacionales, tales como las bombas de Bruselas y los ataques terroristas en París, han destacado la importancia de los asuntos relacionados con el terrorismo, la seguridad personal y la inestabilidad en el turismo. Jordania, como destino turístico muy importante de Oriente Medio, es relativamente seguro. Sin embargo, su industria turística se ha visto negativamente afectada por la inestabilidad política y la constante sucesión de crisis geopolíticas en la región de Oriente Medio. Una de las principales estrategias para responder a este desafío es invitar a escritores occidentales a experimentar Jordania y promover el destino a través de artículos de viajes. Así, utilizando Jordania como caso, el propósito de este estudio era examinar la representación de Jordania como destino en los medios de viaje y discutir los roles de los escritores de viajes como brokers de riesgo en tiempos de inestabilidad. Se empleó un análisis *framing* (análisis de encuadre) cualitativo en artículos de fondo sobre viajes publicados en cinco periódicos nacionales de cinco países (EE.UU. de América, Canadá, Reino Unido, Nueva Zelanda y Australia) en un periodo temporal de 10 años. Los resultados del análisis revelaron que Jordania era enmarcada como un destino típico de turismo patrimonial, provisto de recursos naturales y culturales. Los resultados además revelaban que la seguridad emerge como uno de los asuntos clave sobre los que mostraban preocupación los artículos de viaje contemporáneos. Basándose en los resultados, se aborda el rol de los escritores de viajes como brokers de riesgo. El artículo también discute la importancia para los responsables políticos del turismo de enfatizar la gestión de riegos durante tiempos inestables.

RÉSUMÉ

Les récents événements internationaux tels que les bombardements à Bruxelles et les attaques terroristes à Paris ont souligné l'importance des problèmes liés au terrorisme, à la sécurité personnelle, et de l'instabilité sur le tourisme. La Jordanie, en tant que destination touristique majeure au Moyen-Orient, est plus ou moins en sécurité. Cependant, l'industrie du tourisme y a été affectée négativement suite à l'instabilité politique et à la recrudescence des crises géopolitiques dans la région du Moyen-Orient. L'une des principales stratégies pour faire face à ce défi est d'inviter des écrivains de voyage occidentaux pour vivre l'expérience jordanienne en vue de promouvoir la destination à travers les récits de voyage. Ainsi, en utilisant la Jordanie comme étude de cas, le but de cette étude était d'examiner la représentation de la Jordanie comme destination dans les récits de voyage et de discuter du rôle des écrivains de voyage entant qu'analystes fiables des risques pendant les périodes d'instabilité. Un cadre d'analyze qualitative a été mené sur des articles à caractère de Voyage et publiés dans cinq journaux nationaux de cinq pays (les EUA, le Canada, le Royaume-Uni, la Nouvelle-Zélande et l'Australie) sur une période de dix ans. Les résultats de l'analyse ont révélé que la Jordanie est perçue comme une destination au patrimoine touristique typique, exhibant des ressources naturelles et culturelles. Les résultats ont également révélé que la sécurité apparaît comme l'un des principaux problèmes dont les récits de voyage contemporains se préoccupent. Sur base des résultats, on s'aperçoit que le rôle des écrivains de voyage en tant qu'analystes objectifs des risques a été confirmé. L'article a également discuté de l'importance du fait que les concepteurs des politiques du tourisme devraient considérer comme priorité la gestion du risque pendant les périodes d'instabilité.

摘要

近来类似布鲁塞尔爆炸、巴黎恐怖袭击的国际事件强调了有关恐怖主义、个人安全和旅游不稳定性等问题的重要性。约旦，作为一个中东主要的旅游目的地是相对安全的。但是，当地的旅游业受到政治不稳定和中东地区经常发生的地理政治冲突的消极影响。一个主要应对策略是邀请西方旅行作家去约旦旅行，感受当地的情况，并通过旅行文章推广当地。因此，以约旦为例，这个研究的目的是审视约旦作为一个旅游目的地是如何在旅游媒体中予以表征的，讨论旅游作家在这样一个不稳定时期作为危机代理的角色。定性的架构分析法被用来分析五个国家（美国、加拿大、新西兰和澳大利亚）的国家报纸中与旅游相关的文章。分析的结果揭示约旦被打造为一个典型的遗产旅游目的地，其特色是拥有自然和文化资源。研究结果进一步说明了安全问题是现代旅游文章关注的一个主要问题。基于这样的研究结果，文章阐释了旅游作家作为危机代理的角色。这篇文章也讨论了旅游政策制订者在不稳定时期强调危机管理的重要性。

Introduction

The tourism industry is one of the most important industries around the globe. However, recent international events such as the Brussels bombing, the terrorist attack in Paris, and the airport attack in Turkey, have stressed the importance of issues related to terrorism, personal safety, and/or instability on tourism. In response to these challenges, there has been an increasing number of Destination Management Organizations (DMO) and tourism policy leaders attempt to use different media strategies to promote their destinations during unstable times (Avraham, 2013; Hall, 2002).

Travel writers and their articles is one of the popular means for destination to promote themselves during/after crises (Milo & Yoder, 1991). Travel writers share stories about destinations, which in turn provide information about specific destinations for potential tourists. Oftentimes these stories aid in creating an image of a place, and this image is part of the decision-making criteria tourists use to evaluate whether traveling to a destination is reasonable or not (Rozier-Rich & Santos, 2011). The image created by the travel narrative plays a critical role in potential traveler's mind regarding the destination. If the destination is portrayed as risky, potential tourists may not elect to travel to that destination. Thus, in reality, a travel writer is in a position of assuming a role as not only a destination promotor but also a risk broker.

When destinations are in crisis or perceived as being unstable, the impact of the travel writer as a risk broker is even greater and more significant. This is mainly due to the fact that tourists rely on the information provided by travel articles to remove their concerns and make informed decisions, and that the positive press surrounding a destination can restore the destination image during unstable times (Avraham, 2013, 2015).

Study background

Jordan best exemplifies the situation where a destination is being affected by an unstable environment. Jordan is a popular destination located within the Middle East region. Within the country, the most important assets are Amman, Petra, the Dead Sea, and other archaeological sites. Tourism is argued to be the second highest earner after the remittances from Jordanians working abroad (*Jordan Times*, 2015). It was estimated that in the year 2014 tourism contributed 14% of Jordan's GDP, which equates to a total of USD 4.4 billion. The tourism sector in Jordan is positioned at the growth phase of the tourism area life cycle, during which stage tourism arrivals are expected to grow tremendously (Samardali-Kakai, 2015). The reality, however, is contradictory. As shown in Figure 1, there had been a strong growth in tourist arrivals between 2005 and 2010, where the number of visitors to Jordan has increased from 2.98 million to 4.20 million,

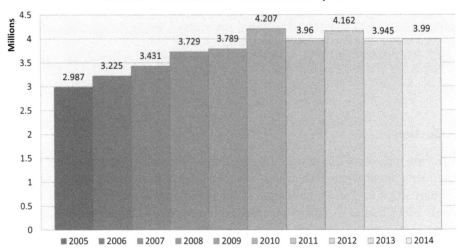

Figure 1. Number of international tourists to Jordan by year.
Source: The Word Bank, 2016, http://data.worldbank.org/

but the number has been fluctuating since then. And Jordan has been losing tourists as well as tourism revenue (*Jordan Times*, 2016).

This is largely due to the geographical location and the unstable environment surrounding Jordan (*Jordan Times*, 2016). Jordan is bordered by Syria and Iraq. The impact of the Islamic State of Iraq and Syria (ISIS) is active in Syria and Iraq (*Daily Mail*, 2015). The unstable condition in these two countries is causing civilians to exit their country and look for refuge in other countries. Due to the geographic proximity, Jordan becomes the major recipient of these refuges. In 2015, Jordan accommodated about 626,357 refugees from Syria and 40,000 refuges from Iraq (RCUSA, 2016).

The long-lasting regional conflicts not only impact the political and social condition of Jordan, but also result in a distorted destination image of Jordan and international tourists' hesitation of visiting the destination (Schroeder, Yilmaz, Liu, Pennington-Gray, & Farajat, 2015). A report published in 1999 revealed that US tourists possessed a positive image towards Jordan (Schneider & Sönmez, 1999). However, more recently a study by Schroeder et al. (2015) found that many US tourists now tend to perceive Jordan as an unsafe destination. Additionally, most US potential tourists express that they will avoid Jordan as a potential destination to travel to (Schroeder et al., 2015). Likewise Liu, Schroeder, and Pennington-Gray (2016) found that under the influences of high risk perception in relation to terrorism, safety concerns become one of the barriers affecting tourists' visitation to Jordan.

With the goal of promoting the destination during special times and remedy a prolonged destination negative image, Avraham and Ketter (2008, 2013) suggest destinations should employ appropriate media strategies. Specifically, the strategy should focus on three aspects: (1) the source of the message (media), (2) the message itself (content), and (3) the target audience (Avraham & Ketter, 2013, p. 149).

Accordingly, in response to the challenge posted by the unstable times, the Jordan Tourism Board (JTB) used travel writers to reach the global market and attract attention from potential travelers (*Travel News Digest*, 2016). Over the past five years, JTB has invited travel writers to visit and write about Jordan on numerous occasions. Travel writers come as part of FAM trips (familiarization trips) and are shown all aspects of the Jordan travel product. It is believed that these ongoing relations can help generate honest and accurate messages, which are the key to maintaining a positive destination image of Jordan during turbulent times. Despite these efforts, the key question, which relates to the image of Jordan framed by travel writers over years, remains unanswered. Thus, by conducting a qualitative framing analysis, the purpose of this study is to explore the destination image of Jordan as framed by travel writers in the major newspapers within the English-Speaking Western markets. In doing so, this study aimed at providing implications for destinations in light of managing destination during unstable times.

Conceptual background

Travel journalism: the new role of travel writer as a risk broker

Travel articles are defined as 'narratives primarily concerned with providing instruction and interpretation of recent travel experiences [which are] written in a non-fictional narrative story from a first-person account and published in regional and national newspapers and magazine' (Rozier-Rich & Santos, 2011, p. 2). Unlike regular news, which tends to be objective, editorial independent, and public relevant, travel articles are normally built upon personal experience and are closely related to advertising (Cocking, 2009; Fürsich, 2002). Newspaper is one of the traditional sources to deliver travel articles (Shaw & Williams, 1995). Normally, the publisher has the message crafted and delivered by paid travel writers, with the goal of introducing and promoting a specific destination.

In spite of the advertising nature, most readers value travel writers' opinions (Rozer-Rich & Santos, 2011; Shaw & Williams, 1995). Tourists' experiences encompass three stages: (1) pre-trip; (2) on-site; and (3) post-trip (Pennington-Gray, Reisinger, Kim, & Thapa, 2005). Throughout these stages, tourists obtain information and knowledge from different sources and integrate them into their travel experiences (Pennington-Gray et al., 2005). Most interactions between tourists' experiences and travel writers take place in the pre-trip stage, where potential travelers read stories on destinations they are considering visiting.

Travel articles have long been used as a way to promote a destination, since it can create the awareness among prospective tourists, offer destination-related information, and improve the publicity of a destination (Loda, Norman, & Backman, 2005). While for destinations, one of the benefits of maintaining a positive relationship with the media is that the destination can work with media personnel to incorporate not only basic information about the destination, but also educational information for the readers. This is especially useful for destinations that are currently or have been impacted by prolonged crises. As suggested by Avraham and Ketter (2013), in order to remedy the negative image of a destination, the messages need to be specific to the issue and deal with the problem directly.

The foci of travel articles may vary by destination, while safety and security is one of the most prominent concerns for both travel writers and prospective tourists (Xiao & Mair, 2006). This holds especially true for destinations like Jordan, whose tourism industry is under the impact of instability. Therefore, contemporary travel writers can undertake the role as a 'risk broker,' who shares information on risk, safety and measures the destination has undertaken to ensure the safety of their 'guests.' However, the concept of travel writers' role as 'risk brokers' is relatively new and remains underexplored within the field of tourism and travel.

Framing analysis in tourism management

Framing analysis is a common research method used to conduct textual analysis of media narratives (Santos, 2005). Unlike content analysis, which mainly focuses on manifest texts, framing analysis attempts to identify the general narrative characteristic and themes in media discourses (Santos, 2005; Stepchenkova, Kirilenko, & Morrison, 2009). It is believed that exploring media frames can allow us 'to advance the conceptual and theoretical discussions regarding tourism narratives production practices and reveal the embedded socio-cultural components of tourism marketing' (Santos, 2005, p. 149).

Framing analysis has been used by a growing body of researchers in tourism management, exploring the media frames surrounding destination attributes (e.g. Liu & Pennington-Gray, 2015), revealing emerging issues, as well as examining the interactions between media discourse and tourism practices (e.g. Santos, 2005). One preliminary theme in this research stream is to explore the image of tourism destinations as framed in mass media. For example, Santos (2005) had analyzed travel news articles from US newspapers and identified two major frames representing the image of Portugal as a tourist destination. Likewise, Hamid-Turksoy, Kuipers, and Van Zoonen (2014) have revealed frames in British news coverage surrounding Turkey as a tourist destination.

With the frequent use of framing analysis in the field of tourism management, contemporary scholars point out that, future research in this area should move towards a new direction, where emphasizes the need to be displayed on 'issue-specific frames related exclusively to a particular topic' (Santos, Tainsky, Schmidt, & Shim, 2013, p. 67). The tourism industry plays an important role in Jordan's economy while the political instability across the region has exerted negative impacts on Jordan's tourism industry. Under such circumstances, understanding media frames surrounding Jordan in travel articles not merely can reveal how different semantic elements of the destination are connected and presented in mass media, but also can offer important managerial recommendations for tourism officials and other relevant organizations within the industry.

Research question

Accordingly, this study set forth the following research questions:

How have traveled writers of major newspapers in the English-speaking Western Markets framed Jordan as a tourism destination in the coverage published in the travel section over the past 10 years? Do they assume a role as a risk broker?

Methods

Research design

The purpose of this study is to understand the media frames surrounding Jordan as a tourism destination during unstable times. Newspapers serve as one of the 'most prominent discursive sites' that enables the researcher to conduct framing analysis and to explore the interaction between media frames, audience perception, and public discourses (D'Angelo & Kuypers, 2010). Specifically, a qualitative framing analysis is employed, given that our goal is to explore the latent content embedded in tourism narratives and to understand the meanings associated with these media messages. Qualitative framing analysis enables researchers to explore fully the underlying meanings of tourism narratives and, therefore, obtain a deeper understanding of the media frames.

Specifically, the thematic framework was developed using a constant comparative method, which is a qualitative analysis technique and allows researchers to discern conceptual similarities as well as to discover patterns (Glaser & Strauss, 1965). The development of major thematic foci was derived from the data while the application of the frames actually followed the practice outlined by previous studies (Santos, 2004). It is believed that the use of contradictory frames (i.e. traditional versus contemporary) can investigate the underlying textual meanings that are beyond the rhetoric, disclose the inherited cultural dimensions, and fully reflect the complexity of the current environment at the destination (Buda, 2015; Santos, 2004).

Data collection

Five newspapers (*The New York Times, The Toronto Star, The Guardian, The New Zealand Herald, and The Sydney Morning Herald*) were selected and news articles published in the travel section were included in the analysis. These five countries (The US, Canada, UK, New Zealand, and Australia) as English-speaking countries are some of Jordan's top source markets (Ministry of Tourism and Antiquities Jordan, 2016), and all the selected newspapers enjoy a large number of leadership in their countries (Lexis Nexis, 2014). Therefore, it is believed that this choice of newspapers can provide an appropriate sample to explore the media frames and to reveal further the representation dynamics surrounding the destination.

The sample was collected as a result of a keyword search of *Lexisnexis® Academic* databases. Using the keyword 'Jordan' appearing in the headline, researchers retrieved the published travel articles. The time frame adopted in this study was between 1 January 2005 and 31 December 2014. We then narrowed our search to feature articles where Jordan was the core story and excluded duplicated news articles. Our final sample consisted of 28 news articles from these 5 newspapers. Although the sample size is small, the selected news articles were deemed appropriate given the representativeness of the regions and the newspaper and the interpretive nature of the analysis.

Data analysis

The coding process followed the constant comparative method, which allows researchers to employ an iterative and inductive approach to developing the thematic framework (Glaser & Strauss, 1965). To analyze the data, one researcher coded all 28 stories independently, while another researcher coded approximately 50% of the articles ($n = 14$) to provide an alternative perspective of the framework. This is an acceptable method of using the secondary researcher for half of the codes according to Creswell (2013). External auditing relies on the assumption that there is a fixed truth which can be accounted for by the researcher and confirmed by an outside auditor. The external auditor was used to foster the accuracy and validity of the research study and findings. This external auditor was also involved with providing feedback to the researcher. Results of the preliminary analyses were used to develop categories representing different aspects of the news stories. Each coding category was exclusive, and one news story might contain several incidents that fit into different categories. Inter-coder reliability was not applicable in such a context, which is due to the interpretive nature of the textual analysis process in this study (Fram, 2013).

Results

Descriptive analysis results

As reported in Table 1, more than one-third of the sample (35.7%, $n = 10$) were published in *The Guardian*, about one-quarter (28.6%, $n = 8$) of the sample were published in the *New Zealand Herald*, and the rest were from the *New York Times* (17.9%, $n = 5$), the *Toronto Star* (10.7%, $n = 3$), and the *Sydney Morning Herald* (7.1%, $n = 2$). The average length of the sample articles was around 770 words. Additionally, very few of the sample articles (14.3%, $n = 4$) were communicated by text only, while the majority (85.7%, $n = 24$) of were accompanied by photographs, offering additional senses of visual enjoyment. Lastly, Figure 2 presents the number of published news articles by year and interestingly, the results indicated that although small, the number of sample news articles was evenly distributed across the time frame.

Results of framing analysis

A framing analysis was conducted to explore the media frames surrounding Jordan and the results are presented in Table 2. The constant comparative method led to a summarization of five common themes: (1) *Wild Jordan*, (2) *Heritage Jordan*, (3) *People*, (4) *Tourism Development*, and (5) *Safety*. And two contradictory frames were utilized to lead the further analysis: (1) *Traditional Frame* and (2) *Contemporary Frame*.

The utilization of these two frames is consistent with previous practices (Santos, 2004) and can reflect the image of Jordan from various angles. Specifically, the traditional frames aim to capture the old-fashioned side of Jordan, revealing its unique heritage resources and the customs and beliefs that have been passed down from generation to generation.

Table 1. Sample characteristics.

Newspaper	Country	Frequency	Percentage
The Guardian	UK	10	35.7
New Zealand Herald	New Zealand	8	28.6
New York Times	USA	5	17.9
Toronto Star	Canada	3	10.7
The Sydney Morning Herald	Australia	2	7.1
Average Length: 770 words			

Format	Frequency	Percentage
Text only	4	14.3
With Photographs	24	85.7

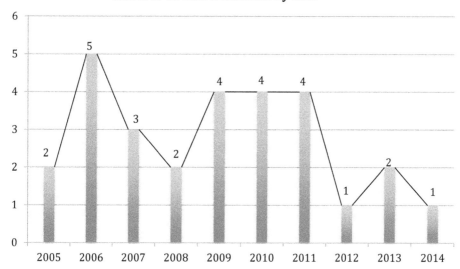

Figure 2. Number of travel news articles by year.

Contemporary frames, on the other hand, attempt to reveal the modern side of Jordan and disclose the transition of Jordan from a historical city to a modernized destination.

Wild Jordan: Jordan is blessed with a diversity of natural resources, which allow Jordan to offer tourists unique sceneries as well as ecotourism opportunities. Via the lenses of traditional frames, most travel articles featured a variety of landscapes in Jordan, such as natural reserves, canyons, mountains, and waterfalls near the Dead Sea, and desert grasslands. As indicated in one article published in *The Guardian*, the writer was amazed by Jordan's 'staggering beauty of the landscape' and, therefore, called Jordan 'the oasis in the desert' and 'the paradise garden.'

Table 2. Results of framing analysis.

Traditional frames	Contemporary frames
Wild Jordan	*Wild Jordan*
Landscape	Ecotourism destination
Scenery	Nature parks
The oasis in the desert	Eco-lodges
The paradise garden	Various nature-based tourist activities
Heritage Jordan	*Heritage Jordan*
UNESCO heritage site	Modernized and popular heritage site
Central to different cultures	Various forms of culture and heritage tourist activities
Architectures	
People	*People*
Friendly local residents	Jordan people want to become modernized
Sex boundaries in the local society	Positive interactions with tour guides
Tourism Development	*Tourism Development*
Tourism as a supporting industry	The government provides continuous support to tourism development
Benefits of tourism development	Conflicts between tourism development and local residents' benefits
	Crisis Impacts on the tourism industry
Safety	
Typical destinations in the Middle East	Relatively safe
	Warmth and welcoming culture

While within a contemporary framework, most travel articles remarked that Jordan is ranked as one of the top ecotourism destinations globally. The dynamics of Jordan's eco-tourism experiences were reflected through (1) the national nature park system, which was regarded as Jordan's best asset and was developed and maintained by the country's Royal Society for the Conservation of Nature (RSCN); (2) the establishments of eco-lodges, which greatly impressed the travel writers as 'local,' 'authentic,' and 'magical'; and (3) various forms of nature-based tourist activities, such as hiking and backpacking in the Jordanian desert and snorkeling, diving, fishing, and spa at the Red sea coast.

Heritage Jordan: Heritage Jordan is another major frame that appeared in selected news articles repeatedly. This was expected given that Jordan is a small country with a rich history and tremendous historic sites. The traditional frames portrayed Jordan as a typical heritage site due to the presence of Petra, a named seven wonder of the ancient world in 2007 as well as a designated UNESCO World Heritage Site since 1985. Besides Petra, many heritage sites in Jordan date from prehistoric times and cover a wide range of cultures, including Nebatean, Roman, Byzantine, Crusader, and Islamic; many of them are considered holy sites for Christians, Muslims, and Jews.

Additionally, the accumulation of culture and history have resulted in distinguished architecture in Jordan, which have been documented by these travel narratives (e.g. Jordan's desert castles, Churches, palaces, and shrines). In one article featured in the *New Zealand Herald*, the journalist said, 'Jordan stunned me with its splendors and its ability to somehow retain its aura of mystery and ancient glory.'

Contemporary frames also addressed the heritage resources of Jordan, but from a modernized perspective. In this context, Jordan was labeled as a popular heritage site that enjoys absolute popularity among modern tourists. One writer commented Petra is 'a rose-red city half as old as time' as well as 'a rose-red city twice as busy as Time Square.' The article further explained that Jordan, as a top attraction in the Middle East 'has gone from being a hard-to-reach World Heritage site that only dedicated travelers ever saw, to an extraordinary popular draw card that puts Jordan on the tourist bus map.' Meanwhile, various forms of modern culture tourism activities were featured, such as the case of new art-themed trips that highlighted the region's ancient cultural heritage, interactions with local art and culture experts and local food, as well as the contemporary art and architecture.

People: People is always an essential element in one's travel experience (Urry, 1990), and therefore, it is not surprising to see that many travel journalists described the people they met or interacted with while in Jordan. Within the traditional framework, some writers might simply say that they were fascinated by the friendliness of the local people while others pointed out that hospitality was embedded within the local culture – 'Hospitality is more than a cup of tea and a mattress in the corner. Their tradition dictates that guests be offered the best – even if that means slaughtering the last horse for food.' And most local residents were 'genuinely glad to have you visit.' Although guests were treated with respect in most cases, some journalists did notice that strict boundaries were maintained between the sexes in Jordan, where women were forbidden to make eye contacts with males, and female workers were less likely hired by local tourism business.

Coming from a different angle, the contemporary frames fully captured local people's desire to become modernized, which was manifested through their changing lifestyles.

As introduced in one article, it was since the 1980s that Jordan people have experienced dramatic changes: 'Before there was no school, no TV, and women had to ask permission to leave the house, now they go to university.' This is an ongoing process, which is due to the government's continuous effort through various projects, the requirements post by the new era, and most importantly, local resident's longings.

Intriguingly, the contemporary frames also highlighted the positive interactions between the travel writer and the tour guide, to whom most journalists attribute the success of the trip. According to their descriptions, these tour guides were local, experienced, and knowledgeable; most of the time they provided detailed and clear explanations of the surroundings, explicated the local culture and traditions, and offered various options of travel plans. Besides the helpfulness, the increasing mention of local guides might partly result from the special condition of Jordan where some areas were sensitive zones, and a visitor was required to have a local guide with them such as the case in Petra and Jerash.

Tourism Development. The tourism industry plays an important role in supporting Jordan's economy. Consistently, the traditional frames tended to address the significance of tourism development for Jordan. For instance, one article from *The Guardian* outlined that, resources such as minerals would soon run out, while tourism, as a sustainable industry, is more viable. In addition, the sample articles discussed the various benefits associated with tourism development, such as the economic income, the employment opportunities, and the support to the development of rural communities.

Although the contemporary frames admired the continuous efforts provided by the government towards tourism development, such as the socio-economic projects and the plans to establish more protected areas and restore deserted villages into facilities; it was noticed that not all communities could benefit directly from these projects. One resident said in the interview 'they take money from tourists and spend it on many things. Not enough money goes to local people.' Lastly, the travel narratives also documented the impacts of recent crises on Jordan's tourism industry. As one article from the *New Zealand Herald* commented, 'the ongoing tension in the region has hurt the tourism-dependent country of six million people.'

Safety: Given the persuasive nature of the travel narratives, negative issues were seldom mentioned. However, safety is a major concern and has frequently been discussed in the media coverage. Safety is a unique topic that has only been mentioned within contemporary frames. Some travel writers, consistent with the general Western media, tended to feature the ongoing conflicts within the region (Avraham, 2015). For example, one article described the landscape of Jordan as 'Yellow grit, the depressing mesh fences of army barracks, and long chains of oil tankers coming in from Saudi Arabia.' Others, interestingly, tried to defend Jordan and portrayed it as a safe destination. For instance, one article published in the *Guardian* addressed that, although protests have been taken places several times in Jordan recently, the demonstrations in Jordan have been very peaceful and in no way compared to other countries in that region. More commonly, travel writers cared about the overall atmosphere rather than safety measures, suggesting that readers should pay attention to the warmth and the welcoming culture of Jordan and consider Jordan thoroughly safe for tourists.

Discussions

Jordan in travel articles

The results of our descriptive analyses showed that when introducing Jordan as a destination, travel writers not merely rely on textual messages, but also include visual demonstrations. Such a combination can create a sense of 'image-scape' and 'experience-scape,' which makes it more appealing to the audience (O'Dell & Billing, 2005; Pan & Ryan, 2009).

In spite of the vivid expressions, we notice that the total number of published articles is relatively small, especially compared with other destinations in the region, such as Turkey, which has attracted approximately 20 designated travel articles every year (Hamid-Turksoy et al., 2014). We also see a small decline in the number of travel articles since 2012, when the Arab Spring had spread through the countries of the Arab League and its surroundings and Jordan's tourism industry had begun experiencing a decline in the number of visitors (*Daily Mail*, 2015). This is in line with previous findings, which signifies the associations between the occurrences of crisis events, the curve of news impact, and the changes in tourism demands (Kim & Wong, 2006).

Framing Jordan as a tourism destination

Our first research question is concerned about the overall destination image of Jordan as framed by the sample articles. As reflected in our results, Jordan is pictured as a typical heritage site, which is characterized by a strong Arabic cultural identity, rich heritage resources and a wide variety of cultural properties. The natural dimension is also featured, including the landscape, the scenery, and the biological diversity. The traditional frames portray Jordan as a static and old nation with diverse natural resources, while the contemporary frames have displayed the dynamic, safe, and energetic aspects of Jordan, whereby the ancient town and modern touristic activities are well intertwined.

Notably, these identified frames are consistent with JTB's marketing campaign, which highlights destination attributes such as History and Culture, Eco and Nature, and Religion and Faith (Jordan Tourism Board, 2016). This demonstrates the effectiveness of JTB's investment in organizing FAM trips and their continuous efforts in creating positive relationship with western travel writers.

Interestingly, the results of our analysis indicate the importance of government during the tourism development process. This is consistent with the tourism literature, which remarks the significance of a supportive government, especially for destinations in the Middle East, which need public investment, pro-tourism policies, and additional marketing efforts (Henderson, 2006). In the early 1990s when Jordan first decided to develop the tourism business, most tourism experts and practitioners agreed that the Jordan government acted as one of the biggest obstacles (Kelly, 1998). Two decades on, the government seems to have undertaken the responsibility and become one of the main forces boosting the development of the tourism industry. This positive transition also underscores the necessity of government's endorsement in long-term crisis management plans, given that Jordan is one of the collateral victims of the Middle East problems and needs extensive and proactive efforts to overcome perceptual barriers in the international market (Beirman, 2002; Henderson, 2006).

Travel writers as risk brokers

Unlike 'hard news,' which is driven by the news value and focuses on political and economic problems, travel journalism is regarded as a type of 'soft news,' which is customer-centered and caters to the interest for specific readerships (Janssen, Verboord, & Kuipers, 2011). During this communication process, travel writers perform as gatekeepers, which filter the places that are worth a visit and provide judgement of taste (Hamid-Turksoy et al., 2014; Hanusch, 2010). Our previous discussions suggest that travel writers can undertake the role of risk brokers by disseminating essential safety information within their articles.

Safety and security is one of the most prominent concerns for prospective tourists (Xiao & Mair, 2006). Travel writers' negative or inaccurate comments may impact the image of the destination, especially for destinations that are culturally different and currently under crisis conditions (Milo & Yoder, 1991; Xiao & Mair, 2006). Consistently, the findings of the current study show that most travel writers display their safety concerns of Jordan within the contemporary framework. The heightened attention to this area is mainly due to the increasing complex sociopolitical environment in Jordan (Buda, 2015). Political instability is one of the most popular news headlines, and the explosion of this type of news content can elevate readers' perceived risk and generate ripple effects, which in turn, affect the entire travel market and the long-term image of the destination (Beirman, 2002).

However, a close examination of our findings reveal that additional efforts are needed to improve travel writers' capacities as risk brokers. Some of the sample articles depict the peaceful environment in Jordan and suggest that the destination is safe in general, but these articles did not provide any specific public safety information for the readers. The findings of a recent study (Liu et al., 2016) showed that prospective tourists' risk perception specific to certain issues (e.g. terrorism) is related to their evaluation of destination-specific safety perceptions. When the level of risk perception is high, prospective tourists especially need safety information to increase their confidence in the destination, remove their concerns, and strength their intentions to visit the destination. This is important for destinations like Jordan, since the majority of readers are not familiar with the destination and have to rely on media as major information resources (Schneider & Sönmez, 1999).

Managerial recommendations

Marketing destinations during unstable times is not an easy task, especially most destinations are reluctant to acknowledge their prolonged negative images (Avraham & Ketter, 2013). In order to overcome such barriers, DMOs and tourism policy leaders need to devise consistent and effective risk/crisis communication campaign (Beirman, 2002; Hall, 2002). Media can influence public opinions and perceptions, and therefore, effective media strategies, can help gradually restore the image of the destination during unstable times (Beirman, 2002; Hall, 2002; Milo & Yoder, 1991). Using Jordan as the case, this study plans to understand how travel media frame Jordan as a destination image and to discuss the potential role of travel writers as 'risk brokers.'

Similar to other destinations in the Middle East, Jordan relies on western travel writers to promote their destination (Avraham, 2015). On one hand, the findings of our study show that the identified frames surrounding Jordan are consistent with JTB's marketing campaign; while on the other hand, the findings of this study indicate that safety, as an important element, has not been fully addressed by the sample articles. Most travel writers who are part of the FAM trips do receive general safety and security information at the JTB's headquarters, but very few of them choose to feature the safety information in their travel articles. The lack of safety information within these travel articles not only limits travel writers' capacities as 'risk brokers,' but also may reinforce the stereotype of Middle East destinations, which are characterized by danger and instability (Avraham, 2015; Liu et al., 2016). Therefore, destinations under the impact of instability should take into account tourists' safety concerns and face the problem directly. Built upon the existing efforts related to FAM trips and travel writers, destinations like Jordan should emphasize risk management and address travel writers' role as 'risk brokers.'

At a practical level, it is essential for the JTB to provide the invited travel writers with timely public safety information and encourage them to share this information in their travel articles. For example, Jordan has employed the Tourism Oriented Policing and Protected Service (TOPPS) program since 2010 and has provided specific training programs for tourism police officers, front-line workers in the tourism industry, and other relevant stakeholders (Arab Turkish Travel Gazette, 2010). Unlike regular police forces, which focus merely on reducing crime rates, TOPPS actually takes into account visitors' interest and undertakes a proactive approach in fighting crime, terrorism activities, and other public safety-related issues (Tarlow, 2014). Thus, creating and sharing travel stories about TOPPS not only can demonstrate how Jordan actively respond to the emerging challenges during unstable times, but also can effectively relieve readers' safety concerns (Liu et al., 2016; Schroeder et al., 2015).

Similarly, the JTB can inform travel writers about the policies Jordan has employed to ensure tourist safety as well as risk reduction behaviors tourists can perform to protect themselves. The safety information can be delivered through multiple forms, such as brochures, factsheets, and websites. Spreading this information can impress the travel writers, as well as display Jordan's open attitude corresponding to emerging challenges.

Additionally, the risk and crisis communication efforts can be extended to the new platform social media. Tactics via social media which demonstrate the safety of the destination should continue to be promoted by both public and private sector in order to mitigate the negative impacts. One of the examples is the recent campaign 'iambassador', which is initiated by the JTB and intends to promote Jordan via disseminating travel writers' comments/impressions of Jordan through social media (*New York Times*, 2013). Built upon this campaign, future programs can maximize the effectiveness of travel writers as 'risk brokers,' focusing on the safety aspects. The goal is to educate prospective tourists about the preventive actions they can engage to against the risk, empower tourists in times of instability, and ultimately, correct the public misperception of Jordan as an unsafe and unstable destination.

Disclosure statement

No potential conflict of interest was reported by the authors.

References

Arab Turkish Travel Gazette. (2010). *JITOA provides specialized training program for Tourist Police.* Retrieved July 18, 2016, from http://www.arabturkishtravel.com

Avraham, E. (2013). Crisis communication, image restoration, and battling stereotypes of terror and wars: Media strategies for attracting tourism to Middle Eastern countries. *American Behavioral Scientist, 57*(9), 1350–1367.

Avraham, E. (2015). Destination image repair during crisis: Attracting tourism during the Arab spring uprisings. *Tourism Management, 47*, 224–232.

Avraham, E., & Ketter, E. (2008). *Media strategies for marketing places in crisis: improving the image of cities, countries, and tourist destinations.* Oxford: Routledge.

Avraham, E., & Ketter, E. (2013). Marketing destinations with prolonged negative images: Towards a theoretical model. *Tourism Geographies, 15*(1), 145–164.

Beirman, D. (2002). Marketing of tourism destinations during a prolonged crisis: Israel and the Middle East. *Journal of Vacation Marketing, 8*(2), 167–176.

Buda, D. M. (2015). Tourism in conflict areas complex entanglements in Jordan. *Journal of Travel Research.* doi:10.1177/0047287515601253

Cocking, B. (2009). Travel journalism: Europe imagining the Middle East. *Journalism Studies, 10*(1), 54–68.

Creswell, J. W. (2013). *Research design: Qualitative, quantitative, and mixed methods approaches.* Thousand Oaks, CA: Sage.

D'Angelo, P., & Kuypers, J. A. (Eds.). (2010). *Doing news framing analysis: Empirical and theoretical perspectives.* New York, NY: Routledge.

Daily Mail. (2015). Ancient Petra sees few visitors as Jordan tourism declines. Retrieved October 28, 2015, from http://www.dailymail.co.uk

Fram, S. M. (2013). *The constant comparative analysis method outside of grounded theory.* Qualitative Report, 18, 1.

Fürsich, E. (2002). How can global journalists represent the 'Other'? A critical assessment of the cultural studies concept for media practice. *Journalism, 3*(1), 57–84.

Glaser, B. G., & Strauss, A. L. (1965). The constant comparative method of qualitative analysis. *Social problems, 12*(4), 436–445.

Hall, C. M. (2002). Travel safety, terrorism and the media: The significance of the issue-attention cycle. *Current Issues in Tourism, 5*(5), 458–466.

Hamid-Turksoy, N., Kuipers, G., & Van Zoonen, L. (2014). "Try a Taste of Turkey": An analysis of Turkey's representation in British newspapers' travel sections. *Journalism Studies, 15*(6), 743–758.

Hanusch, F. (2010). The dimensions of travel journalism: Exploring new fields for journalism research beyond the news. *Journalism Studies, 11*(1), 68–82.

Henderson, J. C. (2006). Tourism in Dubai: Overcoming barriers to destination development. *International Journal of Tourism Research, 8*(2), 87–99.

Janssen, S., Verboord, M., & Kuipers, G. M. M. (2011). Comparing cultural classification. *Kölner Zeitschrift für Soziologie und Sozialpsychologie, 63*(51), 139–168.

Jordan Times. (2015). Urgent plan in the works to 'salvage' tourism sector – minister. Retrieved October 28, 2015, from http://www.jordantimes.com

Jordan Times. (2016). Petra visitors drop by 32% in January. Retrieved July 18, 2016, from http://www.jordantimes.com

Jordan Tourism Board. (2016). *General Information.* Retrieved July 18, 2016, from http://www.visitjordan.com

Kelly, M. (1998). Tourism, not terrorism: The visual politics of presenting Jordan as an international tourist destination. *Visual Anthropology, 11*(3), 191–205.

Kim, S. S., & Wong, K. K. (2006). Effects of news shock on inbound tourist demand volatility in Korea. *Journal of Travel Research, 44*(4), 457–466.

Lexis Nexis. (2014). *Major newspapers.* Retrieved July 18, 2016, from https://www.lexisnexis.com

Liu, B., & Pennington-Gray, L. (2015). Bed bugs bite the hospitality industry? A framing analysis of bed bug news coverage. *Tourism Management, 48*, 33–42.

Liu, B., Schroeder, A., & Pennington-Gray, L. (2016). *Empirically testing the influence of travel safety concerns: Examining alternative models.* Paper presented at the 47th Tourism and Travel Research Association Annual Conference.

Loda, M. D., Norman, W., & Backman, K. (2005). How potential tourists react to mass media marketing: Advertising versus publicity. *Journal of Travel & Tourism Marketing, 18*(3), 63–70.

Milo, K. J., & Yoder, S. L. (1991). Recovery from natural disaster: Travel writers and tourist destinations. *Journal of Travel Research, 30*(1), 36–39.

Ministry of Tourism and Antiquities Jordan. (2016). *Statistics.* Retrieved July 18, 2016, from http://www.mota.gov.jo

New York Times. (2013). Travel blogging today: It's complicated. Retrieved July 18, 2016, from http://www.nytimes.com

O'Dell, T., & Billing, P. (2005). *Experiencescapes: tourism, culture and economy.* Herndon, VA: Copenhagen Business School Press DK.

Pan, S., & Ryan, C. (2009). Tourism sense-making: The role of the sense and travel journalism. *Journal of Travel & Tourism Marketing, 26*(7), 625–639.

Pennington-Gray, L., Reisinger, Y., Kim, J. E., & Thapa, B. (2005). Do US tour operators' brochures educate the tourist on culturally responsible behaviours? A case study for Kenya. *Journal of Vacation Marketing, 11*(3), 265–284.

RCUSA. (2016). *At the breaking point: Refugees in Jordan and Egypt*. A Refugee Council USA Report.

Rozier-Rich, S., & Santos, C. A. (2011). Processing promotional travel narratives. *Tourism Management, 32*(2), 394–405.

Samardali-Kakai, L. (2015). *Obstacles which significantly affect tourism development in Jordan*. Australia: School of Business, Edith Cowan University.

Santos, C. A. (2004). Framing Portugal: representational dynamics. *Annals of Tourism Research, 31* (1), 122–138.

Santos, C. A. (2005). Framing analysis: examining mass mediated tourism narratives. In B. W. Ritchie, P. Burns, & C. Palmer (Eds.), *Tourism research methods* (pp. 149–162). Oxford: CABI Publishing.

Santos, C. A., Tainsky, S., Schmidt, K. A., & Shim, C. (2013). Framing the octagon: An analysis of news-media coverage of mixed martial arts. *IJSC, 6*(1), 66–86.

Schneider, I., & Sönmez, S. (1999). Exploring the touristic image of Jordan. *Tourism Management, 20*(4), 539–542.

Schroeder, A., Yilmaz, S., Liu, B., Pennington-Gray, L., & Farajat, S. A. D. (2015, December 15–19). *Applying the risk-as-feelings hypothesis to tourism: An examination of the influence of perceived comfort and perceived safety on interest in visiting different MENA region destinations*. Paper presented at the 3nd World Research Summit for Tourism and Hospitality.

Shaw, G., & Williams, A. M. (Eds.). (1995). *Tourism and economic development: Western European experiences*. London: Belhaven Press.

Stepchenkova, S., Kirilenko, A. P., & Morrison, A. M. (2009). Facilitating content analysis in tourism research. *Journal of Travel Research, 47*(4), 454–469.

Tarlow, P. (2014). *Tourism security: strategies for effectively managing travel risk and safety*. Oxford: Elsevier.

The World Bank. (2016). International tourism, number of arrivals, Jordan. Retrieved July 18, 2016, from http://data.worldbank.org

Travel News Digest. (2016). Jordan tourism board conducts FAM trip for global media. Retrieved July 18, 2016, from http://www.travelnewsdigest.

Urry, J. (1990). The "consumption" of tourism. *Sociology, 24*(1), 23–35.

Xiao, H., & Mair, H. L. (2006). "A paradox of images" representation of China as a tourist destination. *Journal of Travel & Tourism Marketing, 20*(2), 1–14.

Political instability and trade union practices in Nepalese hotels

Sandeep Basnyat, Brent Lovelock and Neil Carr

ABSTRACT

This paper explores the effects of political instability on trade union practices in the tourism industry by examining how the roles of trade unions alter in relation to changes in the causes of political instability. The data on which this paper is based were collected through unstructured interviews with 22 trade union officials and members employed in hotels in Kathmandu, Nepal from April 2015 to February 2016. The results show that the dominant roles played by the trade unions in the Nepalese tourism industry have changed over the last 25 years from primarily seeking to improve workers' rights and conditions, to being instruments of the political parties, and to protecting the industry. The study contributes to our understanding of the fragility of industrial relations within the tourism industry in Nepal, and how this can be exacerbated in an environment characterized by ongoing instability.

RESUMEN

Este trabajo explora los efectos de la inestabilidad política en la prácticas de los sindicatos en las industria turística examinando cómo los roles en los sindicatos se alteran en relación con los cambios en las causas de la inestabilidad política. Los datos en los que se basa este trabajo fueron recogidos mediante entrevistas no estructuradas con responsables sindicales y miembros empleados en hoteles en Kathmandu, Nepal desde abril 2015 hasta febrero 2016. Los resultados muestran que los roles dominantes que jugaban los sindicatos en la industria turística nepalí han cambiado a lo largo de 25 años desde buscar, principalmente, mejorar los derechos y condiciones de los trabajadores a ser instrumentos de los partidos políticos y a proteger a la industria. Este estudio contribuye a nuestra compresión de la fragilidad de las relaciones industriales dentro de la industria turística en Nepal y cómo esto puede ser exacerbado en un entorno caracterizado por una inestabilidad continuada.

RÉSUMÉ

En examinant les mutations des rôles des syndicats en fonction des facteurs qui sont à la base de l'instabilité politique, cet article explore les effets de l'instabilité politique sur les actions des syndicales dans l'industrie du tourisme. Les données sur lesquelles se base cet article ont été obtenues grâce aux entretiens non structurés menés entre avril 2015 et février 2016 auprès de 22 dirigeants syndicaux et aux syndicalistes employés dans des hôtels à Katmandou au Népal. Les résultats montrent que le rôle primordial des syndicats dans l'industrie du tourisme népalais a connu de grands changements au cours des 25 dernières années, principalement suite aux efforts d'amélioration des droits et des conditions de travail, à la volonté de protection de l'industrie ainsi à la manipulation des syndicats par les partis politiques. Cette étude permet de comprendre la fragilité des relations régissant l'industrie touristique népalaise, et la façon dont cette dynamique relationnelle peut être exacerbée par un environnement opérationnelle caractérisé par d'incessantes instabilités.

摘要
本文通过调查旅游业工会的角色由于政治不稳定导致的变化，探讨政治不稳定对旅游业工会实践的影响。本文所采用的数据来自2015年四月至2016年二月期间，对22位尼泊尔加德满都的工会官员和酒店从业人员的非结构式访谈。结果表明，在尼泊尔旅游业中，工会发挥的主导作用在过去的25年间已经发生改变，从主要寻求改善工人的权利和境况，变成作为政党的工具并保护该行业。这项研究有助于我们了解尼泊尔旅游业内的产业关系的脆弱性，以及它在持续的不稳定环境中如何加剧。

Introduction

This paper explores the effects of political instability on trade union practices in the tourism industry by examining how the roles of trade unions alter in relation to changes in the causes of political instability. Like any other industry, the sustainability of the tourism industry depends upon successful labour–management relations (Lucas, 2004). Trade unions, as representative organizations, advocate and act, in theory, on behalf of employees and assist in managing labour relations (Blyton, Lucio, McGurk, & Turnbull, 2001). However, trade union activities can be influenced by several factors, including their interdependent relationships with political parties and the political condition of the country (Hayward, 1980). Political instability, therefore, has the potential to affect trade unions' practices.

In addition to the struggle for democracy and associated political problems, a myriad of other factors including war, coup d' etats, terrorism, riots, political and social unrest, and general strikes can lead to political instability (Seddighi, Theocharous, & Nuttall, 2002) and potentially affect trade union activities. It is possible that as the sources of political instability change, their effects, individual or collective, on trade union practices may also change. However, existing studies have yet to address this aspect. This paper aims to fill this gap by exploring the effects of political instability on trade union practices in the tourism industry by examining how the roles of trade unions shift in relation to changes in the causes of political instability.

In regard to the tourism and hospitality industry,[1] an important and growing sector in many economies, an important characteristic is that it is very labour intensive (Riley, Ladkin, & Szivas, 2002). Consequently, the effects of political instability on trade union practices may impact the employment conditions of a large number of workers. Political instability can negatively affect the tourism industry in a number of areas ranging from tourist demand to destination management, crisis management, tourism planning and destination marketing (Causevic & Lynch, 2013; Elshaer & Saad, 2016; Ingram, Grieve, Ingram, Tabari, & Watthanakhomprathip, 2013; Som, Aun, & AlBattat, 2015; Sönmez, 1998). Additionally, there is an existing belief that the tourism and hospitality industry is characterized by low wages, poor working conditions, and high levels of seasonal and part-time employment (Zampoukos & Ioannides, 2011). These characteristics may potentially be exacerbated by political instability (Yruela & del Rosal, 1999). Thus, research that can advance our understanding of the roles of unions in politically unstable circumstances may also provide beneficial outcomes for employee well-being and from a sectoral sustainability perspective.

This study is also particularly important in the context of developing Asian countries. In the last two decades, many Asian countries have not only passed through their own internal political turmoil including conflicts and reforms but also have been exposed to the impacts of globalization (Benson & Zhu, 2008). Therefore, there is a need for study of trade union practices in different industries in Asian regions focusing on a variety of political contexts that these countries have experienced. This is even more essential in the context of the tourism and hospitality industry because of the limited research in this sector (Walton, 2012). In addition, research in these settings may also reflect the unique relationships that trade unions have with political parties (Johri, 1967; Ramaswamy, 1969, 1974).

The paper focuses on a study of trade unions in the hotel sector in Nepal, undertaken in Kathmandu, the capital city. Nepal provides a fitting platform for the study because of its experiences of ongoing instability for over 25 years (Upreti, Sharma, Upadhaya, Ghimire, & Iff, 2013). The majority of the hotels in Nepal are situated in Kathmandu, the study site (Ministry of Culture, Tourism and Civil Aviation, Government of Nepal, 2014) which has also been the centre for most of the country's trade union activities (Upreti et al., 2013). For example, Upreti et al. (2013) have argued that a general lack of amicable relationship between managements and trade unions in tourist accommodations has become an inseparable characteristic of the tourism and hospitality industry in Nepal. They noted that economic supremacy of owners and managers of hotels, and the continuing political influence and affiliations of trade unions with political parties as the reasons for the lack of amicable relationships between trade unions and the management. In this context, the next section conceptualizes the role of trade unions in general and in the tourism and hospitality industry in particular, and how their roles are influenced by politics.

Trade unions, politics and tourism

Since Sidney and Beatrice Webb's study *The History of Trade Unionism* identified trade unions as 'a continuous association of wage-earners for the purpose of maintaining or improving the conditions of their working lives' (Webb & Webb, 1920, p. 1), a number of scholars (Allen, 1966; Martin, 1989) have continued to define the roles of trade unions along similar lines. Perlman (1949), for example, introduced the idea of job-conscious unionism and argued that because of the scarcity of jobs, trade unions find opportunities to enrol people into their membership thus affirming the role of trade unions to seeking to establish a form of property rights in jobs.

A more comprehensive approach to understanding the role of trade unions has been prescribed by Hyman (2001) who identifies three models of trade unions; market-oriented, class-oriented and society-oriented. According to Hyman (2001), market-oriented trade unions pursue their goal of improving the well-being of their members through collective bargaining in the labour market. In comparison, class-oriented trade unions focus their attention on improving the welfare of their members through the transformation of society. Finally, society-oriented trade unions pursue their objectives of social reform through social dialogue, operate in democratic contexts, and focus their attention on making employees' voices heard through advocacy and collective bargaining (Hyman, 2001).

Trade union activities are influenced by several factors, and significant among these is their interdependent relationships with political parties (Hayward, 1980). Some scholars have argued that the political party–union relationship is shaped by the party's need to create the broadest electoral base and by the unions' desire to influence all governments, irrespective of the party in power (Ebbinghaus, 1995). Trade union activities are also influenced by the prevailing political conditions (Henry, 2015) and political climate in the country (Cohen, 1990). In Myanmar, for example, the political reforms from 2011 have triggered a rapid growth of legal trade union movements (Henry, 2015). Similarly, research into the impact of political climate on trade union activities in the airline sub-sector of the tourism industry suggests a strong link between political climate and trade union effectiveness (Cohen, 1990). Comparing the Century airline strike of 1932 with the Continental airline strike of 1983–1985 in which the trade union won in the 1930s and lost in 1980s, Cohen argues that despite the similarities between the two strikes, the two outcomes were different because the political climate in the USA favoured trade unionism in the 1930s and opposed it in the 1980s.

Because trade union activities are influenced by their interdependent relationship with political parties, political conditions and political climate, it is reasonable to assume that political instability in a country can correspondingly affect trade union practices. However, this is an area not widely researched, except for a small number of studies which have examined the impacts of democratic movements (Valenzuela, 1989) and political problems (Yruela & del Rosal, 1999) on trade union activities. Valenzuela (1989) examined the consequences of democratic movements and political change on labour management practices and argued that the limitations authoritarian regimes place on the capacities of labour organizations to act in favour of workers' interests lead labour movements to view processes of transition to democracy as singular opportunities to empower their members.

Yruela and del Rosal (1999) argued that trade union relations in Italy tended to reflect the country's political instability. Their study revealed that the instability created by the ideological and political differences among the Christian democrats, social democrats, republicans and communists resulted in the split of the Italian General Federation of Labour (CGIL) into the Italian Confederation of Workers' Trade Unions (CISL), Italian Labour Union (UIL) and CGIL. This split contributed to the inter-union rivalry and sustained political instability.

Although there is a body of literature focused on labour issues in tourism (Baum, 2007, 2008, 2015; Kusluvan, 2003; Ladkin, 2011), relatively little addresses trade unions and their practices (Walton, 2012). Of those works that do, a significant proportion focuses on examining reasons for the low level of unionization in the hospitality industry (Lucas, 2009; Wood, 1997). Some studies have also examined the efforts of trade unions to enhance the working conditions and wages of employees in the tourism industry (e.g. Lloyd, Warhurst, & Dutton, 2013; Waddoups, 2001). For example, Burgess, Connell, and Winterton (2013) have examined the role of trade unions in addressing precarious working conditions and reducing the vulnerability of workers in the hospitality industry. Others have also examined the reasons for industrial disputes in the sector, for example, between airline trade unions and management (e.g. Taylor & Moore, 2014). Studies also exist that have examined employee's (Macaulay & Wood, 1992) and managers' attitudes towards the trade unions (Aslan & Wood, 1993) in Scottish hotels. Additionally, researchers have also explored the role of unions in addressing employee dissatisfaction in the low-cost airline sector (Bamber, Gittell, Kochan, & Von Nordenflycht, 2013). Considering that tourism is an industry that takes place in a broad range of destinations, any one or more of which at any point in time may be subject to various levels of political instability, makes this study apposite. This work will not only contribute to our broad understanding of unions within the tourism sector, but will more specifically enhance our grasp of how political instability impacts union strategies, and thus outcomes for the tourism industry and tourists in such destinations. The next section discusses the causes and impacts of political instability in the tourism industry in Nepal.

Political instability in Nepal and its impact upon tourism

The existing literature points towards democratic movements, the Maoist's insurgency and political disputes as the traditional sources of political instability in Nepal since 1990 (Thapa, 2004). An ongoing border area dispute since September 2015 and an unofficial blockade by India between August 2015 and February 2016 have added to the list. Table 1 lists the most relevant events since 1990 that caused political instability in Nepal.

The first democratic movement against the partyless *Panchayat* system in Nepal started in 1989 and evolved into a full-fledged revolution in 1990 (Basnett, 2009). On 25 April 1990, King Birendra abandoned the *Panchayat* system, established a multiparty democracy, and remained a constitutional monarch (Thapa, 2004). In 1996, the Communist Party of Nepal (CPN-Maoist), one of the political parties in the parliament, went underground and launched a people's war, accusing the Nepali Congress, the Communist Party of Nepal-Unified Marxist-Leninist (CPN-UML) and other political parties of being unable

Table 1. Period and causes of instability in Nepal.

Period of instability	Causes of instability in Nepal
1989–1990	The first democratic movement against the partyless *Panchayat* system
1996–2006	The people's war launched by the underground Communist Party of Nepal (CPN-Maoist)
2002–2006	King Gyanendra's coup d'état and direct rule
2006	The second democratic movement by the political parties and the Maoist rebel against King Gyanendra
2008–2013	Abolition of Monarchy, disputes among the political parties on the inclusion of provisions in the new constitution, failure in drafting new constitution and dissolution of the first constituent assembly
2013	Second constitution assembly election
2015–2016	*Terai* (Nepalese Southern borders) unrest and undeclared blockade of the Nepalese-Indian border by India

to address and resolve pressing economic and social issues of poor and marginalized communities (Basnett, 2009).

In the resultant civil war, more than 15,000 people were killed and 200,000 internally displaced (Upadhayaya, Müller-Böker, & Sharma, 2011). Dissatisfied with the political parties' inability to end the Maoist insurgency, King Gyanendra staged a coup d'état in 2002 and undertook direct rule (Bhandari, 2010). In response to the King's move, the political parties joined the Maoist rebels and started a revolution in 2006. Later that year, the Maoist rebels signed a peace agreement with the political parties which allowed them to join mainstream politics (ILO, 2013).

In 2008, a coalition of the political parties and the Maoists successfully abolished the Monarchy (Bhandari, 2010). In the same year, constitution assembly elections were held in which the Maoist party secured the highest number of votes and became the number one political party in the assembly. The goal of the constituent assembly was to complete the drafting of a new constitution by 2010. Failing to draft the constitution on time, the first constituent assembly was dissolved and a second election occurred in 2013; however, the political deadlock remained (BBC, 2015). Between 2008 and 2013, mass protests, political disputes and nationwide strikes were rampant (BBC, 2015). Shrestha and Chaudhary (2013) reported that 1621 (36.4%) out of 4451 strikes were organized by different political parties between 2008 and 2013. Finally, the constituent assembly completed drafting a new constitution in September 2015 (IANS, 2016). Over this period, between 2008 and 2015, the country experienced seven changes of Prime Minister (Sahayogee, 2016).

Since the promulgation of the new constitution, the United Democratic Madhesi Front, a coalition of several Nepalese Southern borders (*Terai*)-based political parties, has been protesting and demanding a more representative constitution. Several people were killed and injured, property was vandalized, the Nepal-India border was blocked, and indefinite strikes and market closures were organized during the protests (IANS, 2016). However, the *Terai* dispute currently remains unresolved. In the meantime, India imposed an undeclared blockade of the Nepalese–Indian border from August 2015 to February 2016 citing border security reasons because of the *Terai* dispute. This blockade affected the supply of fuel, cooking gas, medicines and other essential items within Nepal (Mahaseth, 2016).

Amidst the ongoing instability, two major earthquakes in 2015 (April 25 and May 12) and their aftershocks caused around 9000 deaths, left 22,000 injured and damaged 800,000 houses (fully and partially) in Nepal (ADB, 2016). Although the earthquakes were not the causes of political instability, the political instability indeed affected the disaster preparedness of Nepal (Domínguez, 2015).

The political instability has affected the tourism industry in a number of ways. For example, as a consequence of the civil war in Nepal, international arrivals decreased by more than 40% between 1998 (463,684) and 2002 (275,468). The impact of the decline in the tourist arrivals was observed on the gross foreign exchange earnings from tourism which also declined from US$119.060 million in the fiscal year 1995/1996 (Open Nepal, 2012) to US$101.628 million in 2001/2002 (MOCTCA, 2015). As the tourist arrivals began to increase after 2007 and reached 803,092 in 2012 (MOCTCA, 2015), the gross foreign exchange earnings from the tourism industry also increased from US$180.165 million in the fiscal year 2006/2007 and reached US$380.374 million in 2011/2012 (MOCTCA, 2015). However, with the increased political instability, visitor numbers have again declined since 2013 (797,616) and reached as low as 538,970 in 2015 (MOCTCA, 2016), exacerbating the fragility of the tourism and hospitality industry (Simone, 2015).

Additionally, the negative effect of political instability was also experienced in the development of hotels in Nepal. The total number of hotels in Kathmandu had increased only by 35 from 464 in 2010 to 499 in 2014 with the number of rooms increasing from 9881 (in 2010) to 11,835 (in 2014). The room occupancy rate of hotels throughout this period remained at around 60% on average (MOCTCA, 2015). In summary, the ongoing political instability has not only adversely affected the demand side (e.g. tourist arrivals and revenue from tourism) but also the supply side (e.g. development of hotels) of the tourism industry in Nepal.

Methods

The data on which this paper is based were gathered from April 2015 to February 2016 via a series of unstructured interviews with 15 trade union officials and seven trade union members employed in hotels of Kathmandu. Trade union officials were selected for interviews because they were the key informants of the trade unions, held positions within the unions, and had a broad understanding of the history and activities of unions in hotels. Trade union members were also selected for interviews in order to gain diverse perspectives. Trade union officials and members were selected using convenience and snowball sampling methods.

Each interview lasted between 30 minutes and 1.5 hours and began with one broad question: 'Tell me something about your experiences of trade union practices in hotels'. This open-ended question enabled trade union officials and members to freely discuss issues they considered important (Ritchie, 2003). As discussion progressed in the interviews, further questions were posed to explore emerging concepts that arose through the participants' description of their experiences such as the reasons for their involvement in the trade unions, activities of the trade unions, factors affecting trade union activities, trade unions' relationships with the political parties, relationships with employers and how such relationships are influencing trade union activities.

Amongst the sample, nine trade union officials were union presidents, three were vice presidents, one was a union-coordinator, one was a union advisor and one was a union secretary in their respective trade unions. They had been in these roles for between 4 and 25 years, while trade union members had been part of a union for between 5 and 12 years. Amongst the sample, three participants were female and the rest were male. It was noticed during the interviews that except in one case, the trade union officials and members usually referred a male participant as a next recruitment for the interview unless explicitly asked about a female. One female participant was recommended by a participant as she was the founding president in a hotel and had provided leadership during the early stage of trade union organization in that hotel around 2006. The participants reported that female participation in trade unions in hotels is a relatively recent phenomenon and suggested that the present research would benefit from recruiting those (male) participants who were experienced in trade union practices.

All the trade union officials had experienced collective bargaining and negotiation processes with the management; 11 of them had experience of strike action. Four trade union members had only participated in union meetings, two had experience of collective bargaining and one had been involved in strike actions.

As indicated in Table 2, three unions are affiliated to their respective federations. All trade union officials and members are ideologically linked to one or the other political party. The trade union officials and members referred to the political party they were affiliated to as their 'mother political party'.

As of April 2015, the All Nepal Hotel, Casino, and Restaurant Workers' Union had branches in over 160 hotels and restaurants in Kathmandu, whereas the Nepal Tourism, Hotel, Casino and Restaurant Workers' Union and Nepal Independent Hotel, Casino and Restaurant Workers' Union had 237 and 70 branches, respectively. The number of branches of the All Nepal Revolutionary Hotel and Restaurant Workers' Union could not be assessed. Even though the federations allowed unions in casinos and restaurants to become their affiliated members, most of the trade union officials and members agreed that above 50% of the membership came from hotels.

The interviews were transcribed verbatim and a three-stage coding process (open, axial and selective) was used. While the constant comparative method was used to analyse the data, the researcher's self-reflective memos (Strauss & Corbin, 1990) aided in integrating contexts with subsequent analysis. The analysis led to the emergence of three distinct themes: seeking to improve workers' rights and conditions, being instruments of the political parties, and recognizing the need to protect the industry. These themes are discussed in the next section.

The changing roles of trade unions with changing causes of political instability

Seeking to improve workers' rights and conditions

A number of trade union officials and members stressed that the reinstatement of democracy through the first democratic movement in the 1990s provided a platform to expand the trade union movements in Nepal. Having a sense of democratic freedom and the

Table 2. Trade union officials and members' affiliations with unions, federations and political parties.

	Name of union	Affiliated federation	Mother political party
Union officials			
3, 4, 7 8, 9, 10, 11, 15	All Nepal Hotel, Casino, and Restaurant Workers' Union	All Nepal Federation of Trade Unions (ANTUF)	United Communist Party of Nepal-Maoist (UCPN-M)
1, 2, 5, 6, 13	Nepal Tourism, Hotel, Casino and Restaurant Workers' Union	Nepal Trade Union Congress (NTUC)	Nepali Congress
14	Nepal Independent Hotel, Casino, and Restaurant Workers' Union (NIHWU)	General Federation of Nepalese Trade Unions (GEFONT)	Communist Party of Nepal-Unified Marxist-Leninist (CPN-UML)
12	All Nepal Revolutionary Hotel and Restaurant Workers' Union		Communist Party of Nepal (Maoist) – Biplav
Union members			
2, 3, 6	All Nepal Hotel, Casino, and Restaurant Workers' Union	All Nepal Federation of Trade Unions (ANTUF)	United Communist Party of Nepal-Maoist (UCPN-M)
4, 5, 7	Nepal Tourism, Hotel, Casino and Restaurant Workers' Union	Nepal Trade Union Congress (NTUC)	Nepali Congress
1	All Nepal Revolutionary Hotel and Restaurant Workers' Union		Communist Party of Nepal (Maoist)- Biplav

enactment of the Labour Act in 1992 provided motivation to the workers to organize trade unions and improve working conditions. Trade union official 2 put it this way,

> Since the Panchayat era, we have felt the necessity of trade unions. At that time, our jobs were totally in the hands of the owners. If they wanted we worked, if they did not, we were fired … we could not speak. We were fearful.

Trade union official 14 provided similar opinion on the same issue by saying,

> After the democratic revolution in 1990, the king also became flexible, people had freedom of speech and there was multi-party democracy in the country. So things became relatively easier for trade unions. Then the labour law came in 1992 which made it even easier for union organization.

Linking motivation for the organization of the unions to improving the rights and conditions of the workers, trade union official 2 remarked,

> We established a union because, then, we could put our demands in every two years with the management and give facilities to the workers, secure their jobs and increase their welfare.

However, trade union officials and members recognized that they needed to feel powerful to pursue the goal of securing the welfare of the workers because of the master–servant attitude of the owners and managers which caused the trade union officials and members to feel inferior and lowered their self-esteem. As trade union member 4 noted, 'I felt like I was being treated like his house servant, but I still could not say anything.'

Several trade union officials and members said that the feeling of powerlessness was also caused by the inflexible and unfriendly nature of some human resource managers. Trade union official 6 noted,

> Normally he [the human resource manager] wanted us to make a note on the time card four times a day. He wouldn't listen to your reasons if you were late even for few minutes. At the end of the month, you would be surprised to see that your salary was deducted or your grades had been stopped … if you break a glass or anything, it would also be deducted from your salary too. If you objected, you would be transferred to some other department.

Motivated to improve the worker's welfare and job security, but constrained by the feeling of powerlessness, the trade unions considered seeking help from their mother political parties. The political parties' support improved trade unions' confidence and their ability to negotiate during collective bargaining, and to stand against management during disputes. As trade union official 1 mentioned, 'When we talked to our party, they assured us that they will help. We became strong during collective bargaining and sometimes we opposed him [the human resource manager] too.'

Almost all of the trade union officials and members believed that the strength and influence of the trade unions diminished from 1996 to 2006 as the country faced the Maoist insurgency. The trade union officials and members who had been working in the hotels for more than 20 years reported that there were very few incidences of strike actions and that collective bargaining practices were infrequent. The issues of wage increments and bonuses became dormant for the trade union officials and members as the hotels were having a difficult time doing business. Some trade union officials also noted that the collective effects of the state of emergency declared by the government of Nepal in 2001 and King Gyanendra's coup d'état of 2002 exacerbated the difficulty of the trade unions to organize meetings and discuss workers' issues because mass gatherings were prohibited.

Being instruments of the political parties

After the second democratic movement of 2006, the Communist Party of Nepal-Maoist, which then was renamed as the United Communist Party of Nepal (UPCN-Maoist) and commonly referred to as the Maoist party, joined mainstream politics ending a decade-long civil war and signing a comprehensive peace agreement with the Nepali Congress-led government (ILO, 2013). The addition of a new player in the formal Nepalese political arena exacerbated the ongoing political instability in the country until 2013. However, the cause of the political instability switched from insurgency to political disputes as the political parties disagreed over the provisions to be included in the new constitution. As trade union member 1 remarked, 'There was marked differences among the political parties of what they wanted to include in the constitution and what they did not and it was always a reason for the street protests.' The inclusion of the type of provisions recommended by any one particular political party in the constitution could have potentially given them an advantage over the others resulting in the likelihood of forming their own government.

The national level of political instability caused by the disputes between the political parties led to a change in the primary role of trade unions from that of seeking to improve workers' conditions to being instruments of the political parties. The political parties extensively used the trade unions during their demonstration of political power, protests and general strikes. The political parties also expanded trade union organizations in hotels so as to provide employment to their political cadres. In exhibiting political power, a vast majority of the trade union officials and members participated in a number of activities organized by their mother political parties ranging from marching in a protest rally to carrying the political parties' flags and taking part in physical clashes, vandalism and violence against other political parties.

Several trade union officials and members affiliated to the Maoist party acknowledged that since the Maoist party came into mainstream politics in 2006, it had extensively used the strategy of organizing trade unions in hotels in order to improve the rights and conditions of the workers. Many trade union officials and members affiliated with Nepali Congress agreed that the Maoist party employed the strategy of organizing trade unions in hotels. However, they refuted the reason provided by the trade union officials and members affiliated with the Maoist party. Instead, they argued that the main reason the Maoist Party organized trade unions in hotels was to provide employment to its political cadres, especially to its militant youth wing – Young Communist League (YCL). Improving workers' condition was of secondary importance.

Once a trade union was organized in a hotel the Maoist party used the affiliated trade unions to pressure the management into providing employment. Trade union official 14 reported that the Nepali Congress and CPN-UML also followed suit; however, they were relatively less successful compared to the Maoists. A number of Nepali Congress and CPN-UML affiliated trade union officials and members believed that employing YCL as trade union members in hotels served two other purposes for the Maoist party: pressuring management for collecting donations and utilizing hotels for organizing the political parties' meetings and annual conventions.

Recognizing the need to protect the industry

Since 2015, two important changes in the causes of political instability have collectively influenced trade union practices in Nepal. The first cause is the ongoing protests being organized by the United Democratic Madhesi Front, a coalition of several Nepalese Southern borders (*Terai*)-based political parties, for a more representative constitution since its promulgation in September 2015. The second cause is the undeclared blockade of the Nepalese–Indian border by India between August 2015 and February 2016 citing border security reasons. The border blockade has since been relaxed on February 2016 but the political instability has remained.

Political instability arising from the above causes had caused the trade unions to reconsider their roles and become more concerned about the survival of the hotels and tourism industry. The majority of the trade union officials and members interviewed stated that there had been a gradual increase of concerns among the trade unions about the future of the tourism industry since 2013 and more particularly since 2015 because of the above causes. As trade union official 12 stated,

> I think now everyone feels that we need to think about whether the hotel where we work or the tourism industry will be able to survive or not? First, it's the company, and then only us. We talk about it and discuss.

The trade union officials and members attributed three reasons for their concern about the survival of the hotels and future of the tourism industry. First, almost all of the trade union officials and members believed that work conditions in hotels in Nepal had improved in the last few years. The majority of the trade union officials and members cited improvements in minimum wages and other benefits such as insurance and allowances among others as examples of their improved situations. As trade union official 10 put it, 'Now even the lowest level of employee takes back home fifteen to twenty thousand rupees every month, which was only a dream until a few years ago.'

On the same issue, trade union official 14 stated,

> We have several other benefits now such as maternity allowance which has increased by more than 100 percent; workers get some money when he or she has to mourn a death at home; best employee award, insurance, and medical allowance.

Second, many trade union officials and members expressed a concern that tourism in Nepal had been sluggish for several years because of the ongoing instability. They realized that the downfall of tourism in Nepal, particularly after the unofficial blockade by India and associated border area unrest, had affected hotels' business significantly. Thus, they did not find it an appropriate time to put additional demands before the management to exacerbate the situation. As trade union member 5 stated, 'Our hotel booking has been confined to 20% what it was last year, and for many, I guess, it is not more than 10% these days.' Trade union 6, on the same issue, said, 'It's probably not a good time to pressure the management. We actually need to think now how will this hotel survive after everything that is going on these days'.

Finally, several trade union officials and members recognized gradual changes in owners' and managers' attitudes in many hotels over the last few years. They reported that some owners and managers were pro-actively fulfilling the trade unions' demands agreed during negotiations, staff layoffs were not common, and some owners followed a system of regular promotions and overtime payments.

Even though there were no outward signs in general, it was noted that trade union offi-cials and members had been impacted in some way by the earthquakes, and had experi-enced the trauma of some kind. This observation became evident as a majority of them reported that they had realized that there should be cooperation among all the trade unions and workers to sustain the industry after the 2015 earthquakes. Some of them even sounded 'protective' as if they wanted to preserve those which had remained after the earthquakes including their jobs or hotels in which they were working.

Discussions/conclusions

This aim of this paper was to explore the effects of political instability on trade union prac-tices in the tourism industry by examining how the roles of trade unions alter in relation to changes in the causes of political instability. The study found that the success of the first democratic movement of 1990 and subsequent enactment of the labour law in 1992 motiv-ated the trade unions to adopt their role as representative organizations of labour, seeking to improve their rights and conditions. However, the feeling of powerlessness among the trade unions while confronting management provided an incentive to actively seek politi-cal parties' support. This analysis is congruent with Ebbinghaus (1995) findings that some-times trade unions are more or less are compelled to rely on the political parties to achieve their aim as some objectives could only be reached with their cooperation.

As the causes of political instability changed from a general quest for democracy to inter-party political disputes, the trade unions became the instruments of their mother political parties to exhibit political power. The trade union officials and members partici-pated in political demonstrations and protests. The political parties also used the strategy of organizing trade unions at hotels in order to provide employment to its political cadres. As explained by Hayward's (1980) Leninist model in which the political party seeks to control the policies and actions of its associated union for its benefits, the inter-est of the political parties to be in, and maintain power, underlay many disputes in Nepal to which the trade unions became the instruments of the political parties they were associated with. This finding is also consistent with Selig Perlman's job-conscious union-ism theory (Perlman, 1949) which notes that the trade unions act as a job provider to its members.

As the demands of the trade unions were being gradually met by the management within the hotel sector, the 2015 earthquakes killed thousands of people and damaged properties, and the causes of instability changed from political disputes to the unofficial blockade by India, and border area unrest since 2015, the trade unions began to recognise the deteriorating condition of hotels and the tourism industry in general. This realization developed their role as a key stakeholder that should be concerned in protecting and assur-ing the future of the industry. The earthquakes as a natural disaster that affected everyone had a unifying effect and changed the focus of the unions from an introspective one that focused on the immediate needs of their members to one that is more strategic and outward looking and aimed to address the future of the industry as a whole.

This changing role of trade unions has important implications. It helps us to recognise that the effects of political instability on trade union practices are not always unidimen-sional. For example, as suggested by Hyman (2001), the initial market-oriented role taken up by the Nepali Congress and CPN-UML trade unions after the first democratic movement shifted towards a class-oriented role as the Maoist party came into mainstream politics after the second democratic movement. Finally, with the eventual realization of the need to protect the industry following a series of changes in the causes of political instability, the society-oriented role of the trade unions has emerged where the sectoral challenges have urged the trade unions to engage in social dialogues.

An alternative argument could also be possible that the trade unions may have multiple objectives at any one point in time and presumably, their priorities simply change over time, but their other roles do not actually disappear. This deduction brings us to an understanding of three distinct roles being played by the trade unions in the tourism industry in Nepal. First, they had been acting as institutions that adhere to the principles behind the organization of trade unions and work and advocate for improving the rights and conditions of workers (Webb & Webb, 1920). Second, by being the instrument of their mother political parties, the trade unions had been effectively playing a role of a mediator in the tourism industry. This was apparent from their efforts to facilitate and achieve the interests of the political parties such as providing employment to its cadres in hotels or collecting donations and utilizing hotels for organizing the political parties' meetings and annual conventions (Ebbinghaus, 1995). Third, the trade unions had been acting as protectors of the industry with a willingness to collaborate with other stakeholders such as the owners, managers and officials and members of the trade unions affiliated to the other political parties to protect the industry in time of need (Hyman, 2001). The successful execution of these roles by the trade unions has had a strong influence on the perception of its members working in the tourism industry: they have developed a notion that the trade unions are an inseparable part of the mainstream political parties and that the trade unions need the political parties' support in executing their agenda

Previous studies of trade unions in the tourism industry (Burgess et al., 2013; Lucas, 2009; Wood, 1997) have mostly focused on aspects of industrial relations in a static context such as examining the roles of trade unions in improving working conditions in a particular hotel within a specified time frame or within a particular political context. While useful, such examinations do little to enlighten us on how the roles of trade unions may vary when the political contexts change or other sources of instability are encountered. This study is distinctive in that it explores longitudinal changes in the roles of the trade unions, in differing political contexts associated with varying causes of political instability. It also contributes to our understanding of the volatility of industrial relations within the tourism industry due to the changing roles of trade unions, and how this volatility can be exacerbated by changes in the causes of the political instability.

The shifting roles of the trade unions in this study have occurred as a by-product of the political instability experienced in Nepal over a period of time. It is possible that the pattern of roles adopted by trade unions may have emerged from the Leninist model to a more general model where even if politically engaged, trade unions refuse any alliance with political parties and are content to improve the wages and conditions of their members (Hayward, 1980), to one which has become more focused on the future of their industry. How dynamic interplays occur among the trade union practices has been indicated, but not been fully covered in this study, and can be a potential topic for future research.

Note

1. Tourism and hospitality are characterized as different but overlapping industries that together are often termed as the 'tourism and hospitality industry' (Leiper, 2008).

Disclosure statement

No potential conflict of interest was reported by the authors.

References

ADB. (2016). Nepal 2015 earthquake: ADB's response. *Countries*. Retrieved from http://www.adb.org/countries/nepal/earthquake-adb-response

Allen, V. L. (1966). *Militant trade unionism: A re-analysis of industrial action in an inflationary situation*. London: The Merlin Press.

Aslan, A. H., & Wood, R. C. (1993). Trade unions in the hotel and catering industry: The views of hotel managers. *Employee Relations, 15*(2), 61–70.

Bamber, G. J., Gittell, J. H., Kochan, T. A., & Von Nordenflycht, A. (2013). *Up in the air: How airlines can improve performance by engaging their employees*. Ithaca, NY: Cornell University Press.

Basnett, Y. (2009). *From politicization of grievances to political violence: An analysis of the Maoist movement in Nepal*. Working paper Series No. 07-78. London: Development Studies Institute, London School of Economics and Political Science. Retrieved from http://www.lse.ac.uk/internationalDevelopment/pdf/WP/WP78.pdf

Baum, T. (2007). Human resources in tourism: Still waiting for change. *Tourism Management, 28*(6), 1383–1399.

Baum, T. (2008). Implications of hospitality and tourism labour markets for talent management strategies. *International Journal of Contemporary Hospitality Management, 20*(7), 720–729.

Baum, T. (2015). Human resources in tourism: Still waiting for change? A 2015 reprise. *Tourism Management, 50*, 204–212.

BBC. (2015). Nepal profile – Timeline. *South Asia*. Retrieved from http://www.bbc.com/news/world-south-asia-12499391

Benson, J., & Zhu, Y. (2008). Trade unions in Asia: Organization, strategy and issues. In J. Benson & Y. Zhu (Eds.), *Trade unions in Asia: An economic and sociological analysis* (pp. 1–10). London: Routledge.

Bhandari, K. (2010). Tourism in Nepal: Post-monarchy challenges. *Journal of Tourism and Cultural Change, 8*(1–2), 69–83.

Blyton, P., Lucio, M. M., McGurk, J., & Turnbull, P. (2001). Globalization and trade union strategy: Industrial restructuring and human resource management in the international civil aviation industry. *International Journal of Human Resource Management, 12*(3), 445–463.

Burgess, J., Connell, J., & Winterton, J. (2013). Vulnerable workers, precarious work and the role of trade unions and HRM. *The International Journal of Human Resource Management, 24*(22), 4083–4093.

Causevic, S., & Lynch, P. (2013). Political (in) stability and its influence on tourism development. *Tourism Management, 34*, 145–157.

Cohen, I. (1990). Political climate and two airline strikes: Century air in 1932 and continental airlines in 1983–85. *Industrial & Labor Relations Review, 43*(2), 308–323.

Domínguez, G. (2015). *How political instability affected Nepal's disaster preparedness*. Retrieved from http://www.dw.com/en/how-political-instability-affected-nepals-disaster-preparedness/a-18411259

Ebbinghaus, B. (1995). The Siamese twins: Citizenship rights, cleavage formation, and party-union relations in Western Europe. *International Review of Social History, 40*(S3), 51–89.

Elshaer, I. A., & Saad, S. K. (2016). Political instability and tourism in Egypt: Exploring survivors' attitudes after downsizing. *Journal of Policy Research in Tourism, Leisure & Events*, 1–20. doi:10.1080/19407963.2016.1233109

Hayward, J. (1980). Trade union movements and their politico-economic environments: A preliminary framework. *West European Politics, 3*(1), 1–9.

Henry, N. (2015). Trade union internationalism and political change in Myanmar. *Global Change, Peace & Security, 27*(1), 69–84.

Hyman, R. (2001). *Understanding European trade unionism: Between market, class and society.* London: Sage.

IANS. (2016). Nepal unrest: No solution in sight, Terai death toll 59. *South Asia.* Retrieved from http://timesofindia.indiatimes.com/world/south-asia/Nepal-unrest-No-solution-in-sight-Terai-death-toll-59/articleshow/50689329.cms

Ingram, H., Grieve, D., Ingram, H., Tabari, S., & Watthanakhomprathip, W. (2013). The impact of political instability on tourism: Case of Thailand. *Worldwide Hospitality and Tourism Themes, 5* (1), 92–103.

International Labour Organization (ILO). (2013). *Decent work country programme 2013–2017 Nepal.* Author Retrieved from http://www.ilo.org/public/english/bureau/program/dwcp/download/nepal.pdf

Johri, C. K. (1967). *Unionism in a developing economy: A study of the interaction between trade unionism and government policy in India, 1950-1965.* Bombay: Asia Pub. House.

Kusluvan, S. (Ed.) (2003). *Managing employee attitudes and behaviors in the tourism and hospitality industry.* New York, NY: Nova Science.

Ladkin, A. (2011). Exploring tourism labor. *Annals of Tourism Research, 38*(3), 1135–1155.

Leiper, N. (2008). Why 'the tourism industry' is misleading as a generic expression: The case for the plural variation, 'tourism industries'. *Tourism Management, 29*(2), 237–251.

Lloyd, C., Warhurst, C., & Dutton, E. (2013). The weakest link? Product market strategies, skill and pay in the hotel industry. *Work, Employment & Society, 27*(2), 254–271.

Lucas, R. (2004). *Employment relations in the hospitality and tourism industries.* London: Routledge.

Lucas, R. (2009). Is low unionisation in the British hospitality industry due to industry characteristics? *International Journal of Hospitality Management, 28*(1), 42–52.

Macaulay, I. R., & Wood, R. C. (1992). Hotel and catering industry employees' attitudes towards trade unions. *Employee Relations, 14*(3), 20–28.

Mahaseth, H. (2016). Nepal is dealing with a massive crisis, and India's 'unofficial' blockade made it worse. *Youth Ki Awaaz.* Retrieved from http://www.youthkiawaaz.com/2016/03/unofficial-blockade-nepal-madhesi-rights/

Martin, R. M. (1989). *Trade unionism: Purposes and forms.* New York: Oxford University Press.

Ministry of Culture, Tourism and Civil Aviation, Government of Nepal (MOCTCA). (2014). *Tourism employment survey 2014.* Nepal: Author. Retrieved from http://www.tourism.gov.np/images/download/Tourism_Employment_Study_Draft_Report_integrated.pdf

Ministry of Culture, Tourism and Civil Aviation, Government of Nepal (MOCTCA). (2015). *Nepal tourism statistics 2014.* Nepal: Author. Retrieved from http://www.tourism.gov.np/images/download/Nepal_Tourism_Statistics_2014_Integrated.pdf

Ministry of Culture, Tourism and Civil Aviation, Government of Nepal (MOCTCA). (2016). *Nepal tourism statistics 2015.* Nepal: Author. Retrieved from http://tourism.gov.np/images/download/Nepal_Tourism_Statistics_2015_forwebsite_edited.pdf

Open Nepal. (2012). *Gross foreign exchange earnings from tourism by fiscal year.* Retrieved from http://data.opennepal.net/content/gross-foreign-exchange-earnings-tourism-fiscal-year.

Perlman, S. (1949). *A theory of the labor movement.* New York, NY: AM Kelley.

Ramaswamy, E. (1969). Trade unions and politics. *Sociological Bulletin, 18*(2), 137–147.

Ramaswamy, E. (1974). The role of the trade union leader in India. *Human Organization, 33*(2), 163–172.

Riley, M., Ladkin, A., & Szivas, E. (2002). *Tourism employment: Analysis and planning* (Vol. 6). Clevedon: Channel View.

Ritchie, J. (2003). The applications of qualitative methods to social research. In J. Ritchie & J. Lewis (Eds.), *Qualitative research practice: A guide for social science students and researchers* (pp. 24–46). London: Sage.

Sahayogee, J. (2016). Name list of prime ministers of Nepal. *Articles about Nepal.* Retrieved from http://www.imnepal.com/prime-ministers-of-nepal/

Seddighi, H., Theocharous, A., & Nuttall, M. (2002). Political instability and tourism: An empirical study with Special reference to the microstate of Cyprus. *International Journal of Hospitality & Tourism Administration, 3*(1), 61–84.

Shrestha, M. B., & Chaudhary, S. K. (2013). *The economic cost of general strikes in Nepal.* NRB Economic Review. Research Department. Nepal Rastra Bank. Kathmandu. Retrieved from http://nrb.org.np/ecorev/pdffiles/vol26-1_art1.pdf

Simone, A. (2015). Nepal says it's open for business, but tourists are still staying away. *Global Politics.* Retrieved from http://www.pri.org/stories/2015-12-11/nepal-says-its-open-business-tourists-are-still-staying-away

Som, A. P. M., Aun, O. C., & AlBattat, A. R. (2015). Tourists' perception of crisis and the impact of instability on destination safety in Sabah, Malaysia. *Tourism & Environment, Social and Management Sciences,* 96–103. doi:10.5829/idosi.aejaes.2015.15.s.213

Sönmez, S. F. (1998). Tourism, terrorism, and political instability. *Annals of Tourism Research, 25* (2), 416–456.

Strauss, A., & Corbin, J. (1990). *Basics of qualitative research (Vol. 15).* Newbury Park, CA: Sage.

Taylor, P., & Moore, S. (2014). Cabin crew collectivism: Labour process and the roots of mobilization. *Work, Employment & Society, 29*(1), 79–98.

Thapa, B. (2004). Tourism in Nepal. *Journal of Travel & Tourism Marketing, 15*(2–3), 117–138.

Upadhayaya, P. K., Müller-Böker, U., & Sharma, S. R. (2011). Tourism amidst armed conflict: Consequences, copings, and creativity for peace-building through tourism in Nepal. *The Journal of Tourism and Peace Research, 1*(2), 22–40.

Upreti, B. R., Sharma, S. R., Upadhaya, P. K., Ghimire, S., & Iff, A. (2013). *Making business count for peace: Reflections from tourism sector in Nepal*: South Asia regional coordination office of the Swiss national centre of competence in research (NCCR) North-South, department of development studies-Kathmandu University and Nepal Center for Contemporary Research.

Valenzuela, J. S. (1989). Labor movements in transitions to democracy: A framework for analysis. *Comparative Politics, 21*(4), 445–472.

Waddoups, C. J. (2001). Wages in Las Vegas and Reno: How much difference do unions make in the hotel, gaming, and recreation industry? *UNLV Gaming Research & Review Journal, 6*(1), 7–21.

Walton, J. K. (2012). 'The tourism labour conundrum' extended: Historical perspectives on hospitality workers. *Hospitality & Society, 2*(1), 49–75.

Webb, S., & Webb, B. (1920). *The history of trade unionism.* London: Longmans, Green.

Wood, R. C. (1997). *Working in hotels and catering.* London: International Thomson Business Press.

Yruela, M. P., & del Rosal, R. S. (1999). The national industrial relations contexts. In M. Rigby, R. Smith, & T. Lawlor (Eds.), *European trade unions: Change and response* (pp. 37–52). London: Routledge.

Zampoukos, K., & Ioannides, D. (2011). The tourism labour conundrum: Agenda for new research in the geography of hospitality workers. *Hospitality & Society, 1*(1), 25–45.

Evaluating the dynamics and impact of terrorist attacks on tourism and economic growth for Turkey

Julio A. Afonso-Rodríguez

ABSTRACT

Turkey is one of the most advanced economies in the MENA region and one of the most important tourist destinations in the world, but with a long lasting history of terrorism that has significantly increased during the last years after the Syrian Civil War. This paper uses an updated sample of quarterly data on GDP, inbound tourism and terrorism to explore the relationship between tourism and economic growth adding information on terrorist activity. Different specifications of cointegrating regressions are used to quantify the impact of terrorism on the relationship between tourism demand and economic growth, including the novelty approach of a threshold cointegrating regression, where the stationary transition variable is given by a standard measure of terrorist activity. Results show that, with a delay between three to six months, and even for a relatively small number of estimated terrorist attacks, there is a negative impact of terrorism on real GDP of around 10% through a reduction of the contribution of tourism demand on economic growth.

RESUMEN

Turquía es una de las economías más avanzadas en la región MENA (Medio Oriente y Norte de África) y uno de los destinos turísticos más importantes del mundo, pero con una duradera historia de terrorismo que se ha incrementado significativamente en los últimos años tras la Guerra Civil Siria. Este trabajo utiliza una muestra actualizada de datos trimestrales del PIB, la llegada de turistas y terrorismo para explorar la relación entre turismo y crecimiento económico añadiendo información sobre la actividad terrorista. Se utilizan diferentes especificaciones de regresiones cointegradas para cuantificar el impacto del terrorismo en la relación entre la demanda turística y el crecimiento económico, incluyendo la novedosa perspectiva de un umbral de regresión cointegrada, donde la variable de transición permanente es dada por una medida estandarizada de la actividad terrorista. Los resultados muestran que, con un retraso de entre tres y seis meses, e incluso para un número relativamente pequeño de ataques terroristas estimados, hay un impacto negativo del terrorismo en el PIB real de alrededor del 10% a través de una reducción de la contribución de la demanda turística al crecimiento económico.

RÉSUMÉ

La Turquie est l'un des pays les plus développés sur le plan économique dans la région du Moyen-Orient et d'Afrique du Nord (MOAN) et l'une des destinations touristiques les plus importantes du monde, mais dont la longue histoire du terrorisme a été exacerbée par la guerre civile syrienne au cours des dernières années . Cet article utilise un échantillon mis à jour des données trimestrielles sur le PIB, des arrivées des touristes et du terrorisme en vue d'explorer la relation entre le tourisme et la croissance économique vis-à-vis des informations sur les activités terroristes. Différentes spécifications des régressions de cointégration ont été utilisées pour quantifier l'impact du terrorisme sur la relation entre la demande touristique et la croissance économique, y compris la nouveauté de l'approche du seuil de la régression de cointégration, où la tension stabilisée variable s'obtient par une mesure standard de l'activité terroriste. Avec un retard de trois à six mois, et même pour un nombre relativement faible d'attaques terroristes estimés, les résultats montrent qu'il y a un impact négatif du terrorisme sur le PIB réel d'environ de 10% à cause de la réduction de la contribution de la demande touristique sur la croissance économique.

摘要

土耳其是中东及北非地区经济最发达的国家之一，也是世界上最重要的旅游目的地之一，但是在叙利亚内战结束之后，该国恐怖主义活动加剧。本文通过恐怖主义与更新的入境旅游GDP季度数据，研究在恐怖活动影响下旅游与经济增长的关系。通过不同的协整回归规范，量化恐怖主义对旅游需求与经济增长间关系的影响，包括门限协整回归的新途径，给定一个标准的平稳转移变量以测量恐怖活动。研究结果显示，即便是规模相对较小的恐怖袭击，在其发生后的三到六个月之间，由于旅游需求下滑，恐怖活动对实际GDP的负面影响大约在10%左右。

1. Introduction

The theoretical and empirical analysis of economic growth and its potential determinants have a long history in economics and econometrics.[1] A large amount of the potentially influential factors on economic development and growth has to do with some measures of the process and degree of openness of an economy through time. There seems to be substantial evidence that many developing countries (and also for some developed ones) have promoted economic policies for stimulating international tourism and export expansion as a potential source of economic growth. The characterization and measure of the relationship between trade openness (the sum of exports and imports over GDP), and economic growth has led to the formulation of the export-led growth hypothesis (ELGH) which appears to crucial to explain economic growth in many emerging and developing economies.[2]

Closely related to the ELGH, the importance of tourism receipts, together with the analysis and measure of their effects on GDP, has also lead to a large number of papers about this question. The consideration of the tourism receipts as an alternative form of export that can contribute to improve a country's balance of payments, favour employment and generate additional tax revenues, and hence to have positive influence on the economy as a whole, has led to formulate the so-called *tourism-led growth hypothesis* (TLGH).[3] From an empirical perspective, there exist mixed evidence on the degree of satisfaction of this postulate depending on the sample used and the methodology applied (cross-sectional data, time series or panel data). Among this variety of results, an important conclusion has to do with the fact that the relation between tourism and growth depends on various factors, the main one being the country's degree of specialization in the tourist sector.

Large part of the empirical evidence for both the ELGH and TLGH using time series data is based on the examination of statistical causality via exclusions restrictions tests, impulse response function analysis and forecast error variance decompositions. However, as shown in Giles and Williams (2000, 2001) for the ELGH case, the results based on standard causality techniques are not typically robust to different specifications and the properties of the series involved in the analysis. Particularly, these authors emphasize that different non-causality outcomes are easy to obtain in applications, implying that results on the empirical literature on these two questions must be interpreted with caution. In view of these methodological problems, this paper follows a more basic and standard approach to test the TLGH based on the estimation of different specifications of a regression model involving both persistent (i.e. integrated of order one) and stationary variables.

Tang and Abosedra (2016) highlight the scarcity of empirical works on the relationship between tourism and economic growth on Middle-East and North Africa (MENA) region. As part of the MENA region, comprising at least 30 countries extending from Morocco to Iran and including all Middle Eastern and Maghreb countries, Turkey is one of the main country of the region being part of the G-20 major economies and a founding member of the OECD. Turkey represents more than 20% of the population of MENA region, and at the present time, has the world's 17th largest real GDP (18th largest GDP in nominal terms). Moreover, tourism sector largely contributes to Turkish GDP representing a direct and total contribution of 5% and 12.9%, respectively. However, although Turkey is one of the most developed countries on the MENA region, it also suffers from large instability and violence in the form of terrorist attacks which can seriously damage its economic growth in general, and its tourism sector in particular. The main aim of this study is to analyse the impact and timing of the terrorist activity in Turkey on economic growth, after controlling for the tourism effect, using a sample of data covering a large period of time and making use of a univariate regression model as the main tool for the analysis.

As will be described in more detail in Section 3, there is significant evidence on the non-stationary behaviour of the basic series for this analysis, namely the real GDP and the seasonally adjusted series of tourist arrivals (as a proxy for tourism demand), so that any existing standard procedure could be used to perform a cointegration analysis between these two series. However, for the series measuring terrorist activity (number of terrorist attacks) we found evidence of being stationary, so that this fact restricts the possibility of using any of these procedures without modifications unless we introduce some additional restrictions that can be directly tested using a new proposal to estimate cointegrating regressions. Together with this application, one of the major empirical contributions of this paper is the estimation of a threshold version of the standard cointegrating regression model relating GDP and tourism arrivals, where the stationary transition (or threshold) variable is the series of terrorist attacks. With this specification we get a very flexible and useful way to quantify the impact of terrorist activity on economic growth, both in terms of magnitude and timing.

The rest of the paper is organized as follows. Section 2 contains an overview of the literature on the effects of terrorism on economic activity and on the relationship between tourist demand and economic growth, with particular emphasis in the Turkish case. We mainly highlight the great amount of different, and even contradictory, results concerning the empirical evidence of the existence, extent and magnitude of these links. Section 3 contains the empirical analysis and description of the results, and Section 4 concludes with the summary and main conclusions of the study.

2. Review of the literature

The two main topics jointly analysed in this paper are the extent of the relationship between tourism demand and economic growth for Turkey and the possible existence of an indirect negative effect on growth, with the quantification and timing of the impact, of terrorist activities damaging the tourist industry in this country.

A large number of studies over the last two decades have established that internal conflicts can have significant economic consequences in terms of reduced growth, both for countries directly affected by these conflicts and also for some neighbouring countries.[4] The empirical literature investigating the effects of terrorism activities on several economic indicators can be grouped by the econometric techniques employed and its object of analysis. First, time series analysis has been used to assess the impact of terrorist events on specific activities such as tourism (Enders & Sandler, 1991; Enders, Sandler, & Parise, 1992), foreign investment (Enders & Sandler, 1996) and the stock market (Abadie & Gardeazabal, 2003). See also Enders and Sandler (2002) for an extensive use of a variety of time series techniques for characterizing the patterns of transnational terrorist incidents, including an intervention analysis based on significant policy and political impacts. Second, intervention analysis, in which the number of terrorist incidents are regressed on indicators of policy intervention, has been applied to evaluate which anti-terrorism policies have worked best in reducing terrorism (Enders & Sandler, 1993; Enders, Sandler, & Cauley, 1990; and Pestana Barros, 2003, among others).

Based on previous works by Blomberg and Hess (2002) and Blomberg, Hess, and Weerapana (2004a, 2004b), Blomberg, Hess, and Orphanides (2004) perform an extensive empirical analysis based on a large unbalanced panel data set with annual observations of 177 countries from 1968 to 2000, and find an economically significant negative average effect of terrorism on growth, although it is considerably smaller and less persistent than the associated with either external wars or internal conflicts. Moreover, these authors remark that these findings suggest important differences regarding both the incidence and the economic consequences of terrorism among different sets of countries. The papers by Sandler and Enders (2004) and Enders and Sandler (2005) provide a survey of some crucial insights gained from applying an economic perspective to the study of terrorism (particularly focussed on transnational terrorist activities), and also an updated analysis of trends and cycles, policy-induced externalities, collective action responses and hostage negotiation strategies. Accounting for the differences between direct and equilibrium impacts of terrorist through the mobility of productive capital in an open economy, Abadie and Gardeazabal (2008) show that terrorism may have a large impact on the allocation of productive capital across countries, increase uncertainty and reduces the expected return to investment, even when terrorism is only a small fraction of the overall economic risk.[5]

Sandler and Enders (2008) make an extensive overview of the potential economic consequences of terrorism, both in developed and developing countries. They identify a number of possible ways in which terrorism impose costs on a targeted country as well among neighbouring countries, namely diverting foreign direct investment (FDI), destroying infrastructure, redirecting public investment funds to security, or limiting trade. If a developing country loses enough FDI, which is an important source of savings, then it may also experience reduced economic growth. The size and the diversity of an economy have much to do with the ability of a country to withstand terrorist attacks without showing significant economic effects. Also, these authors indicate that the distinction between direct and indirect costs that could be drawn from terrorism losses is not really necessary to characterize the economic impact of terrorism, which can be represented in terms of some well-defined macroeconomic (e.g. real per capita GDP growth) or microeconomic variables (e.g. reduced tourist receipts).

The armed conflict with Kurdistan's separatist movement, the role of Turkey as the endpoint of the NATO (North Atlantic Treaty Organization) in the Middle-East and the recent participation on the Syrian civil war has made Turkey an active focus of terrorist activity for more than thirty years. The recent work by Bilgel and Karahasan (2016) tries to estimate the economic effects of PKK (Kurdistan Worker's Party) terrorism in Turkey in a causal framework through the creation of a synthetic control group reproducing the Turkish real per capital GDP before emerging of terrorism in the second half of the 1980s. The authors estimate a 0.62 percentage point higher annual growth rate over the period 1988–2008 if Turkey would have not been exposed to PKK terrorism. This paper is also very useful for an updated review of the literature on the economic effects of particular terrorist organizations and specific cases of political violence all over the world in recent decades.

Given the existing literature on the relationship between tourism and economic development (see Sinclair, 1998 for a Survey), and on the TLGH, we then focus on the literature related to the analysis of the tourist sector in Turkey.[6] As described in Saray and Karagöz (2010), Turkey is one of the main tourist destinations in the world, occupying a position among the top 10 highest revenue earned countries and with a tourism sector that has gained great importance in the Turkish economy. Halicioglu (2004) study aggregate tourism demand function for Turkey using time series data for the period 1960–2002, where total tourist arrivals into Turkey are related to world income, relative prices and transportation costs. The results indicate that income is the most significant variable in explaining total tourist arrivals to this country and that there exist a stable tourism demand function. Aslan, Kaplan, and Kula (2008) take into consideration both demand and supply determinants of tourism and estimate a dynamic panel data model for Turkey with respect to its major partners, finding a small degree of persistence in the consumer decision in favour to this destination, while Saray and Karagöz (2010) find significant effects on tourist inflows of economic size, population and distance of origin countries from the estimation of a panel gravity model.

Regarding the empirical analysis of the TLGH for Turkey results seem to be inconclusive. Katircioglu (2009) using annual data for the period 1960–2006 does not find significant evidence of long-run relationship (cointegration) between international tourism and economic growth, thus rejecting the TLGH for the Turkish economy, while that Coskun and Özer (2014) find evidence of the existence of a reciprocal causal relationship using quarterly data for the period 1992:Q1 to 2014:Q1. Also, GARCH-type measures of the volatility of tourism receipts and economic growth are identified as useful predictors of tourism and economic growth, both in the short and in the long-run. Finally, Terzi (2015), using annual data for the period 1963–2016 and three different econometric techniques to the analysis of statistical causality, find strong evidence for unidirectional and positively significant causality running from tourism receipts to economic growth, thus supporting the empirical validity of the TLGH for the Turkish economy. Again, different econometric procedures and data sets produce a number of different and even contradictory results.[7]

Drakos and Kutan (2001) study the regional effects of terrorism on competitors' market shares in tourism sector through a seemingly unrelated regression model which is based on a consumer-choice model developed by Enders et al. (1992). The empirical evidence, based on three competitors (Greece, Israel and Turkey) and covering the period January 1996–December 1999, mainly indicates that the tourism industry in Israel and Turkey are more sensitive to terrorism incidents than in Greece and there are also significant regional contagion effects of terrorism. Additionally, these authors find that a higher level of terrorist incidents in Greece is associated with an increase in the relative market share of Israel, while terrorism in Israel benefits Turkish market share.

It is also documented evidence that the location (urban versus rural) and the intensity of terrorist incidents play an important role in the decision-making process of tourists for choice of destinations. The unpublished paper Karagoz (2008) investigate the effects of terrorism on Turkey's tourism sector using techniques of time series analysis, particularly tests for non-stationarity with structural breaks, and found two separate periods of terrorism which statistically have a significant negative effect on tourist arrivals. However, this conclusion must be take with care given the small sample size analysed (annual data from 1961 to 2006), and the possible drawback introduced by the assumption of known break points. Finally, and more recently, Raza and Jawaid (2013), also using annual data for the period 1980–2010 and cointegration techniques, find long-run relationships between terrorism and tourism for Pakistan. Results indicate the significant negative impact of terrorism on tourism both in the short- and long-run. However, one might have some doubts on the reliability of these results given that the small number of sample observations could not be sufficient for the long-run analysis.

In this research, the TLGH is revisited for the case of Turkey by incorporating information on terrorist attacks. As previously mentioned, time series analysis is used to study the dynamic properties of the series representing the terrorist activity in Turkey but using a longer period of time and many more observations since quarterly data is considered than in Raza and Jawaid (2013) for Pakistan. Once obtained reliable evidence on the proper characterization of this series, we next perform the study of the long-run relationship between tourism demand, measured by the total number of foreign arrivals and economic growth incorporating the expected non-negligible effect of terrorism.

3. Data, methodology and empirical results

Considering annual data from the World Travel and Tourism Council for the period 1988–2016 (Figure 1), we get that the average contribution of travel and tourism sector to GDP is 10.25% for the whole period, with an average contribution of 7.77% up to 1999 increasing to 11.99% from 2000 to 2016, and levels above 12% in the last three years. The maximum level of the relative contribution of tourism to GDP in this period was in 2001 (14.52%), representing an increase of approximately 92% and 37% from the previous two years, respectively.

This simple information is used to justify the sample period under analysis in the present study (from 1977 to 2014), both because the long span of time covering, the relatively large number of observations (we will use quarterly data as described below) and the expected stability of the relation between the variables of interest in the long-run. To estimate the relationship between economic growth and a measure of tourism demand, we specify a regression model including data on quarterly real GDP (expenditure approach) in millions of 2010 US dollars and foreign tourist arrivals per quarter for Turkey and the period 1977:Q1 to 2014:Q4 (see Figure 2).[8]

Figure 2 shows the evolution of time series for these two variables, both for the original values and for its logarithmic transformation. For the empirical analysis of this relationship, alternative measures for the volume of international tourism could be used, such as tourism receipts. However, due to data availability and the fact that a multicollinearity problem emerges when tourism receipts are used together with GDP, we follow the standard approach of using total international tourist arrivals. Given the seasonal pattern of the quarterly series of tourist arrivals, in what follows we use seasonally adjusted values.

As a proxy for terrorism, we use the number of terrorist attacks per quarter obtained from the Global Terrorism Database (GTD).[9] Figure 3 shows both this original series and its first differences, that is, the difference in the value of the series between each two consecutive quarters. For the sample of the variable measuring terrorist activity, we have a total of 3042 terrorist attacks over the period considered, with an average of 20

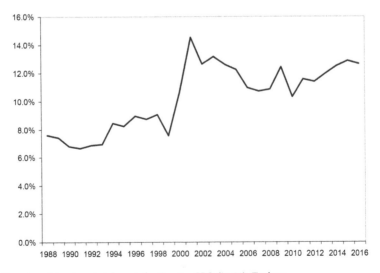

Figure 1. Travel and tourism total contribution to GDP (in %), Turkey.

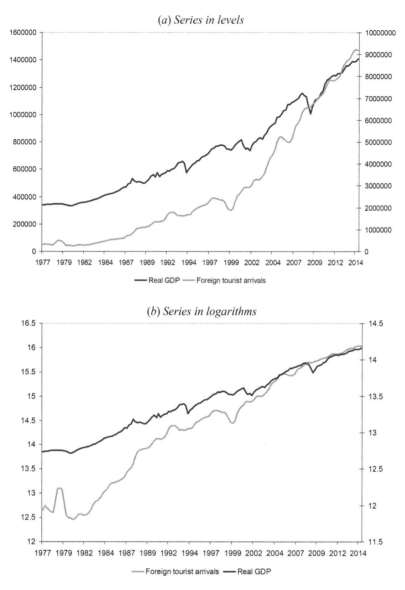

Figure 2. Real GDP and foreign tourist arrivals for Turkey, 1977:Q1-2014:Q4 (a) Series in levels (b) Series in logarithms.

attacks per quarter, a maximum of 186 attacks in the third quarter of 1992 and only 16 of 152 quarters without such events.

From the same database, we also get the registry of the number of fatalities in these events, with a correlation of over 0.8 between these two variables for the period analysed. This high correlation between the two series makes us to decide to include only the first variable as a measure of terrorist activity. As an indicator of the intensity of terrorist activity, Figure 4 plots the evolution of the ratio of number of killed people by number of terrorist attacks per quarter. From this complementary variable of killed people in attacks, we have a maximum of 478 fatalities in the second quarter of 1994, with a total

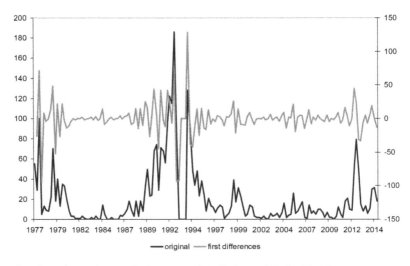

Figure 3. Number of terrorist attacks (by quarter) in Turkey, 1977:Q1-2014:Q4.

of 5178 people killed over the sample period and an average of 34 deaths per quarter. As can be seen from Figure 4, the degree of intensity measured by mortality rate per number of terrorist actions displays a high level of heterogeneity over the sample period and where the highest levels do not correspond to the periods of greater number of attacks.

To obtain initial evidence of the dynamics underlying the series of terrorist attacks in our sample period, we consider the estimation of the autocorrelation structure through the usual sample autocorrelation function (SACF). Table 1 presents the estimated coefficients from lags 1 to 10. The first two columns, labelled as raw series and OLS-demeaned, show the estimated values based on the original series and on the adjusted series by OLS (Ordinary Least Squares) estimation of a constant term, indicating a high degree of persistence in both cases and in the sense of a slow declining of this measure of linear dependence through time. However, this pattern could be a spurious consequence of some outlying or influential observations such as the ones that can be identified in Figure 3.

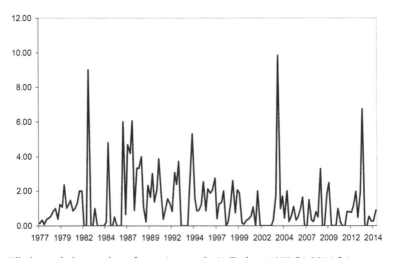

Figure 4. Killed people by number of terrorist attacks in Turkey, 1977:Q1-2014:Q4.

Table 1. Series of terrorist attacks: SACF.

Lag	Raw series	OLS-demeaned	Filtered series by OLS fitting with AO dummies					
			AO(1)	AO(2)	AO(3)	AO(4)	AO(5)	AO(6)
1	0.770	0.664	0.572	0.586	0.442	0.498	0.555	0.564
2	0.638	0.473	0.468	0.519	0.540	0.408	0.414	0.393
3	0.559	0.360	0.363	0.419	0.316	0.336	0.366	0.336
4	0.486	0.254	0.298	0.328	0.332	0.337	0.368	0.298
5	0.490	0.259	0.285	0.230	0.276	0.269	0.279	0.263
6	0.609	0.432	0.285	0.301	0.296	0.352	0.306	0.301
7	0.560	0.360	0.328	0.249	0.245	0.202	0.214	0.258
8	0.566	0.371	0.336	0.270	0.301	0.174	0.158	0.197
9	0.538	0.334	0.322	0.266	0.203	0.185	0.203	0.184
10	0.464	0.231	0.242	0.239	0.191	0.193	0.183	0.085

Note: The columns labelled as AO(j), $j = 1, \ldots, 6$ indicates the SACF computation based on locations of AO's detected using the Vogelsang's procedure in Table 3.

The estimated values of the autocorrelation function in the first two columns of Table 1 show a relatively slow decay of this measure of linear dependence, and hence a certain degree of persistence, but with an estimated value of the SACF of order one well above the limiting unit value. However, as was shown in Chan (1995), the SACF is seriously affected by the existence of large additive outliers (AO) that pushes the SACF towards zero for all lags with an extremely large magnitude of just one AO. The rest of the columns show the SACF computed for OLS-demeaned observations and including some potentially influential observations, detected employing the procedure proposed by Vogelsang (1999) in the context of robust testing for a unit root under AO's. Once adjusted by such events, the estimated pattern of serial correlation displays a less persistent behaviour given the faster decay of these estimated coefficients.

The first part of the next subsection is devoted to a more detailed statistical analysis of the characterization of this series through the use of existing robust procedures for testing the persistence properties under AO contamination. The rest of the subsection includes a more standard analysis for determining the persistence properties of the other two series implied in the cointegration analysis in subsection 3.2.

3.1. Unit root tests

For any of the three variables under analysis, we use the usual representation $x_t = d_t + \eta_t$, with d_t and η_t the deterministic and stochastic components, where d_t could be zero (no deterministic) or, more generally, could be given by a linear trend function of the form $d_t = a_0 + a_1 t$. For the stochastic component we assume it is given by $\eta_t = \alpha \eta_{t-1} + \varepsilon_t$, with coefficient taking values on the interval $-1 < \alpha \leq 1$, and where the zero mean error term ε_t could contain some remaining autocorrelation. The case $\alpha = 1$ identifies the case of a non-stationary autoregressive unit root process, while that the case $|\alpha| < 1$ implies the stationarity of the observed variable around the deterministic component. Tables 2–4 contain the results of a battery of testing procedures for the null hypothesis of a unit root, $\alpha = 1$, against the alternative of stationarity for our three series, and also, for complementing these results we present the estimated values of the so-called KPSS statistic (Kwiatkowski, Phillips, Schmidt, &

Table 2. Series of terrorist attacks: Unit root and stationarity tests.

	No deterministic	Constant term
OLS-estimated a	0.765	0.661
DF_1	-35.746 [(a)]	-51.509 [(a)]
DF_2	-4.579 [(a)]	-5.615 [(a)]
$ADF_2(q)$	$-3.759(2)$ [(a)]	$-9.789(2)$ [(a)]
$IV(q)$-estimated a	1.002	1.018
$IV_1(q)$	0.306	2.782
$IV_2(q)$	0.020	0.065
Breitung, VR	0.129	0.005 [(a)]
KPSS-level	3.779 [(a)]	0.189
KPSS-first difference	0.097	0.097

Notes: Superscripts [(a),(b),(c)] indicates rejection at 1%, 5%, and 10% significance levels, respectively. The number of lags, q, for ADF test is selected by the MAIC criteria proposed by Ng and Perron (2001), while that for IV-based tests we take $q = q_T = [1.25 \cdot T^{1/2}]$. Critical values for KPSS test are taken from Hobijn, Franses, and Ooms (2004), and it is computed with a kernel-type estimator of the long-run error variance based on the Bartlett kernel and sample-size dependent bandwidth given by $[8(T/100)^{1/4}]$.

Shin, 1992) for testing these two same hypothesis, but in reverse order, that is for testing the null hypothesis of (trend) stationarity against the alternative of a unit root. The class of IV-based statistics (instrumental variable) for testing the null hypothesis of a unit root proposed by Hall (1989)[10] are computed from the following estimator of the first-order autocorrelation coefficient

$$\hat{\alpha}_T(q) = \frac{\sum_{t=1}^{T} w_{t,q} \eta_t}{\sum_{t=1}^{T} w_{t,q} \eta_{t-1}} = \frac{\sum_{t=q+1}^{T} \eta_t \eta_{t+q}}{\sum_{t=q+1}^{T} \eta_t \eta_{t+q-1}} = \alpha + \frac{\sum_{t=q+1}^{T} \eta_t \varepsilon_{t+q}}{\sum_{t=q+1}^{T} \eta_t \eta_{t+q-1}},$$

where the instrumental variable $w_{t,q}$ is given by $w_{t,q} = \eta_{t-q}$, with $q \geq 1$, and $\varepsilon_{t+q} = \eta_{t+q} - \alpha \eta_{t+q-1}$. The $IV_{j,T}(q)$ test statistics, for $j = 1, 2$, are defined as

Table 3. Series of terrorist attacks: Unit root tests with AO's.

Panel A. Vogelsang's tests

				No deterministic component		
				DF-AO's		ADF(q)-AO
	No det.	Constant	Constant and linear trend	DF_1	DF_2	$ADF_2(2)$
Iteration, $k = 1$	5.79 (63)	6.46 (63)	6.46 (63)	$-45.39^{(a)}$	$-5.89^{(a)}$	$-2.57^{(b)}$
2	4.22 (69)	4.51 (69)	4.52 (69)	$-45.39^{(a)}$	$-6.75^{(a)}$	$-2.54^{(b)}$
3	4.25 (61)	4.57 (61)	4.56 (61)	$-50.13^{(a)}$	$-7.47^{(a)}$	$-3.75^{(a)}$
4	4.24 (62)	4.58 (62)	4.57 (62)	$-54.15^{(a)}$	$-7.79^{(a)}$	$-3.75^{(a)}$
5	3.86 (3)	4.11 (3)	4.05 (3)	$-56.51^{(a)}$	$-8.73^{(a)}$	$-2.39^{(b)}$
6	3.98 (60)	4.27 (60)	4.26 (60)	$-60.09^{(a)}$	$-9.67^{(a)}$	$-3.32^{(a)}$

Panel B. Perron and Rodríguez's (2003) tests

	No det./Constant	Linear trend	DF_1	DF_2	$ADF_2(2)$
Iteration, $k = 1$	5.06 (3)	5.06 (3)	$-37.55^{(a)}$	$-4.89^{(a)}$	$-3.24^{(a)}$
2	5.29 (69)	5.29 (69)	$-37.55^{(a)}$	$-5.56^{(a)}$	$-3.43^{(a)}$
3	6.02 (63)	6.02 (63)	$-47.39^{(a)}$	$-7.49^{(a)}$	-1.41
4	4.01 (4)	4.01 (4)	$-41.57^{(a)}$	$-6.71^{(a)}$	-1.36
5	4.32 (9)	4.33 (9)	$-42.65^{(a)}$	$-7.13^{(a)}$	-1.38
6	4.01 (63)	4.01 (63)	$-42.65^{(a)}$	$-7.13^{(a)}$	-1.38

Notes: Numbers between brackets indicates the estimated locations in the sample of potential AO's, that is, $T_k = [T \cdot \tau_k]$, $k = 1, \ldots, m$, at each iteration of these two procedures. For computing the ADF statistic at each iteration, ADF(q)-AO, the number of lags is fixed at $q = 2$ (see Table 2). Superscripts [(a), (b), (c)] indicates rejection at 1%, 5%, and 10% significance levels, respectively.

Table 4. Unit root tests for GDP and tourist arrivals, 1977:Q1-2014:Q4.

	Series: Real GDP		Series: Foreign tourist arrivals	
	Constant	Linear trend	Constant	Linear trend
Estimated a	1.0002	0.8794	0.9980	0.9615
DF_1	0.0369	$-18.3329^{(c)}$	-0.3025	-5.8504
DF_2	0.0543	$-3.2620^{(c)}$	-0.4562	-1.6808
$ADF_2(q)$	0.0041(1)	$-3.9538(3)^{(b)}$	$-0.4471(1)$	$-3.9597(2)^{(b)}$
$IV(q)$-estimated a	0.9972	0.4976	0.9983	0.8650
$IV_1(q)$	-0.4324	$-76.3635^{(a)}$	-0.2519	$-20.5141^{(c)}$
$IV_2(q)$	-0.5848	$-3.8636^{(b)}$	-0.4057	$-4.2772^{(a)}$
Breitung, VR	0.0989	$0.0024^{(b)}$	0.0977	0.0073
Stationarity tests against a unit root				
MLH_1	$3.9876^{(a)}$	0.5333	$3.9319^{(a)}$	$1.9431^{(b)}$
KPSS	$1.7677^{(a)}$	0.0629	$1.7398^{(a)}$	$0.1582^{(b)}$

Notes: Superscripts $^{(a),(b),(c)}$ indicate rejection at 1%, 5%, and 10% significance levels, respectively. $DF_1(IV_1)$ and $DF_2(IV_2,$ $ADF_2)$ denotes the Dickey–Fuller type tests based on the normalized bias statistic and the T-ratio test statistic, respectively. The number of lags, q, for ADF test is selected by the MAIC criteria proposed by Ng and Perron (2001), while that for IV-based tests we take $q = q_T = [0.75 \cdot T^{1/2}]$. For the KPSS stationarity test we use the Bartlett kernel and sample-size dependent bandwidth given by $[12(T/100)^{1/4}]$.

$T_k = [T \cdot \tau_k]$ and $IV_{2,T}(q) = (\hat{\alpha}_T(q) - 1)/\sigma_{\hat{\alpha}_T(q)}$, with $\sigma_{\hat{\alpha}_T(q)}$ the standard error of the estimator $\hat{\alpha}_T(q)$, where the standard Dickey–Fuller (DF) statistics are given by $DF_{j,T} = IV_{j,T}(1)$, $j = 1$, 2 (see Dickey & Fuller, 1979). The results of the DF tests are only reliable under lack of serial correlation in the error term ε_t, while that the variance ratio (VR) statistic proposed by Breitung (2002) is robust to the degree of serial correlation in ε_t. The augmented DF (ADF) statistic (see, e.g. Said & Dickey, 1984) is a modified version of the DF_2 statistic that incorporates a parametric correction for this source of distortion in the distribution of the standard DF tests. Following Harris, McCabe, and Leybourne (2003) and McCabe, Leybourne, and Harris (2006), it can be shown that taking $q = q_T = [c\sqrt{T}]$, with $c > 0$ and where $[x]$ denotes the integer part of x, the IV-based tests are also robust to neglected serial correlation in this error term.[11]

First, for the series of terrorist attacks, the results in Table 2 contain contradictory evidence on the persistence characterization of this variable. The IV-based tests, the VR and the results for the KPSS tests (both for the level and the first differences, see also Figure 3) clearly indicate evidence in favour of no stationarity, that is, unit root, while that the DF and ADF tests reject the null hypothesis of a unit root against the alternative of stationarity.[12] Given the very different properties of all these testing procedures, the mixed contradictory evidence in Table 2 implies that there could be some type of alternative explanation besides the possible effect of the serial correlation.

The analysis in Franses and Haldrup (1994) and Vogelsang (1999), among others, indicates that the presence of systematic AO biases many commonly used unit root tests (particularly DF and ADF-type tests) towards over-rejection of the null hypothesis of a unit root in favour of the alternative of stationarity acting like a negative MA component. Conversely, many stationarity testing procedures such as the KPSS, could produce spurious over-rejections of the null hypothesis of stationarity in presence of outlying observations, such as those that appear to be present in this series. To try to clarify these contradictory results, we use the iterative procedures in Vogelsang (1999)[13] and Perron and Rodríguez (2003) to test the null hypothesis of a unit root under possible contamination by AO.

These two procedures are based on testing for $\alpha = 1$ in the following modified augmented auxiliary regression

$$x_t = d_t + \alpha x_{t-1} + \sum_{j=1}^{q} \phi_j \Delta x_{t-j} + \sum_{k=1}^{m} \sum_{j=0}^{q+1} \omega_{kj} I_{t-j}(\tau_k) + v_t, \quad t = q+2, \ldots, T,$$

where $I_t(\tau_k)$ are indicator functions defined as $I_t(\tau_k) = I(t = [T\tau_k])$, $k = 1, \ldots, m$, representing the location of a potential AO with magnitude ω_k, where the difference between the two procedures is in the way to identify the influential observation. The results obtained for the series of terrorist attacks are presented in the following Table 3.

Once adjusted in the indicated way for the occurrence of these influential observations in the outcomes of the ADF unit root test,[14] the results clearly indicates in almost all the cases the evidence of stationarity of the series of terrorist attacks. With this evidence, in what follows this series will be treated as being generated by a stationary process, possible contaminated by some outlying observations, but it will not be filtered by the influence of these point events that could be as informative as the rest of 'normal' observations.

The stationary nature of this series implies that any stochastic shock is transitory (that is, it will have only a limited impact in time measured by the autocorrelation structure of the series), although for the other two series, real GDP and tourist arrivals, the results in Table 4 mostly agree in characterizing these series as being generated by a stochastic trend component around a given deterministic component, that is, by a non-stationary unit root process,[15] implying that the random shocks have a permanent effect on the underlying level of these series. For the real GDP series, we find evidence of non-stationarity around a fixed level, while that for the series of tourist arrivals the empirical evidence points to non-stationarity around a constant level or, alternatively, a constant term and a linear trend function.

Based on these empirical findings, the final stage of our empirical study is dedicated to the analysis of the stability of the long-run relationship between GDP growth and tourist arrivals, but with the inclusion of a stationary additional regressor which is given by our measure of terrorist activity. The chosen basic framework for this analysis is a univariate cointegrating regression model, which at the end of the next subsection will be extended to a nonlinear specification treating the stationary regressor as the responsible of the possible differences in the contribution of tourism demand to GDP growth in Turkey.

3.2. Cointegration analysis

Once obtained empirical evidence on the persistent nature of the main variables in the analysis of the relationship between tourism and growth (TLGH), one has to decide which approach is used to perform the analysis in the context of possibly cointegrated integrated variables. In all the existing procedures based on a VAR (vector autoregression) system, the complete set of variables are treated symmetrically, as opposed to the standard univariate regression models that usually have a clear interpretation in terms of exogenous and endogenous variables. Other drawbacks of the VAR system approach are related to the interpretation of the results and the formulation of hypothesis, the use of many degrees of freedom, and the fact that all the variables are modelled at the same time, which could be a problem in situations where the relation for some variable is defective possibly biasing the estimation of the whole system. In this latter case, a better option could be conditioning on that variable, and specify a standard linear cointegrating regression model following the initial postulate made by Engle and Granger (1987) in the analysis of such type of long-run relationships. To that end, we formulate a log-linear specification of a standard cointegrating regression as follows

$$\log(GDP_t) = d_t + \beta_1 \log(T_t) + \beta_2 TA_t + u_t,$$

where, as before in Section 3.1, d_t represents the deterministic component, usually only a constant term $d_t = \alpha_0$ or a constant term and a linear trend function, $d_t = \alpha_0 + \alpha_1 t$, and u_t is the regression error term, which is assumed to have zero expectation. Also, following Park (1992), and under stationarity of the regression error term u_t, the case $\alpha_1 = 0$ (i.e. inclusion of only a constant term) is known as deterministic cointegration, while the inclusion of a constant term and a linear trend component ($\alpha_1 \neq 0$) is known as stochastic cointegration. Thus, we specify four competing models depending on the specification of the deterministic trend component: models 1 and 3, in which $d_t = \alpha_0$ ($\alpha_1 = 0$), and models 2 and 4, where $d_t = \alpha_0 + \alpha_1 t$, with the difference between models 1-2 and 3-4 being the inclusion of the stationary regressor TA. However, as cited before, our estimation problem is not a standard one in this literature due to the inclusion of the stationary regressor in a regression model where both the dependent variable and the rest of regressors are non-stationary. In the general case, this fact will cause serious changes in the limiting distributions of the estimators of the model parameters under cointegration, implying that the usual standard inference is not longer valid. Fortunately, Phillips (1995) (see Theorem 4.1(b)) has shown that the fully modified OLS (FM-OLS) estimator developed by Phillips and Hansen (1990) will retain its asymptotic optimality properties for the non-stationary parameters in the cointegrated regression whenever the stationary regressors be predetermined or weakly exogenous, that is, uncorrelated with the regression error terms. Also, the stationary parameters are estimated consistently at the usual rate with asymptotically standard normal distribution.

This same result can be proved for the OLS and other existing alternative estimators providing consistent and asymptotically efficient estimates of the model parameters under cointegration and the exogeneity requirement for a stationary regressor included in a cointegrated regression.[16] For that reason, Table 5 provides the OLS estimation results and empirical evidence on the stationarity of the regression error terms of the specified cointegrating regression model through the Phillips and Ouliaris (1990) tests and other complementary testing procedures for the null of cointegration. For model 3, including only a constant term and the two regressors, we obtain large support for the existence of a stable long-run relationship between real GDP and inbound tourism, with a significant and negative (as expected) estimated impact of a unit change on the number of terrorist attacks on the expected change in real GDP. The estimation of model 4, including a constant and a linear trend, also provides economic and statistically significant results (with the parameter β_2 being statistically not different from 0), and also large support to the evidence of cointegration and structural stability of the linear specification.

Given the questionable validity of the inferential results from OLS estimation under general conditions on the integrated regressor, we compare these results with that of FM-OLS estimation in Table 6 below. Globally, there are not large differences with the

Table 5. OLS estimation of the cointegrating regression.

		Terrorist attacks not included ($\beta_2 = 0$)		Terrorist attacks included	
		Model 1	Model 2	Model 3	Model 4
Panel A. Model estimation					
Parameters					
	a_0	7.7667 (48.022)	10.9491 (25.308)	7.7944 (55.987)	10.8727 (22.686)
	a_1		0.0066 (7.511)		0.0065 (6.534)
	β_1	0.3925 (34.992)	0.1359 (3.915)	0.3918 (40.055)	0.1422 (3.676)
	β_2			−0.0009 (−2.282)	−0.0001 (−0.378)
	Adjusted $R2$	0.9789	0.9921	0.9819	0.9921
Panel B. Cointegration tests					
Z-tests					
	$Z_{1,T}$	−16.7183	−28.0847[b]	−25.3731[b]	−28.4221[b]
	$Z_{2,T}$	−2.8491	−3.8935[b]	−3.5964[b]	−3.9143[b]
AR(1) residual-based	OLS modified	0.9049	0.8281	0.8431	0.8272
estimates		0.8900	0.8152	0.8331	0.8130
Shin's test	C_T	0.2018	0.0607	0.1723	0.0627
MLH test	H_T	1.0645	−0.9514	0.0446	−0.9838
Hansen's test	$L_{c,T}$	0.7299 (0.00)	0.2111 (0.43)	0.8468 (0.00)	0.3334 (0.24)

Notes: The numbers between brackets are the *T*-ratio statistics for testing null significance of the corresponding parameter. For the cointegration tests in Panel B, [a],[b],[c] indicates rejection at 1%, 5%, and 10% significance levels, respectively. *Z*-tests denote the DF-type tests proposed by Phillips and Ouliaris (1990) for the null hypothesis of no cointegration, based on the modified estimation of the AR(1) residual coefficient. C and H denote the tests proposed by Shin (1994) and McCabe et al. (2006) for the null hypothesis of cointegration. Finally, $L_{c,T}$ denotes the L_c test proposed by Hansen (1992) to test the null hypothesis of structural stability under cointegration against the alternative of time-varying regression coefficients following a martingale process (in parenthesis estimated *p*-values from Table 3, p. 52 in Hansen's paper).

above results, with stronger evidence in favour of the specification in Model 4, including a constant term and a linear trend in the deterministic part.

Also, as a robustness check of these specifications, Tables 5 and 6 contain Hansen's (1992) test for structural stability under cointegration of the estimated models. The empirical evidence provides significant evidence for the validity of these specifications,

Table 6. FM-OLS estimation of the cointegrating regression.

		Terrorist attacks not included ($\beta_2 = 0$)		Terrorist attacks included	
		Model 1	Model 2	Model 3	Model 4
Panel A. Model estimation					
Parameters					
	a_0	7.7263 (46.802)	10.8289 (24.973)	7.7673 (56.644)	10.7778 (22.521)
	a_1		0.0064 (7.219)		0.0063 (6.353)
	β_1	0.3953 (34.523)	0.1455 (4.183)	0.3940 (41.558)	0.1497 (3.876)
	β_2			−0.0011 (−3.163)	−0.0001 (−0.186)
	Adjusted $R2$	0.9790	0.9919	0.9811	0.9918
Panel B. Cointegration tests					
Z-tests					
	$Z_{1,T}$	−16.2909	−27.1668[b]	−31.7221[a]	−27.7376[b]
	$Z_{2,T}$	−2.8287	−3.8321[b]	−4.1352[a]	−3.8746[b]
AR(1) residual-based	OLS modified	0.9100	0.8299	0.7946	0.8251
estimates		0.8928	0.8213	0.7913	0.8175
Shin's test	C_T	0.1624	0.0609	0.1296	0.0615
Hansen's test	$L_{c,T}$	0.6277 (0.02)	0.2089 (0.44)	0.6909 (0.01)	0.4199 (0.15)

Notes: See Table 5 for a description of the quantities appearing. The FM-OLS estimation is performed using kernel-type estimates of the required long-run variances and covariances, with the Bartlett kernel and deterministic bandwidth given by $[8(T/100)^{1/3}]$. Superscripts [a],[b],[c] indicate rejection at 1%, 5%, and 10% significance levels, respectively.

including the two cases where the stationary regressor is included. As a by-product of these estimates, Table 7 contains the estimated values of the sample cross-autocorrelation function (SCACF) up to lag 10 between the stationary regressor and the OLS residuals (and also the SCACF between the two regressors). This simple evidence points out to the weak exogeneity of the stationary regressor TA, supporting the assumed validity of the standard inference under cointegration of the OLS estimates.

Alternatively, we consider the estimation of our cointegrating regressions by a method recently proposed by Vogelsang and Wagner (2014), based on applying OLS to the so-called integrated modified (IM) cointegrating regression given by

$$\sum_{j=1}^{t} \log (GDP_j) = \sum_{j=1}^{t} d_j + \beta_1 \sum_{j=1}^{t} \log (T_j) + \beta_2 \sum_{j=1}^{t} TA_j + \gamma_1 \log (T_t) + \gamma_2 TA_t + Z_t,$$

where $Z_t = U_t - (\gamma_1 \log (T_t) + \gamma_2 TA_t)$, with $U_t = \sum_{j=1}^{t} u_j$. The OLS estimation of the IM cointegrating regression (IM-OLS), provides almost asymptotically efficient estimates under cointegration with limiting distribution of the estimates free of nuisance parameters without requiring the choice of any tuning parameter.

Note that the parameter γ_2 in the specification of the IM regression allows to directly measuring the degree of endogeneity of the corresponding regressor, TA. The results of the IM-OLS estimation are presented in Table 8.

Again, as under OLS estimation, the most consistent results are obtained with the inclusion of only a constant term in the deterministic component (deterministic cointegration), with a significant negative impact of the number of terrorist attacks on changes in the real GDP, and sample evidence of exogeneity of the stationary regressor ($\gamma_2 = 0$). However, all this evidence is based on static specifications of the relationship between economic growth, tourism demand and terrorist attacks. Thus, to obtain some insight on the dynamic relation between the terrorist activity and changes in the real GDP, adjusted by the influence of tourist arrivals, we choose the specification and estimation of a threshold cointegrating regression as follows

$$\log (GDP_t) = \alpha_0 + \alpha_1 t + \beta_1 \log (T_t) + (\phi_0 + \phi_1 t + \lambda_1 \log (T_t))I(TA_{t-d} > \gamma) + \varepsilon_t,$$

Table 7. Sample evidence of weak exogeneity of TA regressor and linear relationship between T and TA.

| | A. Estimated SCACF between TA and u (sample evidence of weak exogeneity of TA) | | | | B. Estimated SCACF between T and TA | | | |
| | Terrorist attacks supressed | | Terrorist attacks included | | Corr(T_{t-h}, TA_t) | | Corr(T_t, TA_{t-h}) | |
Lag	Constant	Constant and linear trend	Constant	Constant and linear trend	Constant	Constant and linear trend	Constant	Constant and linear trend
0	−0.3201	−0.0487	0.0000	0.0000	0.1653	−0.0726	0.1653	−0.0726
1	−0.2969	0.0110	−0.0889	0.0392	0.2548	0.0242	0.1369	−0.1065
2	−0.2620	0.0572	−0.1180	0.0741	0.2434	0.0198	0.0712	−0.1765
3	−0.2520	0.0554	−0.1473	0.0658	0.1810	−0.0538	0.0844	−0.1617
4	−0.2609	0.0651	−0.1942	0.0686	0.1478	−0.0886	0.2195	−0.0155
5	−0.3035	0.0312	−0.2375	0.0342	0.1708	−0.0632	0.2110	−0.0247
6	−0.3154	0.0385	−0.1866	0.0517	0.2067	−0.0238	0.1821	−0.0551
7	−0.3094	0.0604	−0.2050	0.0691	0.2430	0.0171	0.1584	−0.1000
8	−0.3267	0.0259	−0.2191	0.0355	0.2748	0.0569	0.0450	−0.2364
9	−0.3303	−0.0096	−0.2389	−0.0019	0.3215	0.1052	0.0282	−0.2517
10	−0.3068	−0.0111	−0.2588	−0.0095	0.2863	0.0705	0.1133	−0.1574

Table 8. IM-OLS estimation of the cointegrating regression.

	Terrorist attacks not included ($\beta_2 = 0$)		Terrorist attacks included	
	Model 1	Model 2	**Model 3**	Model 4
Parameters				
a_0	7.7567	10.8936	**7.9036**	11.2083
	(439.051)	(233.019)	**(567.885)**	(190.419)
a_1		0.0065		0.0072
		(65.529)		(57.794)
β_1	0.3924	0.1403	**0.3848**	0.1144
	(321.399)	(37.163)	**(399.452)**	(23.902)
β_2			−0.0018	0.0002
			(−32.414)	(6.505)
γ_1	0.0385	0.0155	**0.0125**	0.0152
	(9.761)	(9.523)	**(4.213)**	(8.903)
γ_2			0.0003	0.0008
			(1.265)	(5.167)

Notes: The numbers between parentheses are T-ratio statistics for testing the null significance of the corresponding parameters, with kernel-based estimation of the long-run variance of the regression error terms.

where TA_{t-d} is the threshold or transition variable between the two states of long-run equilibrium, if the regression error term u_t is stationary, with time delay $d \geq 1$, and γ is the threshold parameter or required level for the transition variable to act separating both states of the relation.

$$\frac{\partial \log (GDP_t)}{\partial \log (T_t)} = \beta_1 + \lambda_1 I(TA_{t-d} > \gamma).$$

Also note that the above specification of the regression model with threshold effects can also be rewritten as a two regime or threshold regression in the form

$$\log (GDP_t) = (\alpha_0 + \alpha_1 t + \beta_1 \log (T_t))I(TA_{t-d}$$
$$\leq \gamma) + [(\alpha_0 + \phi_0) + (\alpha_1 + \phi_1)t + (\beta_1 + \lambda_1)\log (T_t)]I(TA_{t-d} > \gamma) + \varepsilon_t,$$

where the transition between regimes is driven by the stationary threshold variable TA according the classification rule determined by crossing the threshold value γ. This lead us to identify the two states of the relationship as (when $TA_{t-d} \leq \gamma$) and outer ($TA_{t-d} > \gamma$) regimes. Gonzalo and Pitarakis (2006) propose the use of the supremum of a Lagrange Multiplier (LM) statistic to test for the absence of threshold effects under cointegration. The implementation of the SupLM test for testing the null hypothesis of no threshold effect under cointegration, that is, for joint test of $\phi_0 = \phi_1 = \lambda_1 = 0$, usually assumes 10% trimming at each end of the sample, and given that there is no practical rule for the choice of the delay parameter $d \geq 1$, we perform the analysis for values of $d = 1, \ldots, 5$, corresponding to a potential delayed effect between three and fifteen months. The results are shown in the following Table 9, together with the estimation of the threshold value γ (the number of terrorist attacks forcing a change in the state of the relation) for each value of d (Figure 5).

The quantities appearing between parenthesis in the columns of Table 9 labelled with $\gamma_T(d)$ (the estimated values of the threshold parameter), are the proportion of quarters in the sample with number of terrorist attacks over this estimated value.

Table 9. Tests for threshold effects and estimated threshold value.

	(a) Constant term		(b) Constant term and linear trend	
Delay parameter	$SupLM_T(d)$	$\gamma_T(d)$	$SupLM_T(d)$	$\gamma_T(d)$
$d = 1$	$27.656^{(a)}$	40 (14.47%)	$20.941^{(c)}$	7 (57.89%)
2	$19.951^{(a)}$	7 (57.89%)	$12.889^{(c)}$	3 (76.97%)
3	$14.224^{(c)}$	4 (69.08%)	9.451	7 (57.89%)
4	11.044	4	7.682	5 (66.45%)
5	9.503	55 (10.53%)	8.691	8 (55.26%)

Notes: (a), (b), (c) indicates significant rejection of the null hypothesis of no threshold effects under cointegration at 1%, 5%, and 10% significance levels, respectively. The asymptotic critical values are taken from Andrews (1993), Table 1 (p. 840), with $p = 3$, and $\pi_0 = 0.10$ (18.28(1%), 14.62(5%), 12.81(10%)).

As can be seen from Table 9, there are important differences in the outcomes of this testing procedure depending on the specification of the deterministic component of the threshold cointegrating regression. Particularly relevant are the results from including a constant term and a linear trend component (Table 9(b)), for delays $d = 1$ and 2 quarters (corresponding to three to six months) with a relatively small number of estimated terrorist attacks producing significant changes in the magnitude and sign of the relation. Table 10 contains the OLS estimation results of this specification. Note the particular relevance of the estimates in Panel B, when including a constant term and a linear trend component (the so-called case of stochastic cointegration), with significant and negative estimation of the parameter λ_1, which measures the impact of the magnitude of terrorist activity, for delays $d = 1$ and 2.

Given the specification of the threshold cointegrated regression, the OLS estimates of the inner and outer regimes allowing to explain the conditional expected values of $y_t = \log(GDP_t)$ are given by $\hat{y}_{1,t}(\gamma) = (\hat{d}_{1,t} + \hat{\beta}_{1,T}\log(T_t)) \cdot (1 - I(TA_{t-d} > \gamma))$ and $\hat{y}_{2,t}(\gamma) = (\hat{d}_{2,t} + (\hat{\beta}_{1,T} + \hat{\lambda}_{1,T})\log(T_t)) \cdot I(TA_{t-d} > \gamma)$, respectively, with $\hat{d}_{j,t}, j = 1, 2$, the corresponding estimates of the deterministic trend component for each subset of observations. Figure 6 plots the estimated values of $\hat{y}_{1,t}(\gamma)$ for the inner regime and the estimated corrections for the outer regime, which are given by the quantities $\hat{\Delta}_{2,t}(\gamma) = (\hat{d}_{2,t} - \hat{d}_{1,t} + \hat{\lambda}_{1,T}\log(T_t)) \cdot I(TA_{t-d} > \gamma)$, and for both specifications of the regression model depending on the structure of the deterministic component, only with a constant term or with a constant and a linear trend.

As can be seen from these figures, and although not statistically significant, in all the cases, for delays between $d = 1$ and 5 quarters (i.e. for delays between 3 and 15 months), it is estimated a downward correction on the magnitude of the response of changes in tourism demand on changes in real GDP for Turkey due to the impact of terrorist activity. For a delay between three and six months, and even for a relatively small number of estimated terrorist attacks, we estimate a negative impact around 10% on economic growth. Thereafter, the negative impact of terrorism on economic growth through international tourism dilutes.

4. Summary and main conclusions

As indicated by Baker (2014), given that terrorism is an enigmatic and compelling phenomenon, and its relation with tourism is complex and multifaceted, there could be a number of several alternative factors that could explain tourist's decision-making

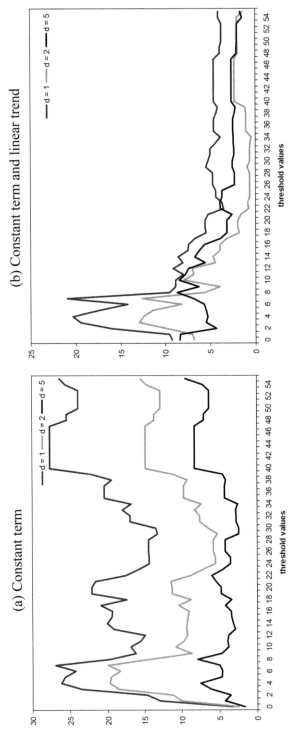

Figure 5. Estimated values of $LM_T(d)$ for $d = 1, 5$, over the set of threshold values (a) Constant term (b) Constant term and linear trend.

74

Table 10. OLS estimation results of the cointegrating regression with threshold effects determined by the estimated value of the threshold parameter for values of the delay parameter $d = 1, \dots, 5$.

Delay parameter, d:	d = 1	2	3	4	5
Panel A. Case of inclusion of a constant term in the deterministic component					
a_0	7.832	8.041	8.050	8.000	7.793
	(106.158)	(77.312)	(66.550)	(65.991)	(100.901)
	[45.443]	[31.583]	[27.018]	[26.157]	[40.593]
β_1	0.389	0.374	0.373	0.377	0.391
	(76.710)	(52.371)	(44.925)	(45.253)	(73.736)
	[32.838]	[21.394]	[18.239]	[17.937]	[29.664]
φ_0	−0.673	−0.568	−0.497	−0.422	−0.381
	(−3.390)	(−4.014)	(−3.302)	(−2.782)	(−1.549)
	[−1.451]	[−1.639]	[−1.341]	[−1.103]	[−0.623]
λ_1	0.042	0.038	0.034	0.028	0.023
	(3.089)	(3.935)	(3.259)	(2.721)	(1.371)
	[1.323]	[1.607]	[1.323]	[1.079]	[0.552]
Panel B. Case of inclusion of a constant term and a linear trend in the deterministic component					
a_0	9.800	10.277	10.520	10.767	10.733
	(32.387)	(27.779)	(33.816)	(31.882)	(36.295)
	[16.767]	[14.522]	[16.980]	[15.925]	[17.595]
a_1	0.004	0.005	0.006	0.006	0.006
	(6.007)	(6.232)	(8.419)	(8.479)	(9.624)
	[3.109]	[3.258]	[4.228]	[4.235]	[4.666]
β_1	0.231	0.192	0.172	0.151	0.154
	(9.459)	(6.423)	(6.837)	(5.558)	(6.467)
	[4.897]	[3.358]	[3.433]	[2.776]	[3.135]
φ_0	1.438	0.882	0.550	0.250	0.278
	(3.511)	(1.963)	(1.291)	(0.574)	(0.651)
	[1.818]	[1.026]	[0.648]	[0.287]	[0.316]
φ_1	0.004	0.002	0.002	0.001	0.001
	(4.129)	(2.422)	(1.724)	(0.963)	(1.127)
	[2.138]	[1.266]	[0.866]	[0.481]	[0.546]
λ_1	−0.119	−0.073	−0.046	−0.021	−0.024
	(−3.592)	(−2.007)	(−1.341)	(−0.609)	(−0.708)
	[−1.859]	[−1.049]	[−0.673]	[−0.305]	[−0.343]

Notes: In parenthesis and brackets, OLS-based T-ratio test statistics based on standard residual variance (estimation of the short-run error variance) and kernel-type estimation of the long-run error variance, respectively. The estimation is performed by OLS using the estimated values of the threshold parameter appearing in Table 9 for each value of d.

process for destination choice. Thus, tourist's risk perception associated with terrorism and the country's level of development and performance in safety could be more informative measures to account for the effect of this phenomenon (see, e.g. Gu & Martin, 1992 and Mansfeld, 1996).

Additionally, there seems to be a quite general consensus among many analysts, experts and entrepreneurs in the tourist sector about the limited impact of terrorist attacks in reducing the number of tourists visiting the affected location, although the magnitude and length of this expected negative effect will depend on a variety of factors, including the stability of the country and the government response. Particularly, it is often argued that natural disasters, diseases or political unrest are worse for tourism than terrorist attacks. However, despite this apparent resilience of the tourist sector to this type of dramatic events, it is of interest to quantify its effects on the whole economy through the modification of the contribution of the tourist activity. This paper address this question for Turkey, one of the leading world tourist destinations, for a quite long time period covering different historical phases, although characterized by high social instability and terrorist activities.

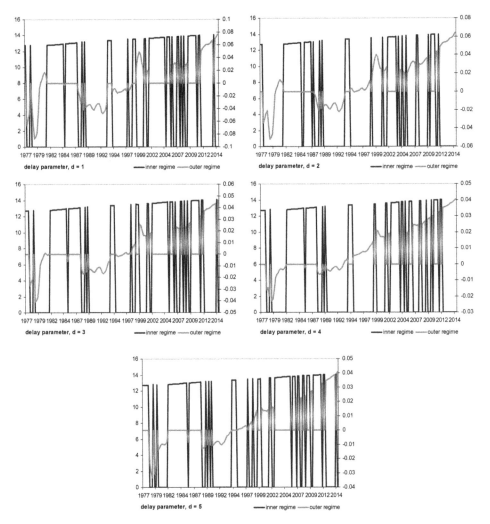

Figure 6. OLS estimates for the inner and outer regimes. Case of inclusion of a constant term and linear trend (Table 10, Panel B).

In this paper, an up-to-date sample period for quarterly data on GDP, inbound tourism and terrorism for the period Q1 : 1977-Q4:2014 are used to explore the relationship between tourism sector and economic growth adding information on terrorist activity. To that end, we employ a standard measure of terrorist activity, namely the number of terrorist attacks per quarter obtained from the GTD, which has also been used in a number of some other studies on the characterization of the economic performance in presence of this type of social and political instability. However, as indicated by Abadie and Gardeazabal (2008), some other indicators of terrorism risk in a country (such as the World Markets Research Centre's Global Terrorism Index (GTI)) could provide more accurate measures of this phenomenon.

Despite the possible drawbacks of the proxy used, we obtain significant and consistent evidence on the negative impact of terrorist activity on economic growth for Turkey through the deterioration of the long-run relationship between tourism and economic growth. Making use of a novelty treatment of this relationship, through the analysis of a threshold cointegrating regression where the stationary transition variable is given by our measure of terrorism, we estimate a negative impact on the contribution of tourism demand on economic growth of around 10% on real GDP for periods where the number of terrorist attacks exceeds a certain level (threshold value), endogenously determined by the procedure. As a by-product of this analysis, we estimate that this negative effect may persist for three to six months (in average terms for the whole sample period), before recovering the level unaffected by the influence of these events.

Consequently, in this paper we have found empirical significant evidence in favour of the TLGH for Turkey, providing further arguments to the inconclusive impact of tourism on economic growth for that country. What is more, terrorism negatively affects the positive impact of international tourism demand on Turkish economic growth. The good news is that the negative impact of terrorism on GDP seems to be concentrated between three and six months after the event and thereafter it vanished. That is, the tourism sector in Turkey seems to be very resilient to terrorism. However, the increasing violence in Turkey and in neighbouring countries after the Arab Spring would compromise its long-run economic growth if policy measures that aim to increase safety and to restore the image after a terrorist attack are not implemented. Also, given the relatively fast estimated impact of terrorist activity of certain intensity, and to avoid possible persistent aftermath, it seems important to highlight the role of the crisis managers in the tourism industry. Among other actions, they must employ creative and clever crisis communications to restore the image of stability and safety in tourist destinations affected by terrorist attacks.

Notes

1. For a review of many of these studies and procedures, see the surveys by Durlauf and Quah (1999) and Durlauf, Johnson, and Temple (2005), as well as the survey by Ehrhart (2009) for the interaction between growth and inequality.
2. For more details on the literature for this phenomenon see, for example, Marin (1992), Giles and Williams (2000, 2001) and Dreger and Herzer (2013) and the references therein.
3. For a review of the literature on this question see for instance the recent surveys by Cortés-Jiménez and Pulina (2006), Brida and Pulina (2010) and Pablo-Romero and Molina (2013).
4. See Table 1 in Sandler and Enders (2008) for a list of many of these macroeconomic empirical studies of the impact of terrorism, with a description of the methodology and the main findings.
5. Differences in the empirical results on the impact of terrorism on macroeconomic variables can be explained by differences in sample of countries and time periods under analysis as well as differences in the indicators or measures of terrorist used. Frey and Luechinger (2003) provide additional possible effects of terrorism activity.
6. For the ELGH, Taban and Aktar (2012) found evidence to support the existence of both a short and long-run bidirectional causality relationship between export growth and real GDP growth for this country and for the period 1980:Q1-2007:Q2.
7. For a complete and updated summary of empirical results on causality analysis between tourism and economic growth for Turkey, see Table 1 (p. 168) in Terzi (2015).
8. The source of these data are Quarterly National Accounts from OECD statistics (https://stats.oecd.org) for real GDP and Turkish Statistical Institute (Turkstat) (http://www.turkstat.gov.tr/Start.do) for tourist arrivals.

9. In this database, maintained by the National Consortium for the Study of Terrorism and Responses to Terrorism (START) which is based at the University of Maryland, terrorism is defined as "the threatened or actual use of illegal force and violence by a non-state actor to attain a political, economic, religious, or social goal through fear, coercion, or intimidation". (https://www.start.umd.edu/gtd)

10. In the basic case, that is, in absence of deterministic component $d_t = 0$, the IV-type estimator is based on the raw observations $x_t = \eta_t$, while that OLS detrended observations are used if $d_t \neq 0$. Originally, this estimator, and the corresponding statistics for testing the null hypothesis of a unit root, is proposed to deal with serially correlated error terms ε_t being generated by a moving average (MA) process of order $q_0 \geq 1$ as $\varepsilon_t = e_t + \sum_{j=1}^{q_0} \theta_j e_{t-j}$, with $e_t \ iid(0, \sigma_e^2)$. For any chosen lag $q \geq q_0$, these test statistics are pivotal with limiting null distributions free of nuisance parameters.

11. Also, following Hansen and Lunde (2014), it can be shown that the unit root tests based on these IV estimators of the first-order serial correlation coefficient α are also robust to measurement errors or aberrant observations in the series.

12. As has been recommended by a referee, the results for the DF tests should not be reported given the need to account for serial correlation in the error terms evidenced by the MAIC criteria in computing the ADF test. This is due to the fact that the true limiting null distribution of the DF statistics has changed and the outcomes of these tests are not longer valid using the usual critical values. However, given that the estimated values of these statistics clearly point in the direction of stationarity, this evidence (being strictly invalid) could still be useful.

13. Although Vogelsang's procedure has the right size under the null hypothesis of no single outlier, Perron and Rodríguez (2003) have shown that when applied in an iterative fashion to select multiple outliers, this test exhibits serious size distortion as an excessive number of outliers will be detected. To avoid this possibility, we use the appropriate limiting distribution of the test at each step of the iterative search obtained by Perron and Rodríguez (2003) and also the modified version proposed by these authors (Panel B of Table 3). It should also be noted that even when the Vogelsang's test is used to detect a single outlier, Haldrup and Sansó (2008) have shown that this procedure is generally inconsistent, with very low power unless the outliers are huge. However, despite the possible unreliable outcomes resulting from this procedure, the results shown in Table 3 indicate close agreement between the two procedures.

14. See footnote 12 for the justification of the inclusion of the results based on the DF test statistics, despite the apparent requirement of serial correlation adjustment.

15. For testing the null hypothesis of stationarity against the alternative of a unit root, in addition to the KPSS test, we also use the MLH_1 test proposed by McCabe et al. (2006), which have the advantage that its limiting null distribution is standard normal and that it is invariant to the particular specification of the deterministic component.

16. Particularly, under exogeneity of a subset of stationary regressors, it can be shown that the no stationary parameters can be consistently estimated by OLS under cointegration with the same limiting distribution as if the stationary regressors are omitted from the estimated regression. As is well known, this distribution is only useful for constructing pivotal test statistics under the additional condition of strict exogeneity of the integrated regressors. In such a case, hypothesis testing for these parameters is standard.

Acknowledgements

We wish to thank two anonymous referees for helpful suggestions and comments that led to a substantial revision of the first draft version.

Disclosure statement

No potential conflict of interest was reported by the author.

References

Abadie, A., & Gardeazabal, J. (2003). The economic costs of conflict: A case study of the Basque country. *American Economic Review, 93*(1), 113–132.

Abadie, A., & Gardeazabal, J. (2008). Terrorism and the world economy. *European Economic Review, 52*(1), 1–27.

Andrews, D. K. W. (1993). Tests for parameter instability and structural change with unknown change point. *Econometrica, 61*(4), 821–856.

Aslan, A., Kaplan, M., & Kula, F. (2008). *International tourism demand for Turkey: A dynamic panel data approach* (Working Paper No. 10601). Munich: MPRA.

Baker, D. Mc. A. (2014). The effects of terrorism on the travel and tourism industry. *International Journal of Religious Tourism and Pilgrimage, 2*(1), 58–67.

Bilgel, F., & Karahasan, B. C. (2016). *Thirty years of conflict and economic growth in Turkey: A synthetic control approach* (LEQS Paper No. 112/2016). London: The London School of Economics and Political Science.

Blomberg, S. B., & Hess, G. D. (2002). The temporal links between conflict and economic activity. *Journal of Conflict Resolution, 46*(1), 74–90.

Blomberg, S. B., Hess, G. D., & Orphanides, A. (2004). The macroeconomic consequences of terrorism. *Journal of Monetary Economics, 51*(5), 1007–1032.

Blomberg, S. B., Hess, G. D., & Weerapana, A. (2004a). An economic model of terrorism. *Conflict Management and Peace Science, 21*(1), 17–28.

Blomberg, S. B., Hess, G. D., & Weerapana, A. (2004b). Economic conditions and terrorism. *European Journal of Political Economy, 20*(2), 463–478.

Breitung, J. (2002). Nonparametric tests for unit roots and cointegration. *Journal of Econometrics, 108*(2), 343–363.

Brida, J. G., & Pulina, M. (2010). *A literature review on the tourism-led-growth hypothesis* (Working Paper 2010/17). Cagliari: Centro Ricerche Economiche Nord Sud (CRENoS).

Chan, W. -S. (1995). Understanding the effect of time series outliers on sample autocorrelations. *Test, 4*(1), 179–186.

Cortés-Jiménez, I., & Pulina, M. (2006). *A further step into the ELGH and TLGH for Spain and Italy* (Nota di Lavoro 118.2006). Milan: Fondazione Eni Enrico Mattei.

Coskun, I. O., & Özer, M. (2014). A reexamination of the tourism-led growth hypothesis under growth and tourism uncertainties in Turkey. *European Journal of Business and Social Sciences, 3*(8), 256–272.

Dickey, D. A., & Fuller, W. A. (1979). Distribution of the estimators for autoregressive time series with a unit root. *Journal of the American Statistical Association, 74*(366), 427–431.

Drakos, K., & Kutan, A. M. (2001). *Regional effects of terrorism on tourism: Evidence from three Mediterranean countries* (ZEI working paper, No. B 26-2001). Bonn: University of Bonn.

Dreger, C., & Herzer, D. (2013). A further examination of the export-led growth hypothesis. *Empirical Economics, 45*(1), 39–60.

Durlauf, S. N., Johnson, P. A., & Temple, J. R. W. (2005). Growth econometrics. In P. Aghion & S. N. Durlauf (Eds.), *Handbook of economic growth* (Vol. 1(A), Chapter 8, pp. 555–677). Amsterdam: Elsevier North-Holland.

Durlauf, S. N., & Quah, D. T. (1999). The new empirics of economic growth. In J. B. Taylor & M. Woodford (Eds.), *Handbook of macroeconomics* (Vol. 1(A), Chapter 4, pp. 235–308). Amsterdam: Elsevier North-Holland.

Ehrhart, C. (2009). *The effects of inequality on growth: A survey of the theoretical and empirical literature* (Working Paper ECINEQ 2009-107). Verona: Society for the Study of Economic Inequality.

Enders, W., & Sandler, T. (1991). Causality between transnational terrorism and tourism: The case of Spain. *Terrorism, 14*(1), 49–58.

Enders, W., & Sandler, T. (1993). The effectiveness of anti-terrorism policies: A vector autoregression-intervention analysis. *The American Political Science Review, 87*(4), 829–844.

Enders, W., & Sandler, T. (1996). Terrorism and foreign direct investment in Spain and Greece. *Kyklos, 49*(3), 331–352.

Enders, W., & Sandler, T. (2002). Patterns of transnational terrorism, 1970–1999: Alternative time-series estimates. *International Studies Quarterly, 46*(2), 145–165.

Enders, W., & Sandler, T. (2005). *Transnational terrorism: An economic analysis* (Non-published Research Reports, Paper 80). CREATE Research Archive. Los Angeles: University of Southern California.

Enders, W., Sandler, T., & Cauley, J. (1990). Assessing the impact of terrorist-thwarting policies: An intervention time series approach. *Defence Economics, 2*(1), 1–18.

Enders, W., Sandler, T., & Parise, G. F. (1992). An econometric analysis of the impact of terrorism on tourism. *Kyklos, 45*(4), 531–554.

Engle, R. F., & Granger, C. W. J. (1987). Co-integration and error correction: Representation, estimation and testing. *Econometrica, 55*(2), 251–276.

Franses, P. H., & Haldrup, N. (1994). The effects of additive outliers on tests for unit roots and cointegration. *Journal of Business and Economic Statistics, 12*(4), 471–478.

Frey, B. S., & Luechinger, S. (2003). *Measuring terrorism* (Working Paper No. 171). Institute for Empirical Research in Economics, University of Zurich.

Giles, J. A., & Williams, C. L. (2000). *Export-led growth: A survey of the empirical literature and some non-causality results. Part 2* (Econometrics Working Paper EWP0002). Department of Economics, University of Victoria.

Giles, J. A., & Williams, C. L. (2001). Export-led growth: A survey of the empirical literature and some non-causality results. Part 1. *The Journal of International Trade and Economic Development, 9*(3), 261–337.

Gonzalo, J., & Pitarakis, J.-Y. (2006). Threshold effects in cointegrating relationships. *Oxford Bulletin of Economics and Statistics, 68*, 813–833.

Gu, Z., & Martin, T. L. (1992). Terrorism, seasonality, and international air tourist arrivals in Central Florida: An empirical analysis. *Journal of Travel and Tourism Marketing, 1*(1), 3–15.

Haldrup, N., & Sansó, A. (2008). A note on the Vogelsang test for additive outliers. *Statistics and Probability Letters, 78*(3), 296–300.

Halicioglu, F. (2004). An ARDL model of international tourist flows to Turkey. In D. Kantarelis (Ed.), *Global business and economics review-anthology* (pp. 614–624). Worcester: B&ESI.

Hall, A. (1989). Testing for a unit root in the presence of moving average errors. *Biometrika, 76*(1), 49–56.

Hansen, B. E. (1992). Tests for parameter instability in regressions with I(1) processes. *Journal of Business and Economic Statistics, 10*(3), 321–335.

Hansen, P. R., & Lunde, A. (2014). Estimating the persistence and the autocorrelation function of a time series that is measured with error. *Econometric Theory, 30*(1), 60–93.

Harris, D., McCabe, B. P. M., & Leybourne, S. (2003). Some limit theory for autocovariances whose order depends on sample size. *Econometric Theory, 19*(5), 829–964.

Hobijn, B., Franses, P. H., & M. Ooms (2004). Generalizations of the KPSS-test for stationarity. *Statistica Neerlandica, 58*(4), 483–502.

Karagoz, M. (2008). *The effect of terrorism on tourism: Evidence from Turkey.* Paper presented at ICM International Conference on Management and Economics, Epoka University.

Katircioglu, S.T. (2009). Revisiting the tourism-led-growth hypothesis for Turkey using the bounds test and Johansen approach for cointegration. *Tourism Management, 30*(1), 17–20.

Kwiatkowski, D., Phillips, P. C. B., Schmidt, P., & Y. Shin (1992). Testing the null hypothesis of stationarity against the alternative of a unit root: How sure are we that economic time series have a unit root? *Journal of Econometrics*, *54*(1–3), 159–178.

Mansfeld, Y. (1996). Wars, tourism and the 'Middle East' factor. In A. Pizam & Y. Mansfeld (Eds.), *Tourism, crime and international security issues* (pp. 265–278). New York, NY: Wiley.

Marin, D. (1992). Is the export-led growth hypothesis valid for industrialized countries? *The Review of Economics and Statistics*, *74*(4), 678–688.

McCabe, B. P. M., Leybourne, S., & Harris, D. (2006). A residual-based test for stochastic cointegration. *Econometric Theory*, *22*(3), 429–456.

Ng, S., & Perron, P. (2001). Lag length selection and the construction of unit root tests with good size and power. *Econometrica*, *69*(6), 1519–1554.

Pablo-Romero, M. del P., & Molina, J. A. (2013). Tourism and economic growth: A review of empirical literature. *Tourism Management Perspectives*, *8*(1), 28–41.

Park, J. Y. (1992). Canonical cointegrating regressions. *Econometrica*, *60*(1), 119–143.

Perron, P., & Rodríguez, G. (2003). Searching for additive outliers in nonstationary time series. *Journal of Time Series Analysis*, *24*(2), 193–220.

Pestana Barros, C. (2003). An intervention analysis of terrorism: The Spanish ETA case. *Defence and Peace Economics*, *14*(6), 401–412.

Phillips, P. C. B. (1995). Fully modified least squares and vector autoregression. *Econometrica*, *63* (5), 1023–1078.

Phillips, P. C. B., & Hansen, B. E. (1990). Statistical inference in instrumental variables regression with I(1) processes. *The Review of Economic Studies*, *57*(1), 99–125.

Phillips, P. C. B., & Ouliaris, S. (1990). Asymptotic properties of residual based tests for cointegration. *Econometrica*, *58*(1), 165–193.

Raza, S. A., & Jawaid, S. T. (2013). Terrorism and tourism: A conjunction and ramification in Pakistan. *Economic Modelling*, *33*(1), 65–70.

Said, S. E., & Dickey, D. A. (1984). Testing for unit roots in autoregressive-moving average models of unknown order. *Biometrika*, *71*(3), 599–607.

Sandler, T., & Enders, W. (2004). An economic perspective on transnational terrorism. *European Journal of Political Economy*, *20*(2), 301–316.

Sandler, T., & Enders, W. (2008). Economic consequences of terrorism in developed and developing countries: An overview. In P. Keefer & N. Loayza (Eds.), *Terrorism, economic development, and political openness* (pp. 17–47). Cambridge: Cambridge University Press.

Saray, O., & Karagöz, K. (2010). Determinants of tourist inflows in Turkey: Evidence from panel gravity model. *ZKU Journal of Social Sciences*, *6*(11), 33–46.

Shin, Y. (1994). A residual-based test of the null of cointegration against the alternative of no cointegration. *Econometric Theory*, *10*(1), 91–115.

Sinclair, M. T. (1998). Tourism and economic development: A survey. *The Journal of Development Studies*, *34*(5), 1–51.

Taban, S., & Aktar, I. (2012). An empirical examination of the export-led growth hypothesis in Turkey. *Journal of Yasar University*, *3*(11), 1535–1551.

Tang, C. F., & Abosedra, S. (2016). Does tourism expansion effectively spur economic growth in Morocco and Tunisia? Evidence from time series and panel data. *Journal of Policy Research in Tourism, Leisure and Events*, *8*(2), 127–145.

Terzi, H. (2015). Is the tourism-led growth hypothesis (TLGH) valid for Turkey? *Dogus University Journal*, *16*(2), 165–178.

Vogelsang, T. J. (1999). Two simple procedures for testing for a unit root when there are additive outliers. *Journal of Time Series Analysis*, *20*(2), 237–252.

Vogelsang, T. J., & Wagner, M. (2014). Integrated modified OLS estimation and fixed-b inference for cointegrating regressions. *Journal of Econometrics*, *178*(2), 741–760.

Travel advisories – destabilising diplomacy in disguise

Aman Deep and Charles Samuel Johnston

ABSTRACT

In developed countries, travel advisories are generally viewed as legitimate by the travelling public. This paper is constructed around the opposite position – the travel advisory often represents an attempt to politically and/or economically destabilise the developing-nation destination through disruption of tourism. As a conceptual paper, we reference academic literature to create a destabilisation-to-re-stabilisation sequence. We examine five aspects. We begin by discussing how the right to travel is guaranteed in international agreements. We develop a typology of the ways travel advisories have been misused, which shows how individual travel decisions can be destabilised. We show how this destabilises developing nations and conclude with a possible strategy to re-stabilise the situation. In the paper, we advance five models we believe help generalise our discussion to a wider range of cases. The paper thus has significant practical implications for countries being adversely affected by politically and economically motivated travel advisories.

RESUMEN

En los países desarrollados, los viajeros ven como legítimos los anuncios públicos de viajes. Este trabajo se construye alrededor de la posición opuesta – los anuncios públicos con frecuencia representan un intento de desestabilizar política o económicamente el destino en la nación en vías de desarrollo a través de la interrupción del turismo. Como trabajo conceptual, nos remitimos a la literatura académica para crear una secuencia desestabilización - reestabilización. Examinamos cinco aspectos. Comenzamos discutiendo como el derecho a viajar está garantizado por acuerdos internacionales. Desarrollamos una tipología de las formas en las que los anuncios públicos han sido manejados que muestra como las decisiones individuales de viaje pueden ser desestabilizadas. Mostramos cómo esto desestabiliza las naciones en vías de desarrollo y concluimos con una posible estrategia para reestabilizar la situación. En el manuscrito avanzamos cinco modelos que creemos que ayudan a generalizar nuestra discusión a un número de casos más amplio. De este modo, el manuscrito tiene relevantes implicaciones prácticas para los países que están siendo negativamente afectados por anuncios públicos de viajes por motivos políticos o económicos.

RÉSUMÉ

Dans les pays développés, les conseils aux voyageurs sont généralement considérés comme objectifs par les voyageurs. Cet article adopte une position différente selon laquelle ces conseils sont souvent influencés par une tentative de déstabiliser politiquement et/ou économiquement les pays en voie de développement à travers la perturbation du tourisme. En empruntant une approche conceptuelle, nous faisons référence aux publications académiques pour créer une séquence de déstabilisation et re-stabilisation. Nous examinons cinq aspects: nous discuter du droit de voyager tel que garanti par les accords internationaux. Nous développons une typologie relative à la manière dont les conseils aux voyageurs sont manipulés, ce qui montre comment certaines décisions de voyager peuvent être basées sur des faits erronés. Nous démontrons comment cela déstabilise les pays en voie de développement et concluons notre analyse avec une stratégie alternative visant à re-stabiliser la situation. Dans cet article nous proposons cinq modèles que nous croyons utiles pour généraliser notre discussion et la rendre applicable à d'autres cas. Cet article a donc des implications pratiques importantes pour les pays ayant été touchés par les conseils aux voyageurs dictés par des motivations politiques et économiques.

摘要

在发达国家，旅行顾问一般被旅行大众认为是合法正当的。这篇文章却是站在一个对立的立场——旅行顾问通常试图通过旅游方式从政治或经济方面干预发展中国家旅游目的地的稳定。作为一篇概念阐述型的文章，我们参照学术文献创造了一个"从削弱稳定到重建稳定"的发展程序。我们探讨了五个方面。首先我们讨论旅游的权利是如何在国际协定中予以保证的。我们建立了一个有关旅行顾问被错误使用的类型学，其说明了个体的旅游决定如何发生变动。我们证明了这将如何危害发展中国家的稳定，并提出一个可能的战略让情况恢复（重建）稳定。在这篇论文中，我们提出了五种模式，我们相信这五种模式有助于将我们的讨论适用于大范围的案例。因此，这篇文章对于政治和经济受旅行顾问影响的国家具有重要的实践意义。

Introduction

Tourism is an integral part of the world political economy and thus also a means through which political and economic objectives can be achieved (Sharpley, Sharpley, & Adams, 1996). One such means is through the issuance of travel advisories. Developed-nation government ministries issuing travel advisories assert that these are always based on threat or security information that is specific, credible and cannot be countered (Bureau of Consular Affairs, 2014). That is, they are proclaimed to be an appropriate means of warning citizens residing in a stable country about instability at potential international destinations. In situations of civil war or political upheaval, travel advisories will routinely be issued as a means of preventing developed-nation citizens from getting in harm's way. Issuing ministries aver that these are merely 'advisory' – they are non-obligatory recommendations, and decisions by tourists to travel to an advised-against destination are still possible (Bureau of Consular Affairs, 2014).

Spokespersons for ministries in the developing world counter that all is not so above board. They assert a hidden political agenda can exist: a developed nation with ulterior motives will use travel advisories as instruments to extract political favours from tourism-dependent developing nations (Lowenheim, 2007). Put another way, spokespersons assert that inappropriate travel advisories (hereafter ITAs) are issued for coercive purposes related to destabilising the economy and/or the polity of developing nations. They further allege that the issuance of such travel advisories contradicts established global regulations, such as the General Agreement on Trade in Services (GATS) agreement, created in part to protect freedom of movement (Henderson, 2004). When tourism adds significantly to a nation's economy, any ITA can cause severe negative economic and political impacts to occur. As a response, developing nations have demanded reforms; for example, that the United Nations World Tourism Organisation (UNWTO) monitor travel advisories for fairness (Dhawan, 2011).

The issuance of travel advisories by developed countries against developing countries has now assumed greater importance in the changing global political context. The situation is not ideal and academic recognition has been slow. The aim of this paper is therefore to critically consider and evaluate the use of travel advisories as political means of coercive diplomacy capable of destabilisation. The paper is conceptual in nature, bringing together relevant academic discussions that have not yet been used to examine instability between nations. The significance of the paper lies firstly in the systematic articulation of the issue – that travel advisories are being inappropriately used as tools of political coercion. Further, we substantiate the start-to-finish aspects of the destabilisation process, thus extending the existing tourism policy literature. To begin, the paper establishes the basis for the guaranteed human right to travel and to have freedom of movement, concentrating on the GATS agreement. Using a typology, we then discuss the range of allegations by developing nations over ITA issuance. This is used to show the ways in which ITAs contravene signed agreements such as GATS. The third section of the paper examines literature on tourist risk assessment as a way of revealing the mechanisms by which ITAs work to destabilise at the individual and industry levels. The following section models how the negative impacts of both tourist decision-making and business-to-business (B2B) industrial relations can destabilise a developing nation's economy and affect the subsequent ability of its government to properly function. Finally, we develop a strategy model for the developing nation to re-stabilise.

The right to travel is guaranteed

There are in existence numerous international treaties and sets of regulations signed by different governments across the world. Many of these contain provisions relating to movement and travel. The obvious example is the United Nations Declaration on Human Rights, which, in Article 13, proclaims that people have the right to freedom of movement both inside and outside their nation. As a different example, the 1975 Helsinki Accords were ostensibly about the inviolability of international borders. However, Fascell (1979) demonstrated that they also required nations to honour the prior U.N.-based human right to freedom of movement across such borders. Of course, as signatories to these documents, governments are required to understand that they must comply with the agreed-to provisions, which may include the right of citizens to travel across international borders (George & Henthorne, 2007).

The GATS agreement came into existence with the completion of the Uruguay Round of talks in 1995 (World Trade Organisation, 1995). Nations signed the agreement in relation to providing and receiving services. However, for these services to be performed internationally, the GATS agreement was required to contain a comprehensive set of provisions concerning human movement and travel. These provisions are linked to four modes of supply of services. It is in the implementation of these services that travel movement becomes important. The first provision is the 'cross-border' supply of services. This provision focuses on services that are being offered from businesses' own territory to another – there should be no trade barrier imposed. As an example, Kuoni Travels (located in Switzerland) should be able to offer its services (the facilitation of tour packages for Switzerland) to citizens in the United Arab Emirates through the Internet without any barrier. The 'consumption abroad' provision requires that people working in the service sector in their own country should be able to offer their services to people from other countries without any barriers. A tourism-related example would be that hotels and restaurants in Kenya should be able to offer their services to visiting citizens of the United Kingdom (U.K.) without any barriers. The third provision – 'commercial presence' – emphasises that an organisation should be able to set up its own business in another country without any barriers. A tourism-related example would be that Hyatt is able to expand their chain of hotels to Fiji. Finally, the 'movement of natural persons' provision is concerned with a person being free to move from one territory to another to offer his or her services. An example would be a CEO of Hyatt group should be able to move to Fiji to oversee Hyatt operations. All members of the World Trade Organisation are of course required to follow the provisions of the GATS Agreement.

Virtually all nations on the planet have, through their association with other nations, signed one or more international agreements that guarantee the right to travel. As of November 2015, 162 nations have, through their membership in the World Trade Organisation, pledged commitment to GATS. To be consistent with the terms of their membership, signatory nations' official travel advice needs to be free from any form of bias or political/economic agenda and most importantly should be solely based on protecting the personal security of citizens, many of whom are travelling as tourists.

Travel advisories – wolves in sheep's clothing?

During the twentieth century, governments increasingly took on the responsibility of warning their citizens about risks at destinations. Lowenheim (2007, p. 210, citing Riesman, 1940) researched the history of the travel advisory system. He noted the U.S. State Department first issued advisories to its general public against travelling to the belligerent European nations during the First World War. He further noted that during the 1980s, governments worldwide began sharing information with their citizens about the potential consequences of travel to certain countries. Lowenheim concluded by noting that travel advisories had become even more frequent with the globalisation of media and the advent of the Internet.

The United Nations World Tourism Organisation resolution A/RES/578 (XVIII) came into effect in 2009 (2009). The document A/18/20 of the General Assembly resolution states that every country has the right to protect its citizens from any form of personal security threats that they may encounter while travelling abroad. Thus, governments have the right to warn citizens about locations where they could potentially be in danger. However, this resolution simultaneously delimits the range of comments governments are allowed to make. Specifically, all issued travel advisories are to be free from bias and the content of travel warnings needs to be discussed with the targeted countries and finalised only after considerable discussion with prominent experts. The resolution also recommends that governments should cancel travel advisories immediately upon a return to normality.

While many travel advisories are issued in the proper spirit, there is also considerable evidence – in the form of protests by developing nations – that developed, tourist-exporting nations have not always complied with the agreements they have signed (Bianchi, 2006; Lowenheim, 2007; Sharpley et al., 1996). There is a sufficiently large body of complaints documented in the academic literature to create a typology of allegations. This is shown in Figure 1. Allegations of abuse of the travel advisory 'privilege' fall into four general categories. Arranged in a sequence from unintentionally to intentionally coercive in motive these are: overstating risks or based on faulty risk assessments (overstatement); based on bias and prejudice (bias); based on ideological hostility (hostility); used as scare tactics and/or political tools (tool). Clearly, the more intentional the ulterior motive, the greater the implied threat concerning destabilisation.

Perhaps as a naïve response by developed nations, travel advisory warnings have at times been based on a faulty interpretation of the situation on the ground or as an overstatement of actual risks posed to their citizens. The research by Fletcher and Morakabati (2008) showed that following the Mombasa attack on Israeli hotels in the year 2002, the governments of the U.S., the U.K., Australia, and Germany, issued travel advisories against travelling to Kenya based on the fear of 'potential threat' against western interests. Subsequent research by Wax (2003, as cited in Prestholdt, 2011) revealed that the Kenyan tourism industry had lost more than a million dollars per day, resulting in the closing

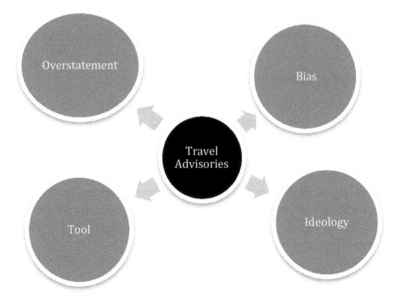

Figure 1. Travel advisories – the range of allegations.

of numerous hotels and restaurants. Were these travel advisories appropriate? The chairman of the Kenya Tourism Federation, Jake Grieves-Cook, issued a statement against the travel advisories:

> We are all aware of the risks of global terrorism in most countries in the world, but there is no greater risk here than in the United Kingdom. For tourists on safari in Kenya's parks, the risk of a terrorist attack must be much lower than in British cities. (*National Geographic News*, 2003, as cited in Fletcher & Morakabati, 2008, p. 550)

As an additional example, Freedman's (2005) research showed that in the past the Thailand Foreign Ministry has criticised developed nations for issuing travel advisories on the basis of speculation rather than intelligence. Freedman also noted the Thailand Foreign Ministry has also alleged that overstated and faulty travel advisories are the result of personnel working in ministries of developed countries seeking to protect themselves against possible charges of negligence, should significant threats materialise. Travel advisories of this type have the potential to destabilise, but this might not be an intention of the issuing nation.

Data collected on travel advisories issued by the U.S. in the last 18 years suggests the existence of bias. Between 1996 and 2014, the U.S. government issued 896 travel warnings against 80 countries (Shankman, 2015). Notably, the majority of the travel advisories were issued against developing nations; hardly any advisories were released that concerned other developed countries.

Lowenheim (2007) presented examples that developed nations can act in a biased way. He observed that the British Foreign and Commonwealth Office (FCO) did not issue an advisory against travel to the U.S. following the 9/11 attacks (2001) but instantly issued a travel advisory against Indonesia during the Bali Bombings (2002). According to Lowenheim, the U.S. then paid back the favour by not issuing a travel advisory during the 2005 London bombings. Lowenheim concluded that such distinct treatment towards 'allies' strengthens the impression of the existence of political bias. For this type of ITA, the motive to destabilise likely varies from case to case.

Ideological hostility governing travel advisory releases has been documented. Travel advisories issued by the U.S., U.K., New Zealand, and Australian governments against Fiji following the 2000 military coup have been interpreted as being based on ideological hostility against Commodore Frank Bainimarama (King & Berno, 2006). Fletcher and Morakabati (2008) asserted that the travel advisories against Fiji were proof that political interests were embedded. These authors showed that besides issuing travel advisories that directly impacted the tourism of Fiji, these governments warned their citizens and tour operators from engaging in any business activity related to Fiji.

Not surprisingly, Cuba has been a target, both directly and indirectly. Bianchi (2006), for example, showed that the U.S. government considered Cuba to be less safe than the nation of Colombia, despite the latter having a far higher crime rate. Cuban protests against this status went unheard. According to the Cuban government, travel advisories issued against travelling to Cuba have been based on the ideological hostility of the U.S. government against communism, not because of danger to American tourists. Sharpley et al. (1996) highlighted the incident when the U.S. government issued a travel advisory against Jamaica on the basis that its prime minister, Manley, had been working to improve ties with the government of Cuba and not because of any security threat to the

American tourists within territorial Jamaica. This type of travel advisory is clearly politically strategic with the ulterior motive of having a destabilising negative impact being only thinly disguised, if disguised at all.

The developed nations have perhaps been most criticised for using travel advisories as political tools for extracting favours. The issuance of a travel advisory by the U.S. government against the Philippines during a relatively peaceful and safe period was seen as a political move to pressurise the Philippines into signing the U.S. Bases Treaty (Richter, 1995, as cited in Bianchi, 2006, p. 70). In another incident, highlighted by Sharpley et al. (1996), the travel advisory issued by the British FCO against the Gambia (a nation whose economy heavily depended on British holiday package tourism) – despite the Gambia having a politically stable government – was interpreted as being a political move to put pressure on the Gambian military regime. Following the issuance of the advisory, British and Scandinavian tour operators quickly ceased their operations, which resulted in the closure of many hotels and massive job losses in the Gambia.

Developing nations' governments have lastly been critical of the developed nations for using travel advisories coercively. The Union Tourism Minister of India, Subodh Kant Sahay, has referred in the past to the travel advisories issued by the U.K., U.S., Australia and New Zealand governments against India as scaremongering (Dhawan, 2011). Kenya's Foreign minister, Kalonzo Musyoka, has also previously protested against the U.S. and the U.K. governments for using travel advisories to instil fear in tourists (Fletcher & Morakabati, 2008). Kenya's President, Uhuru Kenyatta, recently hit back at travel advisories issued by the U.K. and Australia, stating: 'We are now fed up with these threats that we keep getting in travel advisories, Kenya is as safe as any country in the world' (Wangalwa, 2015). A tourism website in Indonesia in the past has criticised the U.S. State Council for often using 'travel advisories to whip Indonesia and other countries into shapes more acceptable to the Bush Administration and thus offending the dignity of the sovereign nations' (Freedman, 2005, p. 395). The intention to destabilise is clearest in this type of travel advisory.

The typology of ITAs, substantiated above, provides strong evidence to support developing nations' claims that the original purpose of travel advisories – to help citizens make informed travel decisions – has become somewhat subverted. Figure 2 combines these specific examples with the four GATS provisions concerning supply of services. When travel advisories are issued inappropriately – the centre oval – they run counter to the spirit of signed agreements such as GATS. In spite of being inappropriate, these warnings are likely to be highly effective. Sharpley et al. (1996) asserted that tourists seek impartial and reliable sources of information about travelling to other countries. Trusting their own governments, tourists are heavily influenced by travel advisories, not understanding that these may be politically motivated. Lowenheim (2007) showed that many tourists from developed nations regularly access government web sites before undertaking travel, and choose to avoid destinations against which a travel advisory has been issued. The destabilising effect of ITAs begins in the developed nations that provide the tourists and the travel system.

In consequence, developing nations have, for some time, been demanding the formation of a formal international agency within the UNWTO to prevent developed nations from exploiting travel advisories (Sonmez, 1998) to achieve ulterior motives that destabilise. According to Myers (2012, p. 7), 'the Mexico Tourism Board has long advocated that travel advisories should abide by three key tenants: context, clarity and

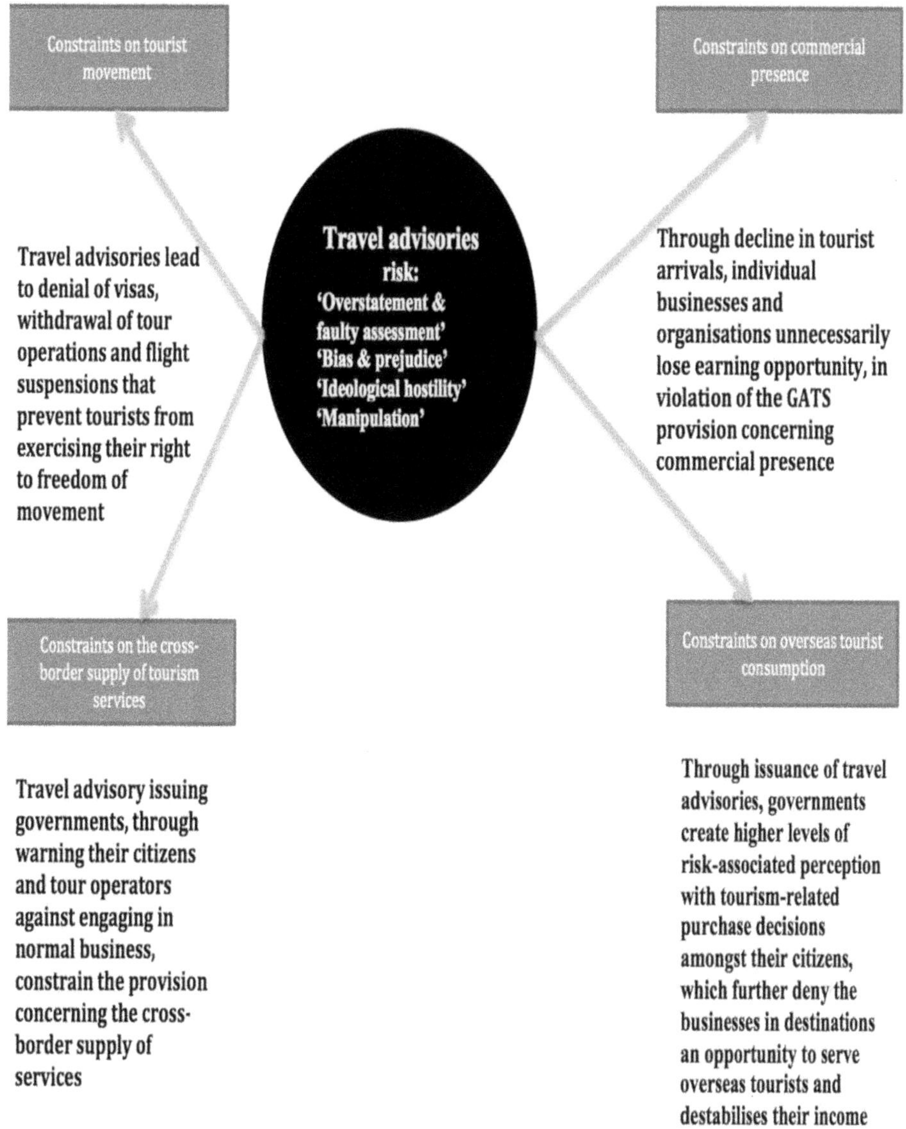

Figure 2. Travel advisories contravene GATS obligations.

specificity'. The Foreign Ministry of India has also raised the issue of travel advisories in G20 summits and has emphasised that travel advisories can contravene the WTO charter of free trade (Dhawan, 2011). Kenya's Tourism Minister, Najib Balala, has urged the UNWTO to consider issuing statements that parallel the travel advisories of developed nations (Allafrica, 2011).

Destabilising the individual travel decision

Tourism analysts emphasise that tourists feel vulnerable to all forms of perceived security threats (Pizam & Mansfeld, 1996, as cited in Bianchi, 2006, p. 69). The literature further shows that such perceived risks adversely affect tourist decision-making, which in turn affects a destination's fate (Schroeder & Pennington-Gray, 2014; Sharpley et al., 1996). Prior research has not attempted to model the direct effects that the travel advisories have on tourists' behaviour, on their decision-making, or on the resulting destabilisation in the destination. In this section, the paper develops a conceptual model that explains tourist attitude and decision-making behaviour in relation to personal security. This framework models the process by which a travel advisory will impact a tourist's decision-making and thus potentially destabilise the tourism industry in the destination. Figure 3 shows the immediate effect of travel warnings on the tourists' threat perception and their subsequent decision-making. This is modelled as a four-step process.

Step 1

A government issues an ITA to its citizens through its official website. A follow-the-leader exercise can occur, when additional governments also issue travel advisories.

Step 2

There is a public response to the ITA. This has three main dimensions. Upon learning of the ITA, tour operators respond by pulling their advertised tour packages and promotions. Their concern is not with patriotism or even the safety of their customers. They are worried about their own economic security. Cavlek (2002) has shown that insurance companies will not cover property or health-related damage claims arising from the crisis. It is 'best practice' for tour operators to strictly adhere to travel advisories – cancelling trips rather than facing the consequences of lawsuits (Lowenheim, 2007). An individual traveller's private travel insurance may also be revoked for travellers visiting advised-against nations (Avari, 2004 and Tunnah, 2005, as cited by Lowenheim, 2007, p. 217).

Negative media coverage also occurs. Media companies will not often oppose government travel advisories even if they themselves consider the destination safe for travel. For one thing, bad news sells. Research by Atkinson, Sandler, and Tschirhart (1987, as cited in Sonmez, Apostolopoulos, & Tarlow, 1999, p. 14) showed that the media is much more interested in promoting negative news. The 'new information' will be in the form of organic and induced images; potential tourists may be influenced by both the ITA itself and the consequent imagery (Gunn, 1972, as cited in Gartner, 1994, p. 205). Organic images are the result of the information that the tourists receive through non-official and/or non-commercial sources (Camprubi, Guia, & Comas, 2001). For potential tourists, this image may remain positive in spite of the supposedly negative incidents occurring in the destination country. Induced images, by contrast, are created by official and commercial sources to intentionally manipulate the perception of the potential tourist towards the destination (Camprubi et al., 2001). In the extant tourism literature, research on induced imagery typically focuses on the marketing efforts of the destination country to create an excessively favourable image that does not jibe with the reality of life in the country. With ITA issuance, this is reversed. In Step 2, the government-issued ITA, in combination with travel webpages and media stories, creates an image that travel to the destination is no longer sufficiently safe (Bierman, 2003, as cited in Bologlu & Mangaloglu, 2001; Schroeder & Pennington-Gray, 2014, p. 228).

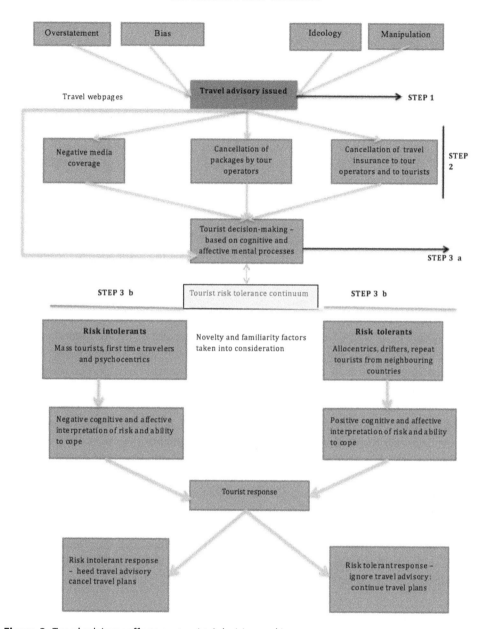

Figure 3. Travel advisory effects on tourists' decision-making.

Step 3a

We have broken Step 3 into 3a and 3b for ease of explanation. Step 3a applies to all people because after receiving new information all individuals go through a valuation process (Schroeder & Pennington-Gray, 2014; Wall, 2006). Conflict between the organic and induced images can result in an extensive information search by the potential tourist (Roehl & Fesenmaier, 1992, as cited in Schroeder & Pennington-Gray, 2014, p. 226) that can be confirmed in the negative by the continuing negative media coverage (Cavlek, 2002; Rittichainuwat & Chakraborty, 2009) and the cancellation of packages by tour operators. The decision to visit, however, is made only after both cognitive and affective mental processes have synthesised the imagery in relation to the likelihood of the threat occurrence (Slovic, Peters, Finucane, & MacGregor, 2005).

Through his discussion of protection motivation theory, Beck (1984) has stressed the role of the cognitive system in the risk decision-making process: the tourist through cognition determines the probability of risk occurrence, the severity of the risk and the efficacy of the coping response. Affective mental activity occurs simultaneously with cognitive activity. The affective component of touristic decision-making is based on holistic feelings associated with the destination. Zajonc (1980) states that these feelings and emotions are based on socio-psychological factors, which includes an individual's personal values, ideas, and intentions. Finucane, Alhakami, Slovic, and Johnson's (2000) research shows that tourists evaluate the perceived benefits and the risks associated with the destination based on the positive or negative feelings they get when thinking about the destination. These authors further show that when the potential risks outweigh the perceived benefits then the destination is considered more risky to visit.

Step 3b

Step 3b occurs at the same time as 3a but is modelled separately because individuals will vary in their tolerance of risk (Villegas et al., 2013). At this step, we have adapted Plog's (1972) continuum, based on novelty, to account for perception of risk. The tourist risk-tolerance continuum models the reality that individual tourists vary along a continuum between the extremes of risk avoidance and risk acceptance. The left column under Step 3b in Figure 3 focuses on risk intolerant people, who, as a result of their overall evaluation, will consider the destination to be highly risky. Categories of risk intolerants in the literature include mass tourists, psychocentric/traditionals and first-time travellers (Beck, 1984; Best Trip Choices, n.d.; Plog, 1972; Sonmez & Graefe, 1998). This segment might cancel their plans immediately or wait for further information. In contrast, the right column includes groups who are more risk tolerant. Tourists in these groups – allocentrics/venturers and drifters (Best Trip Choices, n.d.; Cohen, 1972; Lepp & Gibson, 2003; Plog, 1972) – look forward to novelty in destinations and their experiences in them. This segment may not consider the travel advisory to be significant unless other information confirms it as accurate.

The destabilising process of travel advisories on destinations

Research has shown that travel advisories, once imposed, are often not quickly lifted (Sonmez et al., 1999). Further, Wall (2006) has shown that even when issued legitimately, a continuing impact of the advisory is felt by risk avoiders. Destinations catering to the more conservative segments of tourists can experience a destabilising impact that extends in time from the immediate to the delayed.

Figure 4 models the destabilisation process between nations (international). After the issuance of an ITA, tourism (at the industry level and tourists, themselves) from the developed country drops or ceases altogether. In the developing nation, this has immediate and delayed impacts on both the tourism industry and on government. International B2B linkages decay and arrival numbers drop (Cavlek, 2002; Wall, 2006). Investors lose interest in the destination and development plans are shelved (Sonmez, 1998). The ongoing negative image created by the ongoing imposition of the ITA expands the range of tourist types affected, as the negative perception of the destination continues to increase (Stafford, Yu, & Kobina Armoo, 2006) (shown as a two-way arrow to emphasise iterative impacts). Cumulatively, loss in direct and indirect tax revenues begins to destabilise governmental ability to function (Henderson, 2004).

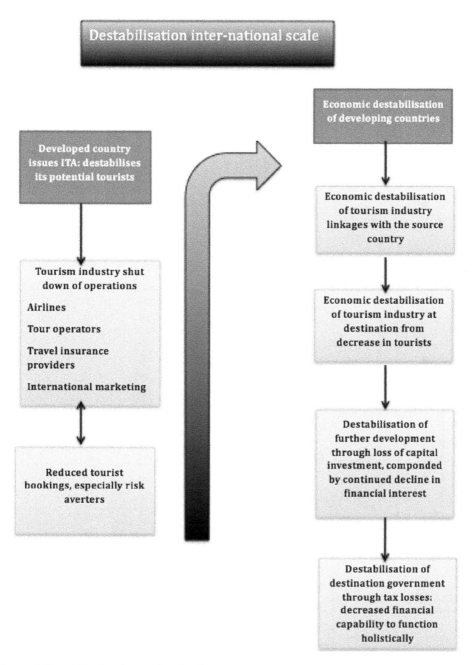

Figure 4. Destabilisation: international scale.

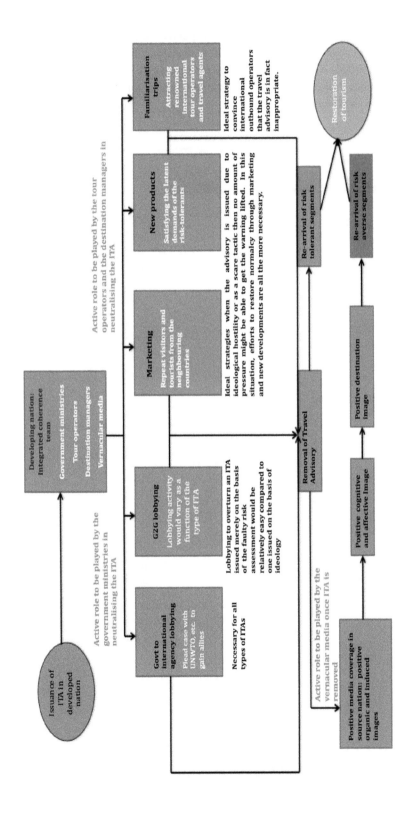

Figure 5. From destabilisation to restabilisation.

Strategies to neutralise impacts of ITAs

Because ITAs from developed nations are a source of destabilisation for tourism-dependent economies, appropriate measures are needed to re-stabilise the situation. Neutralising ITAs connected to political agendas is an important topic for future research because of the use of this tactic by an increasing number of nations (see 'Chinese tourists abandon Vietnam,' 2014). For this paper, Figure 5 is offered as an initial conceptual framework.

King and Berno (2006) discussed how, in the context of Fiji, an integrated approach was required to deal with travel advisories and the negative media. They noted such an approach requires an effective 'coherence team' working together on multiple fronts. According to the authors, the ideal team should include members from diversified backgrounds and different fields. Figure 5 provides an example in which destination managers, tour operators, local ministries, and the vernacular media work together as a team to create 'one voice one message' that is consistent and effective. Obviously, the members of such a team would vary between ITA situations.

The goals for the developing nation, especially one relying on tourism, are to remove the ITA and to restore tourism. These will not happen easily – strenuous efforts are required by all stakeholders (Cavlek, 2002). The coherence team will need to work simultaneously on multiple fronts.

Destination governments looking to overturn the adverse effects of the ITAs must be actively involved at two levels. First, the government must go to official international agencies, such as the UNWTO or PATA, and plead the case that the travel advisory has been issued inappropriately. Success at this level brings the international agencies on-side as allies; the developing nation is no longer fighing alone. The second level is government-to-government (G2G) (Mansfeld & Pizam, 2006), though the developing nation would likely want private sector assistance to increase the number of battlefields on which lobbying could be fought at a given time. The lobbying team would be a function of the type of ITA. Success at lobbying to overturn an ITA that was issued merely on the basis of misinformation would likely be relatively easy compared to success against one issued on the basis of ideology. The developing nation would likely need to demonstrate that visitation was in fact safe and the ITA should therefore be cancelled. For an ITA issued on the basis of politics or ideology, the G2G effort by the developing nation would likely need to be much more intense. Earlier in the paper we noted that ITA issuance contravened GATS. Putting G2G pressure on the developed nation – by asserting that one arm of its government had been acting in violation of signatory responsibilities – might be a successful strategy for rescinding the ITA.

When a developed nation issues an ITA, business consequences occur within the developed nation. Tour operations would slow and perhaps cease altogether. Travel insurance companies would refuse to provide insurance to either tourists or businesses. B2B lobbying at the international scale must therefore be as intense as G2G lobbying, in order to restore the daily functioning of the tourism industry. Inbound tour operators have an especially important responsibility to convince outbound operators that the travel advisory is in fact inappropriate. One way to do this is through a stepped-up programme of familiarisation trips, showing first hand that the situation is better than the ITA would indicate.

A marketing strategy would be to target repeat visitors (who know the country) and tourists from neighbouring countries (who have a more informed image). The return of these can be used to show a different, and more positive, reality.

The coherence team also has the related task of initiating projects – new developments – that expand the existing resource base of the developing country. These should be of a sort that can attract the more risk tolerant segments (Stafford et al., 2006) because this group would be less fearful of an ITA. The initiation process will be easier if products for which there is already latent demand can be identified (Mansfeld & Pizam, 2006).

In addition to activity between governments and business, the destination's vernacular media must be very active. A new set of induced images, reassuring in nature, needs to be created in order to render obsolete the conditions the released ITA was supposedly addressing. Such marketing efforts must be fought on multiple fronts. On one front, reassuring and welcoming images must be generically produced for all types of tourists. Simultaneously, other marketing efforts should be specifically tailored to the types of tourists who have stopped visiting but are likely to return quickly (Wall, 2006). In general, repeat visitors and the tourists from neighbouring regions might be appealed to first because they know the country the best and will have knowledge about the destination that contradicts the ITA (Rittichainuwat & Chakraborty, 2009). However, such marketing efforts will need assessment on a case-by-case basis.

Proper marketing strategies and newly created tourist products will have a tendency to neutralise the ITA. Once the developed government has been persuaded to lift the advisory, the return to normalcy at the destination could be relatively smooth. Risk tolerant segments may begin to re-visit almost immediately. New, positively slanted stories by the vernacular media will lead to renewed positive organic and induced image production, which will further result in positive cognitive and affective images in the minds of the tourists. With the supposed crisis resolved, media in the developed country would again be able to take a positive slant when discussing the destination. Improved images in the developed nation will mean the return of the risk averse segments. Tourism can be said to be fully restored when all previously visiting segments have begun to return.

Conclusion

This paper began by documenting the human right to movement, as provided through the signing of a multitude of treaties and conventions, such as GATS. Evidence was then presented that this right to travel was being subverted when a developed nation, by inappropriately issuing a travel advisory, attempted to gain economic and/or political hegemony over a developing nation. The range of situations in which this occurs has become sufficiently diverse to enable the creation of a typology of ITA motives (Figure 1). These motives suggest that an intention to destabilise is more apparent in some types of ITAs than in others. The paper next examined the process by which destabilisation occurred at the level of the individual tourist. The issuance of the ITA sets in motion a series of actions in the developed nation that effectively removes the potential tourist's desire to travel to that particular developing nation. Figure 4 then modelled the cumulative impact of individual tourist decisions, showing that destabilisation would occur in both the private and public sectors of the developing nation. The final section of the paper focussed on finding a general solution for the developing nation. This must, of necessity, be conceptual in nature because every situation would need to vary according to the nature of the relationship between the developed and developing nation and the nature of the travel advisory that was issued.

To date the relationship between inappropriate issuance of travel advisories and consequent impacts on developing-nation tourism has not been adequately examined. Future research could fruitfully focus on a number of topics. Among them: Do patterns of ITA issuance exist, suggesting a deeper level of intentionality to destabilise? Does the consequent tourism disruption indirectly assist terrorism, or cause the developing nation's government to lose control of the situation? Does post-ITA manipulation of media by the developed nation's government occur as a way of intensifying the consequences shown in Step 2 of Figure 3 – the cancellation of tours and travel insurance – thus reinforcing the decline in tourism to the developing nation?

A limitation of the paper is that we have relied solely on academic documentation. This enabled theorisation and the creation of models but limited the case material we could draw upon. Future research that examines evidence reported in the popular media would undoubtedly turn up far more instances of destabilisation than we have mentioned here. As an example that came to light during the writing of the paper, China has been accused of using tourism as a weapon against Vietnam with regard to political issues in the South China Sea ('Chinese tourists abandon Vietnam,' 2014). We finish by noting it is apparently very easy for a government to use one hand to sign a document guaranteeing its citizens the right to freedom of movement, but then use the other hand to hold up their movement for coercive motives that create economic and political destabilisation. Discouragingly, the day when such duplicity in international relations comes to an end seems far into the future.

Disclosure statement

No potential conflict of interest was reported by the authors.

References

Allafrica. (2011). *Balala wants UNWTO to issue travel advisories.* Retrieved June 12, 2015, from http://ezproxy.aut.ac.nz/login?url=http://search.proquest.com/docview/1012125159?accountid=8440

Beck, K. H. (1984). The effects of risk probability, outcome severity, efficacy of protection and access to protection on decision making: A further test of protection motivation theory. *Social Behavior and Personality: An International Journal, 12*(2), 121–126.

Best Trip Choices. (n.d.). *What's your travel personality?* Retrieved from http://besttripchoices.com/travel-personalities/quiz/

Bianchi, R. (2006). Tourism and globalisation of fear: Analysing the politics of risk and (in) security in global travel. *Tourism and Hospitality Research, 7*(1), 64–74.

Bologlu, S., & Mangaloglu, M. (2001). Tourism destination images of Turkey, Egypt, Greece and Italy as perceived by US based tour operators and travel agents. *Tourism Management, 22*(1), 1–9.

Bureau of Consular Affairs. (2014). *Alerts and warnings.* Retrieved from http://travel.state.gov/content/passports/english/alertswarnings.html

Camprubi, R., Guia, J., & Comas, J. (2001). Destination markets and induced tourism image. *Tourism Review, 63*(2), 47–58.

Cavlek, N. (2002). Tour operators and destination safety. *Annals of Tourism Research, 29*, 478–496.

Chinese tourists abandon Vietnam over bitter maritime row. (2014, July 21). *South China Morning Post.* Retrieved from http://www.scmp.com/news/asia/article/1556891/chinese-tourists-abandon-vietnam-after-oil-rig-row

Cohen, E. (1972). Towards a sociology of international tourism. *Social Research, 39*, 164–182.

Dhawan, H. (2011, October 26). Five countries issue travel advisories against India travel. *The Economic Times*, viewed March 20, 2014.

Fascell, D. B. (1979). The Helsinki accord: A case study. *Annals of the American Academy of the Political and Social Sciences, 442*(1), 69–76.

Finucane, M. L., Alhakami, A., Slovic, P., & Johnson, S. M. (2000). The affect heuristic in judgements of risks and benefits. *Journal of Behavioral Decision Making, 13*(1), 1–17.

Fletcher, J., & Morakabati, Y. (2008). Tourism activity, terrorism and political instability within commonwealth: The cases of Fiji and Kenya. *The International Journal of Tourism Research, 10*, 537–556.

Freedman, L. (2005). The politics of warning: Terrorism and risk communication. *Intelligence and Natural Security, 20*, 379–418.

Gartner, W. (1994). Image formation process. *Journal of Travel and Tourism Marketing, 2*(2), 191–216.

George, B. P., & Henthorne, T. L. (2007). Tourism and the general agreement on trade in services: Sustainability and other developmental concerns. *International Journal of Social Economics, 34*(3), 136–146.

Henderson, J. (2004). Managing the aftermath of terrorism: The Bali bombings, travel advisories and Singapore. *International Journal of Hospitality and Tourism Administration, 4*(2), 17–31.

King, B., & Berno, T. (2006). Fiji Islands: Rebuilding tourism in an insecure world. In Y. Mansfeld & A. Pizam (Eds.), *Tourism, security and safety* (pp. 67–81). New York, NY: Elsevier Butterworth-Heinemann.

Lepp, A., & Gibson, H. (2003). Tourist roles, perceived risk and international tourism. *Annals of Tourism Research, 30*, 606–624.

Lowenheim, O. (2007). The responsibility to responsibilize: Foreign offices and issuing of travel warnings. *International Political Sociology, 1*, 203–221.

Mansfeld, Y., & Pizam, A. (2006). *Tourism security and safety from theory to practice.* Oxford: Butterworth-Heinemann.

Myers, G. N. (2012). Mexico tourism officials praised revised U.S travel warning: Advisory offers state by state security assessment. *Travel Weekly, 71*(7), 7.

Plog, S. J. (1972, October 10). *Why destinations rise and fall in popularity.* Paper presented at the meeting of the Southern California Chapter of the Travel Research Bureau, San Diego, CA.

Prestholdt, J. (2011). Kenya, United States, and counterterrorism. *Africa Today, 57*(4), 3–27.

Rittichainuwat, B. N., & Chakraborty, G. (2009). Perceived travel risks regarding terrorism and disease: The case of Thailand. *Tourism Management, 30*, 410–418.

Schroeder, A., & Pennington-Gray, L. (2014). Perception of crime at the Olympic Games: What role does media, travel advisories, and social media play? *Journal of Vacation Marketing, 20*, 225–237.

Shankman, S. (2015). *What we found in 18 years of U.S. travel warnings*. Retrieved from http://skift.com/2015/04/16/what-we-found-in-18-years-of-u-s-travel-warnings/

Sharpley, R., Sharpley, J., & Adams, J. (1996). Travel advice or travel embargo? The impacts and implications of official travel advice. *Tourism Management, 17*(1), 1–7.

Slovic, P., Peters, E., Finucane, M. L., & MacGregor, D. G. (2005). Affect, risk and decision making. *Health Psychology, 24*(4), S35–S40.

Sonmez, S. F. (1998). Tourism, terrorism and political instability. *Annals of Tourism Research, 25*, 416–456.

Sonmez, S. F., Apostolopoulos, Y., & Tarlow, P. (1999). Tourism in crisis: Managing the effects of terrorism. *Journal of Travel Research, 38*(1), 13–18.

Sonmez, S. F., & Graefe, A. R. (1998). Determining future travel behavior from past travel experience and perceptions of risk and safety. *Journal of Travel Research, 37*, 171–177.

Stafford, G., Yu, L., & Kobina Armoo, A. (2006). Crisis management and recovery: How Washington, D.C. hotels responded to terrorism. *Cornell Hotel and Restaurant Administration Quarterly, 43*(5), 27–40.

United Nations World Tourism Organisation. (2009). *Declaration on the facilitation of tourist travel.* Retrieved from http://www2.unwto.org/sites/all/files/docpdf/ares578xviiideclarationfacilitation2009en.pdf

Villegas, J., Matyas, C., Srinivasan, S., Cahyanto, I., Thapa, B., & Pennington-Gray, L. (2013). Cognitive and affective responses of Florida tourists after exposure to hurricane warning messages. *Natural Hazards, 66*(1), 97–116.

Wall, G. (2006). Recovering from SARS: The case of Toronto tourism. In Y. Mansfeld & A. Pizam (Eds.), *Tourism security and safety: From theory to practice* (pp. 143–152). Oxford: Elsevier Butterworth-Hienemann.

Wangalwa, E. (2015). *Kenyatta's travel advisory hit back backfires amid attack*. CNBC Africa. Retrieved May 28, 2016, from http://www.cnbcafrica.com/news/east-africa/2015/04/02/uhuru-fires-back-travel-advisories/

World Trade Organisation. (1995). *General agreement on trade in services (GATS): Objectives, coverage and disciplines.* Retrieved from https://www.wto.org/english/tratop_e/serv_e/gatsqa_e.htm#2

Zajonc, R. B. (1980). Feeling and thinking: Preferences need no inferences. *American Psychologist, 35*(2), 151–175.

Impacts of political instability on the tourism industry in Ukraine

Stanislav Ivanov, Margarita Gavrilina, Craig Webster and Vladyslav Ralko

ABSTRACT

The purpose of this research paper is to learn about how the tourism industry in Ukraine has been hit by the political instability in the country and how it has reacted to mitigate its negative consequences. The data were collected via a self-administered questionnaire completed by 102 hotel managers and 73 travel agency managers in Ukraine. Mann–Whitney U-test, Kruskal–Wallis χ^2 test, and t-test were used to analyse differences in respondents' answers by category, size, location, region, and chain affiliation of hotels. Mann–Whitney U-test was used to investigate the differences in travel agency managers' responses on the basis of licence type, region, main market segment, and IATA certification of the agency. The findings confirm previous research results that political instability leads to negative impacts on the tourism industry of a country – decreased revenues, plummeting numbers of tourists and overnights, and increased costs. This was valid not only for the regions that were neighbouring the conflict areas, but for the rest of country as well, although the former were more severely hit by the political instability than the latter. The findings further revealed differential effect of the political instability on the accommodation establishments and travel agencies on the basis of their characteristics. This is the first-known survey of the tourism industry in Ukraine following the political turmoil of 2014 that illustrates the impact of the political instability to the tourism industry, as well as elaborates the tactics that hoteliers and travel agency managers in Ukraine are taking to counteract the shock.

RÉSUMÉ

Le but de cette étude c'est de mieux comprendre l'impact de l'instabilité politique qu'a connue l'Ukraine sur l'industrie du tourisme et les mesures mises en place pour en atténuer les conséquences négatives sur le pays. Les données d'analyse ont été recueillies au moyen d'un questionnaire rempli librement par 102 directeurs d'hôtels et 73 responsables d'agences de Voyage en Ukraine. En vue d'analyser les différences entre les réponses des participants rangées par les variables de la catégorie, la taille, l'emplacement, la région et l'affiliation à la chaîne hôtelière, on a fait recours aux tests non paramétriques, dont le test de Mann-

This article was originally published with errors. This version has been corrected. Please see Erratum (http://dx.doi.org/10.1080/19407963.2016.1219091).

Whitney ou le test-U, de Kruskal-Wallis ou le test des χ^2, ainsi que le test-T. Le Test-U de Mann-Whitney a été utilisé pour étudier les différences entre les réponses des responsables d'agences de voyage en fonction du type de licence d'exploitation, de région, de la niche de marché, ainsi que de la certification de l'Association internationale du transport aérien (AITA). Cette étude confirme les résultats des recherches précédentes selon lesquels l'instabilité politique génère les effets négatifs sur l'industrie du tourisme d'un pays, notamment la baisse des revenus, la chute significative du nombre de touristes et de nuitées, et une augmentation des coûts opérationnels. Ce constat a été une évidence, non seulement dans les zones de combat, mais aussi dans le reste du pays, quoique les régions de conflits aient été plus sévèrement touchées par l'instabilité politique qu'ailleurs. En fin de compte, les résultats ont également révélé l'effet différentiel de l'instabilité politique sur les établissements d'hébergement et les agences de voyage en fonction de leurs caractéristiques. Cette étude est la première du genre menée sur l'industrie du tourisme en Ukraine après la crise politique de 2014. Elle souligne l'impact de l'instabilité politique et identifient des tactiques que les hôteliers et les gestionnaires d'agences de Voyage en Ukraine utilisent pour désamorcer le choc.

摘要

这篇文章的目的是探究乌克兰国家政治的不稳定如何给该国的旅游业带来冲击以及旅游业如何对此作出回应以减轻其产生的消极影响。本研究是通过自填式问卷调查的方法收集数据，完成问卷的是乌克兰102位宾馆经理和73位旅行社经理。他们在宾馆的类别、规模、位置、地区以及连锁机构这几个方面给出的不同答案通过Mann-Whitney U检验、Kruskal-Wallis χ2 检验和t检验予以分析。Mann-Whitney U检验被用来调查旅行社经理就执照类型、地区、主要市场分割和旅行社IATA证书方面给出的不同回应。本研究的结果证实了以前的研究成果，即政治不稳定给一个国家的旅游业带来消极影响——收入减少、游客和过夜旅行数量急剧下降以及成本增加。这个研究结果不仅适用于冲突地区的周边地方，也适用于这个国家的其他地区，只不过前者比后者受的政治冲击更严重。本研究还揭示了由于住宿的位置和旅行社的特征，政治不稳定对其会产生不同的影响。本研究是继2014年乌克兰政治骚乱之后第一个针对乌克兰旅游业的问卷调查，其不仅证明了政治不稳定对旅游业的影响，也呈现了乌克兰宾馆经营者和旅行社经理应对这种冲击的策略。

RESUMEN

El propósito de este trabajo de investigación es aprender sobre cómo la industria del turismo en Ucrania ha sido golpeada por la inestabilidad política del país y cómo ha reaccionado para mitigar sus consecuencias negativas. Los datos fueron recogidos mediante cuestionarios auto-administrados completados por 102 directivos de hotel y 73 directivos de agencias de viaje. Los tests de U Mann-Whitney, Kruskal-Wallis χ^2 y la prueba-t se utilizaron para analizar las diferencias en las respuestas por categoría, tamaño, localización, región y cadena de pertenencia de los hoteles. El test U de Mann-Whitney fue utilizado para investigar las diferencias en las respuestas de los directores de agencias de viaje en función del tipo del licencia, región, principal segmento de mercado y la certificación IATA de la agencia. Los resultados confirman los de investigaciones previas que indican que la inestabilidad política conduce a impactos negativos en la industria turística de un país – descenso de los ingresos, desplome del número de turistas y pernoctaciones e incremento de los costes. Esto era válido no sólo para las regiones vecinas a las áreas de conflicto sino también para el resto del país, aunque las primeras eran más duramente golpeadas por la inestabilidad política que las segundas. Los resultados revelaban además un efecto diferencial de la inestabilidad política en los establecimientos de alojamiento y las agencias de viaje en función de sus características. Esta es la primera investigación conocida sobre la industria turística en Ucrania tras el desorden político de 2014 que ilustra el impacto de la inestabilidad política en la industria turística así como la primera que elabora las tácticas que directores de hoteles y agencias de viaje en Ucrania están llevando a cabo para contrarrestar el golpe.

1. Introduction

1.1. Background and rationale

In December 1991, the Soviet Union was dissolved and its 15 constituting republics, including Ukraine, became independent. With this act, millions of people were transformed into minorities overnight in various pockets throughout the former Soviet Union. Newly independent Ukraine was one of the republics with the largest concentration of a Russian-speaking population, especially on the Crimean peninsula and the eastern provinces of the country due to the historical links between the two peoples. Until 2013, the coexistence of the peoples was peaceful.

In November 2013, pro-EU protests (more famously known as 'Euromaidan') started in Ukraine which ultimately led to the resignation of the pro-Russian president, Viktor Yanukovich, on 22 February 2014 and the election of new government. While praised as a victory for democracy in the West, the 'Euromaidan' was considered by the Russian-speaking minority in the country as a de facto coup d'état. As a reaction, on 16 March 2014, after a highly disputed referendum, the Autonomous Republic of Crimea left Ukraine. A few days later, it was accepted as a new federal entity in the Russian Federation. The referendum and the entrance of the Autonomous Republic of Crimea into the Russian Federation were considered illegal by Ukraine and the international community and as a result, the EU, U.S.A., and other countries imposed various sanctions on citizens and companies from Crimea and Russia, which are still active as of today (January 2016). Protests against the new government took place in the eastern regions of Donetsk and Lugansk as well, where the Russian-speaking population was an overwhelming majority of the population. Similar to Crimea, the two regions of Donetsk and Lugansk held referenda and declared independence from Ukraine, but they were not admitted into the Russian Federation. On the contrary, the local separatists and the government forces entered into intensive military fights, which led to nearly one million refugees fleeing the conflict areas – over 730,000 moved to Russia and 117,000 were displaced to other parts of Ukraine (Reuters, 2014).

The political and military events have been a major shock to the entire economy of Ukraine and for tourism, in particular. Table 1 presents some key statistics for the accommodation establishments and travel agencies in Ukraine for the 2011–2014 period. For comparison, the table presents the statistics with and without Crimea. The number of hotels and

Table 1. Key statistics of accommodation establishments and travel agencies in Ukraine.

	2011	2012	2013	2014	2014/ 2013
Number of hotels and similar establishments					
Total, including Crimea	3162	3144	n.a.	n.a.	n.a.
Total, excluding Crimea	2499	2375	3582	2644	−26.19%
Number of beds in hotels and similar establishments					
Total, including Crimea	154,200	162,831	n.a.	n.a.	n.a.
Total, excluding Crimea	120,248	123,713	179,100	135,500	−24.34%
Number of guests staying in hotels and similar establishments					
Total, including Crimea	4,656,800	4,983,585	n.a.	n.a.	n.a.
Total, excluding Crimea	4,194,601	4,420,241	5,467,800	3,814,200	−30.24%
Number of travel agencies					
Total, including Crimea	4793	5346	n.a.	n.a.	n.a.
Total, excluding Crimea	4157	4710	5071	3885	−23.39%
Number of tourists served by travel agencies and other tourist companies, including:					
Total, including Crimea	2,199,977	3,000,696	n.a.	n.a.	n.a.
Total, excluding Crimea	1,840,483	2,693,031	3,454,316	2,425,089	−29.80%
Foreign tourists					
Total, including Crimea	234,271	270,064	n.a.	n.a.	n.a.
Total, excluding Crimea	112,141	167,421	232,311	17,070	−92.65%
Domestic tourists					
Total, including Crimea	715,638	773,970	n.a.	n.a.	n.a.
Total, excluding Crimea	497,550	598,443	702,615	322,746	−54.07%
Ukrainian citizens travelling abroad					
Total, including Crimea	1,250,068	1,956,662	n.a.	n.a.	n.a.
Total, excluding Crimea	1,230,792	1,927,167	2,519,390	2,085,273	−17.23%

Sources: State Statistics Service of Ukraine (2012, 2013, 2015a, 2015c) and authors' calculations.
Notes: (1) Data for 2013 available only for Ukraine excluding the Autonomous Republic of Crimea; data for 2014 exclude the Autonomous Republic of Crimea and parts of Donetsk and Lugansk regions; (2) No data available for the number of over-nights; (3) n.a. – no data available; (4) Crimea includes the regions of the Autonomous Republic of Crimea and the City of Sevastopol.

similar accommodation establishments in Ukraine outside Crimea grew from 2499 in 2011 to 3582 in 2013, while the number of hotel guests increased from 4.2 million in 2011 to 5.5 million in 2013. In the same manner, the number of travel agencies increased from 4157 in 2011 to 5071 in 2013, while the number of the tourists served by them grew from 1.84 million in 2011 to 3.45 million in 2013. In 2014, the situation drastically changed as a consequence from the break-up of the Autonomous Republic of Crimea and its transition to the Russian Federation in March 2014, and the military hostilities in the Donetsk and Lugansk regions. The number of travel agencies, accommodation establishments, and tourists in Ukraine outside Crimea fell dramatically (by 20–30%), especially the number of foreign tourists served by Ukrainian travel agencies who plummeted by 92.65%. These statistics reveal that the Ukrainian tourist companies are experiencing significant shock and they have to adjust their strategies to mitigate its negative consequences on their business.

1.2. Aim and objectives

In light of the above discussion, this paper aims to evaluate the impact of current political instability on Ukraine's tourism industry (the accommodation establishments and the travel agencies). The specific objectives are:

- *Objective 1*: Investigate how the political and military events have influenced the performance metrics of the tourism industry in Ukraine;

- *Objective 2*: Elaborate how managers of tourist companies in the country perceive the various political and economic challenges of the macroenvironment;
- *Objective 3*: Unearth the different methods by which the tourism industry has reacted to the challenges of the new political and economic environment in which it functions;
- *Objective 4*: Identify the role of category, location, region, size, and chain affiliation of the accommodation establishments in: (a) the impacts of political instability on their performance; (b) their managers' perceptions about the political and economic challenges; and (c) the way their managers react to the challenges.
- *Objective 5*: Identify the role of licence type, region, main market segment, and IATA certification of the travel agencies in: (a) the impacts of political instability on their performance; (b) their managers' perceptions about the political and economic challenges; and (c) the way their managers react to the challenges.
- *Objective 6*: Investigate the differences between accommodation establishments and travel agencies in regard to: (a) the impacts of political instability on their performance; (b) their managers' perceptions about the political and economic challenges; and (c) the way their managers react to the challenges.

The specific research questions are elaborated in the appendix. The rest of the paper is organised as follows: Section 2 provides a focused literature review, Section 3 presents the empirical contexts, Section 4 elaborates the methodology, Section 5 analyses the findings, while Section 6 summarises the paper's contribution, managerial and policy implications, limitations and provides future research directions.

2. Literature review

There is a substantial literature that deals with various types of political shocks and their influence in the tourism and hospitality sectors. One of the best known and most influential is Neumayer's (2004) investigation that found that tourism arrivals drop due to a number of different unattractive political factors (human rights violations, conflict, and other political/violent events). These findings support, what many would expect, that tourists avoid unpleasant political realities. Llorca-Vivero (2008), in his investigation of over 130 tourist destinations, found support for Neumayer's (2004) research. All in all, the research from Neumayer (2004) and Llorca-Vivero (2008) empirically illustrates that destinations that are unattractive for their political attributes will largely be avoided by travellers.

Similar to these is the sizable literature that deals with how tourists avoid locations that are associated with violence, such as terrorist attacks (see, for example, Aimable & Rosselló, 2009; Araña & León, 2008; Björk & Kauppinen-Räisänen, 2011; Causevic & Lynch, 2013; Drakos & Kutan, 2003; Feridun, 2011; Ingram, Tabari, & Watthanakhomprathip, 2013; Larsen, Brun, Øgaard, & Selstad, 2011; O'Connor, Stafford, & Gallagher, 2008; Saha & Yap, 2014; de Sausmarez, 2013; Solarin, 2015; Wolff & Larsen, 2014; Yap & Saha, 2013). However, it is not merely terrorist attacks but also much vaguely threatening crises that may impact upon tourism flows (see, for example, Clements & Georgiou, 1998). Much like other political features of a country that tourists would feel are unattractive and would repel them from visiting the country with the terror problem or having recently suffered from a terror attack, the literature generally illustrates that terror is bad for the tourism business, although in a minority of cases the impact may be miniscule (Wolff & Larsen, 2014). There are others who have looked into a related problem, how destinations (countries and destinations within countries) and firms react to political crises that may impact upon the economy (Ivanov, Idzhilova, & Webster, 2016; Jallat & Shultz, 2010; Purwomarwanto & Ramachandran, 2015).

Apart from this literature, there is another literature that is more closely linked with war/international conflict, although many of the works may not clearly delineate between those military conflicts that are clearly within the borders of a country and those that are between two different countries. At any rate, the relationship between political and military events and the study of tourism is nothing new. In fact, in the past few years, substantial edited volumes have concentrated upon related issues. For example, Butler and Suntilkul (2013), in their edited volume, concentrate upon the complex relationship between tourism and war. In a similar manner, Moufakkir and Kelly (2010) focused in their edited volume upon the complex relationship between tourism and peace. Many authors in these works view tourism either as something that is an object/victim that suffers from conflicts or is an active player working to reconcile opposing sides of a conflict.

When looked upon as a victim of political circumstances, the consensus of the literature (for example, Clements & Georgiou, 1998; Llorca-Vivero, 2008; Neumayer, 2004) supports, what common sense informs most of us, that tourists avoid political realities that are unpleasant. However, there is a substantial literature that deals with the role of tourism in a post-conflict environment in terms of encouraging peace and peace-making (Askjellerud, 2003; Anson, 1999), working on the premise of the liberal principle that tourism leads to contacts between peoples who may have reason to conflict and that the contacts lead to peaceful and cooperative interactions. This is even becoming a lively field in which tourism is seen as an active player bringing about peace following political turmoil/violence (D'Amore, 1988, 2009; Khamouna & Zeiger, 1995; Levy & Hawkins, 2009). Indeed, Webster and Ivanov (2014) find evidence for this liberal approach, although certain political preconditions seem to be needed. There are others, as well, who take the proverbial view of making lemons into lemonade, by exploring and extolling the use of ethnic political conflicts as a magnet to attract tourism post-conflict (see, for example, McDowell, 2008). In any way, political instability has a negative impact on the business environment in which the tourist companies operate (Llorca-Vivero, 2008; Neumayer, 2004), because it makes the destination less secure for tourists, and often leads to economic instability as well (inflation, currency devaluation, recession, unemployment, increases in interest rates, etc.).

Here, we investigate two different elements. First, we investigate the extent the political crisis that has been ongoing in Ukraine for some time has impacted upon the tourism and hospitality industries. While there is substantial reason to believe that the impact should be negative to private sector firms operating in Ukraine, as suggested by the literature on the topic (see, for example, Llorca-Vivero, 2008; Neumayer, 2004). This investigation intends to quantify the impact of the crisis. Second, while much of the literature deals with the private sector as a victim of political circumstances, this investigation will look into the private sector as an active player, to learn how the private sector's players react when a political and economic crisis hits, as others have done in the past (Ivanov et al., 2016; Jallat & Shultz, 2010; Purwomarwanto & Ramachandran, 2015).

3. Methodology

3.1. Instrument

In order to answer the research questions and achieve research objectives, two research populations were formulated (the managers of accommodation establishments and the managers of travel agencies in Ukraine), a survey was selected as the research approach and a questionnaire was used as the data collection instrument. Two questionnaires were prepared by the authors – one for each research population in line with prior research (Ivanov et al., 2016). Most of the questions in them overlapped in order to facilitate the comparison of the responses of the two populations. The questionnaires consisted of several blocks of questions. The first block (related to Objective 1 and RQ1) measured the dynamics of selected operational statistics in 2014, when the political tension and military activities in the eastern provinces escalated, compared to 2013. The second and the third blocks (related to Objective 2 and RQ2) included questions regarding the importance and the impact of various factors influencing the tourism business, resulting from the political instability. The fourth and the fifth blocks (related to Objective 3 and RQ3) evaluated the level of agreement with statements about the impacts of the political instability on the company's business and the ways to mitigate the negative consequences of the political instability. A separate block of questions (related to Objectives 4–6 and RQ4–6) collected data about the characteristics of the accommodation establishments or the travel agencies.

3.2. Data collection

Data collection took place in January–November 2015 by distributing an online questionnaire to the managers of accommodation establishments in Ukraine. During the development of the sampling frame, the authors did not find any official comprehensive publicly available lists of the accommodation establishments and travel agencies in Ukraine and their contact details. That is why the authors had to develop their own database with contact details of 1001 accommodation establishments and 2108 travel agencies in the country. The sampling frame did not include companies in the Autonomous Republic of Crimea and the regions of Donetsk and Lugansk for two reasons. First, during the time of data collection, the Autonomous Republic of Crimea was already admitted as a member of the Russian Federation, and although this political act was not recognised by the international community, it was and still is a political reality. Second, during the time of data collection, hotels in the regions of Donetsk and Lugansk were closed, without electricity and water, some of them even destroyed. The two regions themselves were not accessible for tourists and were and still are under separatist control. The questionnaire was sent to the managers of all accommodation establishments and travel agencies in the sampling frame. In order to stimulate participation in the survey and increase the response rate, three reminders were sent to the potential respondents. Furthermore, following Illum, Ivanov, and Liang (2010, p. 340) advice, every participant received a link to a complimentary copy of an e-book written by the first author as an incentive to complete the questionnaire. The book publisher provided prior permission to use this incentive during the data collection stage. Ultimately, 102 hotel managers and 73 travel agency managers completed the questionnaire, yielding a 10.19% and 3.46% response rates, respectively. The response rates were similar to the response rates of tourism industry representatives in other surveys in Eastern Europe (Ivanova & Ivanov, 2015; Ivanov, Stoilova, & Illum, 2015). The samples' characteristics are presented in Table 2.

3.3. Data analysis

The results of the Kolmogorov–Smirnov z-test showed that the distributions of the answers of the managers of the accommodation establishments and the managers of the travel agencies were statistically different from normal for most of the questions. That is why the differences in respondents' opinions were analysed with non-parametric tests (Baggio & Klobas, 2011). In particular, the Kruskal–Wallis χ^2 test was used to identify the differences in the responses of hoteliers on the basis of the category (1–2 stars, 3 stars, 4–5 stars), size (up to 50, 51–100, and over 100 rooms) and location (urban, seaside, mountain, rural/countryside) of their properties. The Mann–Whitney U-test was adopted to identify differences in the opinions of hotel managers on the basis of the chain affiliation of the hotels (affiliated vs. independent hotels) and the region where the hotel was located (in regions neighbouring the conflict areas vs. the rest of Ukraine). Furthermore, the Mann–Whitney U-test was used to identify the differences in the opinions of travel agency managers on the basis of licence type (tour operator or travel agent), region where the agency is located (in regions neighbouring the conflict areas vs. the rest of Ukraine), IATA certification (IATA-certified vs. non-certified), and main market segment (groups vs. individual tourists) of the agency. Finally, the Mann–Whitney U-test was used to evaluate the differences in the responses of the managers of the accommodation establishments and travel agencies. The regions neighbouring the conflict areas (the Autonomous Republic of Crimea, Donetsk, and Lugansk) were identified as: Dnipropetrovsk, Harkiv, Herson, Zaporizhzhya, Mykolaiv, and Odessa. These

Table 2. Sample characteristics.

	Grouping criteria	Groups	Number of respondents
Accommodation establishments ($N = 102$)	*Category*	1–2 stars	33
		3 stars	43
		4–5 stars	26
	Location	Urban	71
		Seaside	14
		Mountain	12
		Rural/countryside	5
	Region	Neighbouring the conflict areas[a]	35
		Rest of Ukraine	67
	Size	Up to 50 rooms	70
		51–100 rooms	26
		Over 101 rooms	6
	Chain affiliation	Part of a chain	20
		Independent	82
Travel agencies ($N = 73$)	*Licence*	Tour operator	26
		Travel agent	47
	Region	Neighbouring the conflict areas[a]	17
		Rest of Ukraine	56
	Main market segment	Groups	10
		Individual tourists	63
	IATA certification	IATA-certified agency	12
		Not IATA-certified agency	61

[a]Includes the regions of Dnipropetrovsk, Harkiv, Herson, Zaporizhzhya, Mykolaiv, and Odessa.

regions border the conflict areas directly either by land or by sea. A paired samples t-test was used to identify the differences in respondents' answers to some questions.

4. Discussion of findings

4.1. Impacts of the political instability on the performance metrics

4.1.1. Accommodation establishments' perspective

The impacts of the political instability in Ukraine on the operational statistics of hotels are reported in Table 3(a) (RQ1.1). Results reveal that the hotels were put under serious financial pressure: their revenues plummeted by −15.39%, the number of guests decreased by −15.49%, overnights by −14.02% and the average length of stay by −1.42 nights, while costs surged on average by 12.75%. Therefore, not surprisingly, the hotel managers considered that the political instability had a distinctively negative impact on their business ($m = 1.74$) and hired 2% less employees in 2014 than in 2013. The Kruskal–Wallis χ^2 test did not reveal any statistically significant difference in respondents' answers on the basis of the category (RQ4.1) and location (RQ4.2) of the properties, but only on their size. The total costs of the smallest hotels (up to 50 rooms) increased on average by 14.36%, of midsized properties (51–100 rooms) – by 9.81%, and of large hotels (over 100 rooms) by 6.67%, and these differences were statistically significant ($\chi^2 = 7.181$, $p < .05$), showing that the large hotels enjoyed some efficiencies of the economies of scale. A similar situation was observed regarding the total employee costs: the total employee costs of the small hotels increased by 3.29%, of midsized hotels – by 1.73%, while the employee costs of large hotels actually decreased by −2.50% ($\chi^2 = 4.983$, $p < .10$).

The region of the hotels was an important factor, influencing the changes in the performance metrics of the hotels. The hotels located in the regions neighbouring the conflict areas were more severely hit by the political instability than hotels in the rest of Ukraine. Expectedly, they lost more guests, had much lower prices, less revenue and shorter length of stay of their guests than hotels in the rest of Ukraine. These results confirmed previous research findings (Llorca-Vivero, 2008; Neumayer, 2004) that political instability in a country had detrimental effects on its economy, in general, and tourism, in particular. Surprisingly, chain affiliated hotels turned out to be more vulnerable to political instability than independent hotels. For example, chain hotels had fewer guests, less number of overnights and worked with fewer employees in 2014 than in 2013 compared to independent properties. This result was not expected, because prior literature identified the hotel chain's brand as one of its most important advantages and most sought-after chain attribute by the managers of independent hotels when they evaluate whether to affiliate their property to a chain or not (Ivanova & Ivanov, 2015). One possible explanation is that the chain hotels were more dependent on foreign tourists than the independent properties. With the increased political instability, the outbreak of military actions in the regions of Donetsk and Lugansk and the separation of the Autonomous Republic of Crimea, the number of foreign tourists staying in accommodation establishments in Ukraine plummeted from 990,997 in 2011 to 551,519 in 2014 (State Statistics Service of Ukraine, 2012, 2015a). However, future research needs to confirm or reject this suggestion.

Table 3. Impact of the political instability on the operational statistics.

Operational statistics	Total mean	Standard deviation	Kruskal–Wallis χ^2 test				Mann–Whitney U-test
			Category	Size	Location	Region	Chain affiliation
(a) Accommodation establishments							
Differences by category, size, location, region, and chain affiliation							
How would you evaluate the magnitude of the impact of current political instability on your business in general?[a]	3.75	0.898	0.054	1.041	2.081	928.5*	624.5*
How would you assess the direction of the impact of current political instability on your business in general?[b]	1.74	0.770	0.124	1.806	2.917	1024.0	707.5
How did the number of your guests change in 2014 compared to 2013?[c]	−15.49	11.092	0.345	3.334	4.508	832.0***	610.0*
How did the number of overnight of your guests change in 2014 compared to 2013?[c]	−14.02	9.926	1.244	0.706	1.998	1046.0	605.0*
How did the average price per room per night change in 2014 compared to 2013 year?[c]	−0.69	11.081	3.545	1.954	4.999	652.5***	694.0
How did your total revenues change in 2014 compared to 2013?[c]	−15.39	11.447	2.247	1.194	3.406	861.0**	671.5
How did your total costs change in 2014 compared to 2013?[c]	12.75	9.689	1.096	7.181**	1.029	1103.5	814.5
How did your total employee costs (salaries, social security payments, employee insurances etc.) change in 2014 compared to 2013?[c]	2.55	9.894	2.885	4.983*	4.524	1017.0	621.0*
How did the total number of your employees change in 2014 compared to 2013?[c]	−1.99	4.463	0.425	3.229	0.956	1042.0	601.5**
How did the average stay for your guests change in 2014 compared to 2013?[d]	−1.42	1.031	2.474	1.011	3.979	878.5**	711.0

Notes: Grouping of respondents: *Size* (up to 50, 51–100 and over 100 rooms), *Location* (urban, seaside, mountain, rural/countryside), *Category* (1–2 stars, 3 stars, 4–5 stars), *Region* (neighbouring the conflict areas, rest of Ukraine), *Chain Affiliation* (affiliated to a chain, independent hotels).

Measurement scales:

[a]1 – no impact, 5 – very high impact.
[b]1 – very negative, 5 – very positive.
[c]In percentage points.
[d]In number of overnights.
***Significant at 1% level.
**Significant at 5% level.
*Significant at 10% level.

Table 3. Continued

(b) Travel agencies

Operational statistics	Total mean	Standard deviation	Mann–Whitney U-test			
			Licence type	Region	Main market segment	IATA certification
Differences by licence type, region, main market segment, and IATA certification						
How would you evaluate the magnitude of the impact of current political instability on your business in general?[a]	3.74	0.943	535	381	283	339
How would you assess the direction of the impact of current political instability on your business in general?[b]	1.99	0.790	460.5**	302***	230	303.5
How did the number of your tourists change in 2014 compared to 2013?[c]	−19.59	11.048	578.5	446.5	279.5	300
How did your total revenues change in 2014 compared to 2013?[c]	−17.19	12.304	555.5	475.5	305.5	216**
How did your total costs change in 2014 compared to 2013?[c]	5.62	16.603	555.5	377.5	278.5	336
How did your total employee costs (salaries, social security payments, employee insurances etc.) change in 2014 compared to 2013?[c]	1.85	14.518	585.5	426.5	313.5	360
How did the total number of your employees change in 2014 compared to 2013?[c]	−3.80	6.321	563	449	294	290

Notes: Grouping of respondents: *Licence* (tour operator, travel agent), *Main market segments* (groups, individual tourists), *IATA certified* (IATA-certified agency, not IATA-certified agency), *Region* (neighbouring the conflict areas, rest of Ukraine).
Measurement scales:
[a]1 – no impact, 5 – very high impact.
[b]1 – very negative, 5 – very positive.
[c]In percentage points.
***Significant at 1% level.
**Significant at 5% level.
*Significant at 10% level.

Operational statistics	Mann–Whitney U-test	Explanation
(c) Accommodation establishments vs. Travel agencies		
How would you evaluate the magnitude of the impact of current political instability on your business in general?	3704	
How would you assess the direction of the impact of current political instability on your business in general?	3051.5**	H < TA
How did the number of your tourists change in 2014 compared to 2013?	2801.5***	H > TA
How did your total revenues change in 2014 compared to 2013?	3308.5	
How did your total costs change in 2014 compared to 2013?	2952.5**	H > TA
How did your total employee costs (salaries, social security payments, employee insurances, etc.) change in 2014 compared to 2013?	3451	
How did the total number of your employees change in 2014 compared to 2013?	3349	

Notes: H indicates the average value of the responses of the hotel managers. TA indicates the average value of the responses of the managers of travel agencies.
*Significant at 10% level.
**Significant at 5% level.
***Significant at 1% level.

110

4.1.2. Travel agencies' perspective

Table 3(b) presents the changes in travel agencies' operational statistics in 2014 compared to 2013 (RQ1.2). Similar to the accommodation establishments, the performance of Ukrainian travel agencies deteriorated. The number of their customers decreased on average by −19.59%, the revenues dropped by −17.19%, while costs surged by 5.62%. Not surprisingly, the travel agency managers considered the political instability as important for their business ($m = 3.74$) and with predominantly negative impact ($m = 1.99$). The main market segment of the agency (RQ5.3) had no impact on its performance while licence type (RQ5.1), region (RQ5.2), and IATA certification (RQ5.4) had marginal influence. The travel agents and the agencies located in regions neighbouring the conflict areas assessed more negatively the impact of the political instability on their business, while the revenues of IATA agencies fell more significantly than the revenues of other agencies. The results are to be expected: the travel agents work on commission basis and sell the products (package tours, tickets, etc.) of other companies. The tour operators work on mark-up basis, create their own products, may sell through an extensive agent network and thus are more flexible than agents and more resilient to negative developments in the external environment. The IATA agencies sell flight tickets and are highly vulnerable to shifts in air travel. In 2014, the number of air passengers in Ukraine decreased from 8,107,200 to 6,473,300 (State Statistics Service of Ukraine, 2015b). It is possible that the drop in the air travel could have resulted in decrease in the flight tickets sales and the revenues of the IATA agencies. However, our data do not allow us to confirm or reject this conjecture.

4.1.3. Accommodation establishments vs. travel agencies

Comparing the agencies and the accommodation establishments (RQ6), we see that the revenues of the travel agencies dropped more than the revenues of the accommodation establishments ($p < .01$), while their costs increased less – see Table 3(c). Therefore, we see that the agencies' and accommodation establishments' financial results are deteriorating, but by different reasons: agencies' profits drop mostly due to decrease in their revenues, not so much on the increase in their expenses, while the hotels experience significant effects of both events. Moreover, the accommodation establishments are geographically and, at least in the short term, product bound – their location cannot be changed while changing the product requires time. Furthermore, travel agencies can change their product offering and react to changes in demand and external environment much more easily than the accommodation establishments. This might explain why the managers of travel agencies evaluated the impact of the political instability as slightly less negative than the managers of the accommodation establishments.

4.2. Factors influencing the business, resulting from the political instability

4.2.1. Accommodation establishments' perspective

Table 4(a) illustrates hotel managers' opinions about the importance and the direction of the impact of various factors, resulting from the political instability in Ukraine (RQ2.1). The military hostilities in Eastern Ukraine were considered as the most important factor influencing the hotel business ($m = 4.39$) and the paired samples t-tests with the other factors revealed that its level of importance was statistically different from the levels of importance of each of the other factors at $p < .01$. Surprisingly, the entry of the Autonomous Republic of Crimea into the Russian Federation was rendered as one of the least important factors, influencing the hotel business in Ukraine, but we could only speculate on the reasons. Probably, the hotel managers considered this as a one-off event with limited repercussions on their business, while the military actions in the eastern provinces of the country had a more enduring effect on hotel customers' perceptions of the riskiness of the destination. Category (RQ4.6), size (RQ4.9) and region (RQ4.8) of hotels did not influence managers' assessment of the importance of the analysed macroenvironment factors. On the other hand, location (RQ4.7) and chain affiliation (RQ4.10) had some impact. For example, managers of rural/countryside and seaside hotels were more concerned with the annexation of Crimea ($\chi^2 = 9.956$, $p < .05$) and the continuing military hostilities in Eastern Ukraine ($\chi^2 = 7.939$, $p < .05$) rather than the managers of urban and mountain hotels. Additionally, managers of independent properties put greater emphasis on the tax level than the managers of chain affiliated hotels.

In regard to RQ2.2, the military activities in Eastern Ukraine were evaluated as having the most negative impact on the hotel business ($m = 2.43$), followed by the annexation of Crimea ($m = 2.62$) and the tax level ($m = 2.65$). In contrast, the process of integration of Ukraine into the EU and the speed of this process were perceived as having neutral rather than positive impact on the business ($m = 3.25$ and $m = 3.07$, respectively). Expectedly, the paired samples t-tests showed that the differences between the perceived impacts of the first three and the second two factors were all significant at $p < .01$. The managers of low category 1–2 star hotels felt more negatively about the current political situation in the country than the luxurious 4–5 star hotels (RQ4.6), same as the managers of hotels in conflict neighbouring regions compared to the managers of the hotels in the rest of Ukraine (RQ4.8). Probably both groups of respondents did not feel that the government was doing enough to end the military hostilities, decrease the political tension and lead the country into peaceful waters. On the other hand, managers of rural/countryside properties reported less negative impacts of the hostilities in Eastern Ukraine than the managers of other hotels, probably because they relied more on domestic tourists than the rest of the hotels.

4.2.2. Travel agencies' perspective

Table 4(b) presents travel agency managers' perceptions about the factors, influencing the business. The military hostilities in Eastern Ukraine were considered as the single most important factor ($m = 4.15$) and the paired samples t-tests with the level of importance of the other factors were all significant at $p < .01$ (RQ2.3). The tax level ($m = 3.71$) and the annexation of the Crimean peninsula ($m = 3.58$) were considered as less important. In regard to the direction of the impacts the ordering of the factors looked the same: the continuing military hostilities were evaluated as having the highest negative impact factor ($m = 1.84$) and the paired samples t-tests with the evaluation of the other factors were all significant at $p < .01$, while the annexation of Crimea ($m = 2.22$) and the tax level ($m = 2.44$) were the second and third factors with highest negative influence (RQ2.4).

Travel agency characteristics had a marginal role in its manager's perceptions of the macroenvironmental factors. The managers of tour operators, for example, evaluated the acts of terrorism/war in Eastern Ukraine more negatively than the managers of travel agents (RQ5.5); the managers of agencies in conflict neighbouring regions assessed

Table 4. Factors, influencing the business, resulting from the political instability.

Factors	Total mean	Standard deviation	Kruskal–Wallis χ^2 test			Mann–Whitney U-test	
			Category	Size	Location	Region	Chain Affiliation
(a) Accommodation establishments							
Differences by category, size, location, region, and chain affiliation							
Level of importance of the factors influencing the business, resulting from the political instability							
Annexation of the Crimean peninsula	3.24	1.329	2.701	3.797	9.956**	1053.5	771.5
Acts of terrorism/ war in Eastern Ukraine (Donetsk, Lugansk)	4.39	0.997	4.225	0.140	7.939**	1041.0	687.0
Change of political government in 2013	3.41	1.213	0.128	1.157	4.598	975.5	814.0
Current political situation and governmental structure	3.86	1.025	2.792	0.445	1.137	1081.0	720.0
The process of integration of Ukraine to the EU	3.23	1.151	0.902	0.602	2.069	1019.0	768.5
Speed of the integration process to the EU	3.31	1.177	0.265	0.540	2.723	1081.0	681.0
Tax level	3.66	1.255	0.353	0.649	1.477	1078.5	575.5**
Evaluation of the impacts of the factors influencing the business, resulting from the political instability							
Annexation of the Crimean peninsula	2.62	1.178	2.042	0.601	4.531	1160.5	790.0
Acts of terrorism/ war in Eastern Ukraine (Donetsk, Lugansk)	2.43	1.564	2.110	5.600*	11.085**	993.5	788.5
Change of political government in 2013	3.04	1.297	2.578	3.418	6.360*	911.5*	655.0
Current political situation and governmental structure	2.74	1.226	6.850**	5.462*	3.812	850.5**	767.5
The process of integration of Ukraine to the EU	3.25	1.116	1.002	1.999	1.403	974.5	677.0
Speed of the integration process to the EU	3.07	1.119	1.918	0.793	1.526	966.5	604.0*
Tax level	2.65	1.199	0.062	1.970	0.682	957.0	609.5*

Notes: Measurement scales: *level of importance*: 1 – very unimportant, 5 – very important; *evaluation of the impact*: 1 – very negative, 5 – very positive. Grouping of respondents: *Size* (up to 50, 51–100 and over 100 rooms), *Location* (urban, seaside, mountain, rural/countryside), *Category* (1–2 stars, 3 stars, 4–5 stars), *Region* (neighbouring the conflict areas, rest of Ukraine), *Chain Affiliation* (affiliated to a chain, independent hotels).
***Significant at 1% level.
**Significant at 5% level.
*Significant at 10% level.

Operational statistics	Total mean	Standard deviation	Mann–Whitney U-test			
			Licence type	Region	Main market segment	IATA certification
(b) Travel agencies						
Differences by licence type, region, main market segment, and IATA certification						
Level of importance of the factors influencing the business, resulting from the political instability						
Annexation of the Crimean peninsula	3.58	1.235	602	459.5	173**	296
Acts of terrorism/war in Eastern Ukraine (Donetsk, Lugansk)	4.15	0.981	505	436	293.5	211.5**
Change of political government in 2013	3.25	1.331	599	461	302	248*
Current political situation and governmental structure	3.41	1.311	579.5	465.5	280	277.5
The process of integration of Ukraine to the EU	3.16	1.334	548	416	290	261.5
Speed of the integration process to the EU	3.12	1.394	598.5	428	282.5	283
Tax level	3.71	1.230	473.5*	401	272	286.5

(Continued)

Table 4. Continued.

Operational statistics	Total mean	Standard deviation	Mann–Whitney U-test			
			Licence type	Region	Main market segment	IATA certification
Evaluation of the impacts of the factors influencing the business, resulting from the political instability						
Annexation of the Crimean peninsula	2.22	1.109	510.5	469.5	277	178.5***
Acts of terrorism/war in Eastern Ukraine (Donetsk, Lugansk)	1.84	1.067	453**	429.5	245	248.5
Change of political government in 2013	2.59	1.012	496.5	406.5	309	352
Current political situation and governmental structure	2.55	1.001	490	360.5	291.5	361.5
The process of integration of Ukraine to the EU	3.06	1.039	574.5	373	285.5	279
Speed of the integration process to the EU	2.96	1.111	510	440.5	248.5	216.5**
Tax level	2.44	1.000	486	387.5***	274.5	344

Notes: Measurement scales: *level of importance*: 1 – very unimportant, 5 – very important; *evaluation of the impact*: 1 – very negative, 5 – very positive. Grouping of respondents: *Licence* (tour operator, travel agent), *Main market segments* (groups, individual tourists), *IATA certified* (IATA-certified agency, not IATA-certified agency), *Region* (neighbouring the conflict areas, rest of Ukraine).
***Significant at 1% level.
**Significant at 5% level.
*Significant at 10% level.

Operational statistics	Mann–Whitney U-test	Explanations
(c) Accommodation establishments vs. Travel agencies		
Level of importance of the factors influencing the business, resulting from the political instability		
Annexation of the Crimean peninsula	3193*	H < TA
Acts of terrorism/war in Eastern Ukraine (Donetsk, Lugansk)	3062**	H > TA
Change of political government in 2013	3467	
Current political situation and governmental structure	3042**	H > TA
The process of integration of Ukraine to the EU	3655	
Speed of the integration process to the EU	3469	
Tax level	3633	
Evaluation of the impacts of the factors influencing the business, resulting from the political instability		
Annexation of the Crimean peninsula	3004.5**	H > TA
Acts of terrorism/war in Eastern Ukraine (Donetsk, Lugansk)	3076.5**	H > TA
Change of political government in 2013	2921**	H > TA
Current political situation and governmental structure	3500	
The process of integration of Ukraine to the EU	3382.5	
Speed of the integration process to the EU	3592.5	
Tax level	3482.5	

Notes: H indicates the average value of the responses of the hotel managers. TA indicates the average value of the responses of the managers of travel agencies.
*Significant at 10% level.
**Significant at 5% level.
***Significant at 1% level.

the tax level more negatively (RQ5.6); the annexation of Crimea was more important factor for the managers of agencies serving predominantly groups (RQ5.7); the managers of IATA agencies put greater emphasis on the military hostilities in Eastern Ukraine, and evaluated the annexation of Crimea ($p < .01$) and the speed of Ukraine's integration process to the EU more negatively than non-IATA agencies (RQ5.8). A possible explanation for the findings might be the fact that until 2013, Crimea was a major mass tourist destination on Ukraine – for example, in 2011, the Autonomous Republic of Crimea and Sevastopol generated 16.2% of the overnights in collective accommodation establishments (State Statistics Service of Ukraine, 2012). Therefore, its entry into the Russian Federation in March 2014 was seriously felt by the agencies serving groups. The IATA agencies suffered from the plummet in the number of air passengers mentioned above; hence, their managers perceive more negatively the factors that contribute the decreased air traffic like military hostilities and slow integration of the country into the European Union.

4.2.3. Accommodation establishments vs. travel agencies

The comparison of accommodation establishments' and travel agencies' managers' perceptions about the macroenvironmental factors is presented in Table 4(c) (RQ6). The results indicate that the managers of travel agencies were more negative in their perceptions than the managers of accommodation establishments in regard to the annexation of Crimea, military hostilities and the change of political government in 2013, but they put slightly less importance on the acts of terrorism and the current political situation and government structure. Despite these differences, the respondents from both groups are unanimous that the continuing acts of terrorism/war in Eastern Ukraine is the single most important, with the greatest negative impact, political challenge faced by tourist companies in the country.

4.3. Strategies to mitigate the negative impact of the political instability

4.3.1. Accommodation establishments' perspective

The strategies used by the hotels to mitigate the negative consequences of the political instability are reported in Table 5(a) (RQ3.1). The hotel managers relied mostly on increased marketing efforts ($m = 4.13$) to compensate the loss of tourists to their properties and the paired samples t-tests with the other strategies were all significant at $p < .01$. The intuitive actions of decreasing prices ($m = 3.05$), cutting costs by working with fewer employees ($m = 2.80$), and paying later to suppliers ($m = 2.59$) were less significant options for the managers. It is interesting to note that despite the difficult financial situation, hoteliers did not report actions that were connected with hiding revenues and taxes – requiring more cash payments instead of payments by bank, debit, or credit card ($m = 2.42$), or requiring payments in foreign currency rather than in hryvnia ($m = 2.16$). Category (RQ4.11), size (RQ4.14), and location (RQ4.12) did not reveal any major differences in the responses of the hotel managers. The managers of chain affiliated hotels were more eager to pay later to their suppliers, to work with fewer employees and to increase their marketing efforts than the managers of independent properties. Not surprisingly, the managers of hotels in regions neighbouring the conflict areas were more willing to use price decreases to stimulate demand than the rest of the hotel managers, due to the greater drop in the number of tourists accommodated in their hotels in 2014 compared to 2013 than the decrease in the number of hotel guests in other regions, discussed earlier.

4.3.2. Travel agencies' perspective

Similar to the managers of the accommodation establishments, the managers of travel agencies try to mitigate the negative consequences of political instability by increasing their marketing efforts ($m = 3.33$), while decreasing prices ($m = 3.12$) is the second favourite option – see Table 5(b). The paired samples t-test revealed no statistically significant

Table 5. Level of agreement with statements related to mitigating the negative impacts of the political instability.

Question	Total mean	Standard deviation	Kruskal–Wallis χ^2 test			Mann–Whitney U-test	
			Category	Size	Location	Regions	Chain Affiliation
(a) Accommodation establishments							
Differences by category, size, location, region, and chain affiliation							
Level of agreement with statements related to mitigating the negative impacts of the political instability							
We try to mitigate the impacts of political instability on our business by requiring more cash payments by guests than payments by bank or credit/debit card	2.42	1.048	2.065	0.678	3.412	1128.5	798.0
We try to mitigate the impacts of political instability on our business by requiring more payments in foreign currency (USD/GBP/EUR) than payments in hryvnia	2.16	0.952	4.444	1.396	2.373	1136.5	812.0
We try to mitigate the impacts of political instability on our business by working with fewer employees	2.80	1.186	0.506	3.212	5.188	1006.0	629.0*
We try to mitigate the impacts of political instability on our business by paying later to suppliers	2.59	1.146	0.292	3.750	3.532	1116.0	573.0**
We try to mitigate the impacts of political instability on our business by increased marketing efforts to attract more guests	4.13	0.941	3.099	5.607*	5.656	1102.0	635.5*
We try to mitigate the impacts of political instability on our business by decreasing prices	3.05	1.197	0.665	2.278	5.272	829**	679.0
The political instability endanger our hotel with bankruptcy	3.25	1.338	2.241	3.569	7.342*	1021.0	679.5
Expectations:							
How long do you expect the political instability to continue?	2.52	1.109	0.099	1.501	8.913**	880.5	660.5

Notes: Measurement scales: *level of agreement*: 1 – strongly disagree, 5 – strongly agree; *expectations*: in years. Grouping of respondents: *Size* (up to 50, 51–100 and over 100 rooms), *Location* (urban, seaside, mountain, rural/countryside), *Category* (1–2 stars, 3 stars, 4–5 stars), *Region* (neighbouring the conflict areas, rest of Ukraine), *Chain Affiliation* (affiliated to a chain, independent hotels).
***Significant at 1% level.
**Significant at 5% level.
*Significant at 10% level.

Question	Total mean	Standard deviation	Mann–Whitney U-test			
			Licence type	Region	Main market segment	IATA certification
(b) Travel agencies						
Differences by licence type, region, main market segment, and IATA certification						
Level of agreement with statements related to mitigating the negative impacts of the political instability						
We try to mitigate the impacts of political instability on our business by requiring more cash payments by customers than payments by bank or credit/debit card	2.77	1.125	568.5	403.5	274.5	331.5

(Continued)

Table 5. Continued.

			Mann–Whitney U-test			
Question	Total mean	Standard deviation	Licence type	Region	Main market segment	IATA certification
We try to mitigate the impacts of political instability on our business by requiring more payments in foreign currency (USD/GBP/EUR) than payments in hryvnia	2.69	1.311	596.5	446.5	266.5	262.5
We try to mitigate the impacts of political instability on our business by working with fewer employees	2.38	1.101	599	409.5	263.5	326.5
We try to mitigate the impacts of political instability on our business by paying later to suppliers	1.86	0.887	564	352*	302.5	341.5
We try to mitigate the impacts of political instability on our business by increased marketing efforts to attract more guests	3.33	1.119	477.5	428	278.5	349.5
We try to mitigate the impacts of political instability on our business by decreasing prices	3.12	1.142	555	449.5	290.5	271
The political instability endanger our agency with bankruptcy	3.15	1.340	519	437.5	246.5	351
Expectations:						
How long do you expect the political instability to continue?	3.15	1.684	378	266.5	180	230

Notes: Measurement scales: *level of agreement*: 1 – strongly disagree, 5 – strongly agree; *expectations*: in years. Grouping of respondents: *Licence* (tour operator, travel agent), *Main market segments* (groups, individual tourists), *IATA certified* (IATA-certified agency, not IATA-certified agency), *Region* (neighbouring the conflict areas, rest of Ukraine).
***Significant at 1% level.
**Significant at 5% level.
*Significant at 10% level.

Question	Mann–Whitney U-test	Explanation
(c) Accommodation establishments vs. Travel agencies		
We try to mitigate the impacts of political instability on our business by requiring more cash payments by guests than payments by bank or credit/debit card	3166*	H < TA
We try to mitigate the impacts of political instability on our business by requiring more payments in foreign currency (USD/GBP/EUR) than payments in hryvnia	2899***	H < TA
We try to mitigate the impacts of political instability on our business by working with fewer employees	2997.5**	H > TA
We try to mitigate the impacts of political instability on our business by paying later to suppliers	2406.5***	H > TA
We try to mitigate the impacts of political instability on our business by increased marketing efforts to attract more guests	2173.5***	H > TA
We try to mitigate the impacts of political instability on our business by decreasing prices	3658	
The political instability endanger our company with bankruptcy	3567	
Expectations:		
How long do you expect the political instability to continue?	2382.5**	H < TA

Notes: H indicates the average value of the responses of the hotel managers. TA indicates the average value of the responses of the managers of travel agencies.
*Significant at 10% level.
**Significant at 5% level.
***Significant at 1% level.

differences between the answers to these two questions; hence, we may consider the two approaches as nearly equally preferred (RQ3.2). The other approaches were less popular, and their differences with the increased marketing efforts and decreasing prices were all significant at $p < .01$ or $p < .05$. Licence type (RQ5.9), region (RQ5.10), main market segment (RQ5.11), and IATA certification (RQ5.12) of the agencies do not influence the ways their managers mitigate the negative consequences of the political instability.

4.3.3. Accommodation establishments vs. travel agencies

Table 5(c) shows the comparison between the responses of the managers of the accommodation establishments and travel agencies in regard to the approaches used to mitigate the negative consequences of the political instability. While both groups of respondents rely on increased marketing efforts and decreased prices as their two most used approaches, we see numerous statistically significant differences between the respondent groups. Managers of accommodation establishments rely more on marketing efforts, delaying payments to suppliers and working with fewer employees, while the agencies reported higher values on cash payments and payments in foreign currency. This means that the managers of travel agencies seemed more inclined to be involved in hidden economic activities (associated with payments in cash and in foreign currency) than the hotel managers. Looking back at Table 3(a, b), we see that the accommodation establishments experienced larger cost increases than the travel agencies. Therefore, it is understandable why their managers focus more on delaying payments to suppliers and decreasing the number of employees than the managers of travel agencies. The currency structure of the expenses of the accommodation establishments and the travel agencies is very different: accommodation establishments use predominantly local suppliers to whom they have to pay in local currency. Contrarily, the travel agencies, especially when they are IATA certified and operate on the outgoing tourist market, have a large share of expenses in foreign currency in the form of payments to foreign suppliers. This makes them more vulnerable to currency rate fluctuations. In order to eliminate the currency exchange risk, the companies should have their revenues and expenses denominated in the same currencies. Considering that the travel agencies cannot persuade their foreign suppliers to accept the Ukrainian hryvnia as payment currency, their managers could decrease the currency exchange risk by requesting local customer's payments in the currencies of their foreign suppliers (EUR/USD/GBP, etc.). That is why, we think, the travel agencies in Ukraine needed to request more payments in foreign currency than the accommodation establishments in the country.

5. Conclusion

5.1. Contribution

This paper contributes to the advancement in knowledge in crisis management by analysing the impacts of the political instability and continuing military hostilities in eastern provinces of Ukraine on the tourism industry in the country. Furthermore, it evaluates the differential impact of the above-mentioned factors on the accommodation establishments by their category, location, region, size, and chain affiliation, and the differential impacts on the travel agencies by their licence type, region, main market segment, and IATA certification. Finally, the paper elaborates the practical strategies adopted by industry representatives to mitigate the negative impacts of political instability. The summary answers to the paper's research questions are presented in Table 6.

5.2. Managerial and policy implications

From a managerial perspective, the findings confirm previous research results that political instability leads to negative impacts on the tourism industry of a country (Ivanov et al., 2016; Llorca-Vivero, 2008; Neumayer, 2004) – decreased revenues, plummeting numbers of tourists and overnights, and increased costs. This was valid not only for the regions that were neighbouring the conflict areas, but for the rest of country as well, although the former were more severely hit by the political instability than the latter. The findings further revealed differential effect of the political instability on the accommodation establishments and travel agencies on the basis of their characteristics. However, their managers bravely faced this challenging political and economic environment and increased their marketing efforts to overcome some of the negative consequences of the political instability.

The findings of this research first and foremost echo what is intuitive, that tourism suffers in places that experience violent and other political conflicts. The findings also echo the basic geographical concept of decay, usually used in tourism research in modelling tourist flows (see, for example, McKercher & Lew, 2003; Yan, 2011), as the hotels and agencies that are further from the conflict suffer less from the conflict than those that are closest to it. The results illustrate that not all accommodation establishments in Ukraine have been hurt equally by the political situation and that various characteristics of hotels lead them to using different methods to adjust to the political and economic shocks they experience. Not surprisingly, smaller accommodation establishments seemed to have been hurt more than larger ones. What is not very obvious nor intuitive is the way the chain affiliation of hotels influenced how hotels have experienced the crisis. The results revealed that the chain affiliated hotels were more severely hit by the political instability than the independent properties, that is, the strong brands of the hotel chains, considered to be one for their most important advantage and most sought-after attribute by the managers of potential chain members (Ivanova & Ivanov, 2015), failed to fulfil their promises to the hotel owners in time of crisis. The landslide in the performance metrics of chain hotels means that their managers need to diversify their customer base and decrease their dependence on foreign tourists. Our results provide a hint that they have already started doing this – the managers of chain affiliated establishments reported greater increased marketing efforts than the managers of independent properties. In addition, the findings indicated that the revenues of the travel agencies were more severely hit than the accommodation establishments while their costs did not increase much. This means that the travel agency managers needs to focus on diversifying the product portfolio, especially in the case of IATA agencies, which would help them attract new market segments and generate revenue.

From a tourism policy perspective, the findings reveal that the political environment has major influences on tourist businesses. Public authorities' and tourist companies' efforts in attracting tourists and stimulating a destination's competitiveness would be significantly undermined by political crises because they make the country insecure and, hence, unattractive to tourists. Without peace and political stability, any efforts to attract tourists would be largely in vain. On the other hand, prior research (Moufakkir & Kelly, 2010; Webster & Ivanov, 2014) has indicated that while tourism benefits greatly from the peace in a country, tourism itself can be an instrument to achieve peace, that is, the link between tourism and peace is bidirectional, although it seems that tourism suffers more from the lack of peace in a country than it contributes to its

Table 6. Summary answers to research questions.

Research question	Answer
RQ1: Performance metrics	
• RQ1.1: How have the political and military events influenced the performance metrics of the accommodation establishments in Ukraine?	Performance metrics deteriorated
• RQ1.2: How have the political and military events influenced the performance metrics of the travel agencies in Ukraine?	Performance metrics deteriorated
RQ2: Political and economic challenges	
• RQ2.1: What importance do the managers of accommodation establishments in the country put on the various political and economic challenges of the macroenvironment?	The military hostilities in Eastern Ukraine were considered as the most important factor
• RQ2.2: How do the managers of accommodation establishments in the country evaluate the various political and economic challenges of the macroenvironment?	The military hostilities in Eastern Ukraine were considered as having highest negative impact
• RQ2.3: What importance do the managers of travel agencies in the country put on the various political and economic challenges of the macroenvironment?	The military hostilities in Eastern Ukraine were considered as the most important factor
• RQ2.4: How do the managers of travel agencies in the country evaluate the various political and economic challenges of the macroenvironment?	The military hostilities in Eastern Ukraine were considered as having highest negative impact
RQ3: Mitigating the negative impacts	
• RQ3.1: How do the managers of accommodation establishments in the country mitigate the negative impacts of the various political and economic challenges of the macroenvironment?	The hotel managers relied mostly on increased marketing efforts
• RQ3.2: How do the managers of travel agencies in the country mitigate the negative impacts of the various political and economic challenges of the macroenvironment?	The travel agency managers relied mostly on increased marketing efforts and decreased prices
RQ4: The role of accommodation establishments' characteristics	
• RQ4.1: Does the impact of political instability on an accommodation establishment's performance metrics depend on its category?	No
• RQ4.2: Does the impact of political instability on an accommodation establishment's performance metrics depend on its location?	No
• RQ4.3: Does the impact of political instability on an accommodation establishment's performance metrics depend on its region?	Yes, hotels in conflict neighbouring regions more negatively affected
• RQ4.4: Does the impact of political instability on an accommodation establishment's performance metrics depend on its size?	Yes, costs increased more for smallest than for largest hotels
• RQ4.5: Does the impact of political instability on an accommodation establishment's performance metrics depend on its chain affiliation?	Yes, chain affiliated properties more severely affected
• RQ4.6: Do accommodation establishment's manager's perceptions about the political and economic challenges depend on its category?	Marginal, the managers of 1–2 star hotels felt more negatively about the current political situation in the country than of the 4–5 star ones
• RQ4.7: Do accommodation establishment's manager's perceptions about the political and economic challenges depend on its location?	Marginal, managers of rural/countryside and seaside hotels were more concerned with the annexation of Crimea and the continuing military hostilities in Eastern Ukraine
• RQ4.8: Do accommodation establishment's manager's perceptions about the political and economic challenges depend on its region?	Marginal, the managers of hotels in conflict neighbouring regions felt more negatively about the current political situation than the rest of respondents
• RQ4.9: Do accommodation establishment's manager's perceptions about the political and economic challenges depend on its size?	No

(Continued)

Table 6. Continued.

Research question	Answer
• RQ4.10: Do accommodation establishment's manager's perceptions about the political and economic challenges depend on its chain affiliation?	Marginal, the managers of independent properties put greater emphasis on the tax level
• RQ4.11: Do accommodation establishment's manager's reactions to the political and economic challenges depend on its category?	No
• RQ4.12: Do accommodation establishment's manager's reactions to the political and economic challenges depend on its location?	No
• RQ4.13: Do accommodation establishment's manager's reactions to the political and economic challenges depend on its region?	Marginal, the managers of hotels in regions neighbouring the conflict areas were more willing to use price decreases
• RQ4.14: Do accommodation establishment's manager's reactions to the political and economic challenges depend on its size?	No
• RQ4.15: Do accommodation establishment's manager's reactions to the political and economic challenges depend on its chain affiliation?	Yes, the managers of chain affiliated hotels were more eager to pay later to their suppliers, to work with fewer employees and to increase their marketing efforts
RQ5: The role of travel agencies' characteristics	
• RQ5.1: Does the impact of political instability on a travel agency's performance metrics depend on its licence type?	Marginal, the travel agents assessed more negatively the impact of the political instability on their business
• RQ5.2: Does the impact of political instability on a travel agency's performance metrics depend on its region?	Marginal, the agencies in conflict neighbouring regions assessed more negatively the impact of the political instability on their business
• RQ5.3: Does the impact of political instability on a travel agency's performance metrics depend on its main market segment?	No
• RQ5.4: Does the impact of political instability on a travel agency's performance metrics depend on its IATA certification?	Marginal, revenues of IATA agencies fell more than of non-IATA agencies
• RQ5.5: Do travel agency's manager's perceptions about the political and economic challenges depend on its licence type?	Marginal, tour operators evaluated the acts of terrorism/war in Eastern Ukraine more negatively
• RQ5.6: Do travel agency's manager's perceptions about the political and economic challenges depend on its region?	Marginal, the managers of agencies in conflict neighbouring regions assessed the tax level more negatively
• RQ5.7: Do travel agency's manager's perceptions about the political and economic challenges depend on its main market segment?	Marginal, the annexation of Crimea was more important factor for the managers of agencies serving predominantly groups
• RQ5.8: Do travel agency's manager's perceptions about the political and economic challenges depend on its IATA certification?	Yes, the managers of IATA agencies put greater emphasis on the military hostilities in Eastern Ukraine, and evaluated the annexation of Crimea and the speed of Ukraine's integration process to the EU more negatively
• RQ5.9: Do travel agency's manager's reactions to the political and economic challenges depend on its licence type?	No
• RQ5.10: Do travel agency's manager's reactions to the political and economic challenges depend on its region?	No
• RQ5.11: Do travel agency's manager's reactions to the political and economic challenges depend on its main market segment?	No
• RQ5.12: Do travel agency's manager's reactions to the political and economic challenges depend on its IATA certification?	No
• *RQ6: Accommodation establishments vs. travel agencies*	

(Continued)

Table 6. Continued.

Research question	Answer
• RQ6: Are there statistically significant differences in the responses of accommodation establishments' and travel agencies' managers?	Yes: • Revenues of agencies drop more • Costs of hotels increase more • The managers of travel agencies were more negative in regard to the annexation of Crimea, military hostilities and the change of political government in 2013, but they put slightly less importance on the acts of terrorism and the current political situation and government structure • Accommodation establishments rely more on marketing efforts, delaying payments to suppliers and working with fewer employees; the agencies reported higher values on cash payments and payments in foreign currency

peaceful development. That is why, the political leaders in Ukraine, the rebel provinces and the international community need to focus first and foremost on providing peace and political stability in the country in order to secure its economic development. Ukraine's future entry into the European Union would well serve this purpose.

5.3. Limitations

We expected that if the questionnaire included questions about the absolute values of financial and operational statistics, the potential respondents would be very suspicious to the research and less likely to participate in it. That is why, as a limitation of the research, we could mention the fact that the questionnaire did not collect any financial data and operational statistics in absolute values but as relative percentage changes in 2014 compared to 2013 due to confidentiality reasons. Therefore, the percentage changes of the operational statistics were calculated as simple averages rather than weighted with the revenues of the accommodation establishments and the travel agencies.

5.4. Future research directions

Future research could focus on the long-term impacts of the political instability on the tourism industry in Ukraine through a longitudinal study. We expect that the effects of political instability will decrease in time after a political solution of the crisis is found, but future research needs to confirm or reject this proposition. Additionally, research could concentrate on the impact of the political instability on other tourism characteristic activities like F&B outlets and passenger transport. Finally, future research might shed light on how the public authorities in Ukraine help the tourist companies mitigate the negative impacts of the political instability and the military hostilities.

Disclosure statement

No potential conflict of interest was reported by the authors.

References

Aimable, E., & Rosselló, J. (2009). The short-term impact of 9/11 on European airlines demand. *European Journal of Tourism Research, 2*(2), 145–161.

Anson, C. (1999). Planning for peace: The role of tourism in the aftermath of violence. *Journal of Travel Research, 38*(1), 57–61.

Araña, J. E., & León, C. J. (2008). The impact of terrorism on tourism demand. *Annals of Tourism Research, 35*(2), 299–315.

Askjellerud, S. (2003). The tourist as messenger of peace? *Annals of Tourism Research, 30*(3), 741–744.

Baggio, R., & Klobas, J. (2011). *Quantitative methods in tourism. A handbook.* Bristol: Channel View.

Björk, P., & Kauppinen-Räisänen, H. (2011). The impact of perceived risk on information search: A study of Finnish tourists. *Scandinavian Journal of Hospitality and Tourism, 11*(3), 306–323.

Butler, R., & Suntilkul, W. (Eds.). (2013). *Tourism and war.* Abingdon: Routledge.

Causevic, S., & Lynch, P. (2013). Political (in)stability and its influence on tourism development. *Tourism Management, 34*, 145–157.

Clements, M. A., & Georgiou, A. (1998). The impact of political instability on a fragile tourism product. *Tourism Management, 19*(3), 283–288.

D'Amore, L. (1988). Tourism – the world's peace industry. *Journal of Travel Research, 27*(1), 35–40.

D'Amore, L. (2009). Peace through tourism: The birthing of a new socio-economic order. *Journal of Business Ethics, 89*(4), 559–568.

Drakos, K., & Kutan, A. M. (2003). Regional effects of terrorism on tourism in three Mediterranean countries. *The Journal of Conflict Resolution, 47*(5), 621–641.

Feridun, M. (2011). Impact of terrorism on tourism in Turkey: Empirical evidence from Turkey. *Applied Economics, 43*(24), 3349–3354.

Illum, S. F., Ivanov, S., & Liang, Y. (2010). Using virtual communities in tourism research. *Tourism Management, 31*(3), 335–340.

Ingram, H., Tabari, S., & Watthanakhomprathip, W. (2013). The impact of political instability on tourism: Case of Thailand. *Worldwide Hospitality and Tourism Themes, 5*(1), 92–103.

Ivanov, S., Idzhilova, K., & Webster, C. (2016). Impacts of the entry of the Autonomous Republic of Crimea into the Russian Federation on its tourism industry: An exploratory study. *Tourism Management, 54*, 162–169.

Ivanov, S., Stoilova, E., & Illum, S. F. (2015). Conflicts between accommodation establishments and travel agencies. *Tourism and Hospitality Research, 15*(1), 54–70.

Ivanova, M., & Ivanov, S. (2015). Affiliation to hotel chains: Hotels' perspective. *Tourism Management Perspectives, 16*, 148–162.

Jallat, F., & Shultz, C. J. (2010). Lebanon: From cataclysm to opportunity – crisis management lessons for MNCs in the tourism sector of the Middle East. *Journal of World Business, 46*(4), 476–486.

Khamouna, M., & Zeiger, Z. B. (1995). Peace through tourism. *Parks & Recreation, 30*(9), 80–86.

Larsen, S., Brun, W., Øgaard, T., & Selstad, L. (2011). Effects of sudden and dramatic events on travel desire and risk judgments. *Scandinavian Journal of Hospitality and Tourism, 11*(3), 268–285.

Levy, S. E., & Hawkins, D. (2009). Peace through tourism: Commerce based principles and practices. *Journal of Business Ethics, 89*(Suppl. 4), 569–585.

Llorca-Vivero, R. (2008). Terrorism and international tourism: New evidence. *Defence and Peace Economics, 19*(2), 169–188.

McDowell, S. (2008). Selling conflict heritage through tourism in peacetime Northern Ireland: Transforming conflict or exacerbating difference? *International Journal of Heritage Studies, 14* (5), 405–421.

McKercher, B., & Lew, A. A. (2003). Distance decay and the impact of effective tourism exclusion zones on international travel flows. *Journal of Travel Research, 42*(3), 159–165.

Moufakkir, O., & Kelly, I. (Eds.). (2010). *Tourism, progress and peace.* Wallingford: CABI.

Neumayer, E. (2004). The impact of political violence on tourism: Dynamic cross-national estimation. *The Journal of Conflict Resolution, 48*(2), 259–281.

O'Connor, N., Stafford, M. R., & Gallagher, G. (2008). The impact of global terrorism on Ireland's tourism industry: An industry perspective. *Tourism and Hospitality Research, 8*(4), 351–363.

Purwomarwanto, Y. L., & Ramachandran, J. (2015). Performance of tourism sector with regard to the global crisis: A comparative study between Indonesia, Malaysia, and Singapore. *The Journal of Developing Areas, 49*(4), 325–339.

Reuters. (2014, August 5). *About 730,000 have left Ukraine for Russia due to conflict – UNHCR.* Retrieved September 6, 2015, from http://in.reuters.com/article/2014/08/05/uk-ukraine-crisis-migrants-idINKBN0G517P20140805

Saha, S., & Yap, G. (2014). The moderation effects of political instability and terrorism on tourism development: A cross-country panel analysis. *Journal of Travel Research, 53*(4), 509–521.

de Sausmarez, N. (2013). Challenges to Kenyan tourism since 2008: Crisis management from the Kenyan tour operator perspective. *Current Issues in Tourism, 16*(7–8), 792–809.

Solarin, S. A. (2015). September 11 attacks, H1N1 influenza, global financial crisis and tourist arrivals in Sarawak. *Anatolia, 26*(2), 298–300.

State Statistics Service of Ukraine. (2012). *Collective accommodation establishments in Ukraine in 2011. Statistical Bulletin.* Kiev: Author.

State Statistics Service of Ukraine. (2013). *Tourist activity in Ukraine in 2012. Statistical Bulletin.* Kiev: Author.

State Statistics Service of Ukraine. (2015a). *Collective accommodation establishments in Ukraine in 2014. Statistical bulletin.* Kiev: Author.

State Statistics Service of Ukraine. (2015b). *Passenger transportation by public transport.* Retrieved December 30, 2015, from http://www.ukrstat.gov.ua

State Statistics Service of Ukraine. (2015c). *Tourist activity in Ukraine in 2014. Statistical Bulletin.* Kiev: Author.

Webster, C., & Ivanov, S. (2014). Tourism as a force for political stability. In C. Wohlmuther & W. Wintersteiner (Eds.), *The international handbook on tourism and peace* (pp. 167–180). Klagenfurt/Celovec: Drava.

Wolff, K., & Larsen, S. (2014). Can terrorism make us feel safer? Risk perceptions and worries before and after the July 22nd attacks. *Annals of Tourism Research, 44,* 200–209.

Yan, L. (2011). Uneven distance decay – a study of the tourism market segments of Hong Kong. *International Journal of Tourism Sciences, 11*(1), 95–112.

Yap, G., & Saha, S. (2013). Do political instability, terrorism, and corruption have deterring effects on tourism development even in the presence of UNESCO heritage? A cross-country panel estimate. *Tourism Analysis, 18*(5), 587–599.

Appendix

Research questions

The six research objectives, formulated in the Introduction, are decomposed into six groups of specific research questions as follows:

RQ1: Performance metrics
- RQ1.1: How have the political and military events influenced the performance metrics of the accommodation establishments in Ukraine?
- RQ1.2: How have the political and military events influenced the performance metrics of the travel agencies in Ukraine?

RQ2: Political and economic challenges
- RQ2.1: What importance do the managers of accommodation establishments in the country put on the various political and economic challenges of the macroenvironment?
- RQ2.2: How do the managers of accommodation establishments in the country evaluate the various political and economic challenges of the macroenvironment?
- RQ2.3: What importance do the managers of travel agencies in the country put on the various political and economic challenges of the macroenvironment?
- RQ2.4: How do the managers of travel agencies in the country evaluate the various political and economic challenges of the macroenvironment?

RQ3: Mitigating the negative impacts
- RQ3.1: How do the managers of accommodation establishments in the country mitigate the negative impacts of the various political and economic challenges of the macroenvironment?
- RQ3.2: How do the managers of travel agencies in the country mitigate the negative impacts of the various political and economic challenges of the macroenvironment?

RQ4: The role of accommodation establishments' characteristics
- RQ4.1: Does the impact of political instability on an accommodation establishment's performance metrics depend on its category?
- RQ4.2: Does the impact of political instability on an accommodation establishment's performance metrics depend on its location?
- RQ4.3: Does the impact of political instability on an accommodation establishment's performance metrics depend on its region?
- RQ4.4: Does the impact of political instability on an accommodation establishment's performance metrics depend on its size?
- RQ4.5: Does the impact of political instability on an accommodation establishment's performance metrics depend on its chain affiliation?
- RQ4.6: Do accommodation establishment's manager's perceptions about the political and economic challenges depend on its category?
- RQ4.7: Do accommodation establishment's manager's perceptions about the political and economic challenges depend on its location?
- RQ4.8: Do accommodation establishment's manager's perceptions about the political and economic challenges depend on its region?
- RQ4.9: Do accommodation establishment's manager's perceptions about the political and economic challenges depend on its size?
- RQ4.10: Do accommodation establishment's manager's perceptions about the political and economic challenges depend on its chain affiliation?
- RQ4.11: Do accommodation establishment's manager's reactions to the political and economic challenges depend on its category?
- RQ4.12: Do accommodation establishment's manager's reactions to the political and economic challenges depend on its location?
- RQ4.13: Do accommodation establishment's manager's reactions to the political and economic challenges depend on its region?
- RQ4.14: Do accommodation establishment's manager's reactions to the political and economic challenges depend on its size?
- RQ4.15: Do accommodation establishment's manager's reactions to the political and economic challenges depend on its chain affiliation?

(Continued)

Appendix. Continued

RQ5: The role of travel agencies' characteristics
- RQ5.1: Does the impact of political instability on a travel agency's performance metrics depend on its licence type?
- RQ5.2: Does the impact of political instability on a travel agency's performance metrics depend on its region?
- RQ5.3: Does the impact of political instability on a travel agency's performance metrics depend on its main market segment?
- RQ5.4: Does the impact of political instability on a travel agency's performance metrics depend on its IATA certification?
- RQ5.5: Do travel agency's manager's perceptions about the political and economic challenges depend on its licence type?
- RQ5.6: Do travel agency's manager's perceptions about the political and economic challenges depend on its region?
- RQ5.7: Do travel agency's manager's perceptions about the political and economic challenges depend on its main market segment?
- RQ5.8: Do travel agency's manager's perceptions about the political and economic challenges depend on its IATA certification?
- RQ5.9: Do travel agency's manager's reactions to the political and economic challenges depend on its licence type?
- RQ5.10: Do travel agency's manager's reactions to the political and economic challenges depend on its region?
- RQ5.11: Do travel agency's manager's reactions to the political and economic challenges depend on its main market segment?
- RQ5.12: Do travel agency's manager's reactions to the political and economic challenges depend on its IATA certification?

RQ6: Accommodation establishments vs. travel agencies
- RQ6: Are there statistically significant differences in the responses of accommodation establishments' and travel agencies' managers?

Index

For Product Safety Concerns and Information please contact our EU
representative GPSR@taylorandfrancis.com
Taylor & Francis Verlag GmbH, Kaufingerstraße 24, 80331 München, Germany